Stella's
SEPHARDIC TABLE

Stella's
SEPHARDIC TABLE

Jewish family recipes from the
Mediterranean island of Rhodes

STELLA COHEN

Photography by MARC HOBERMAN

THE GERALD & MARC HOBERMAN COLLECTION
CAPE TOWN · LONDON · NEW YORK

Recipes and text: Stella Cohen, Monique Levy and Claude Levy
Food styling: Stella Cohen
Photography and colour reproduction: Marc Hoberman,
additional photography: Gerald Hoberman
Photography for pages 31, 106, 130, 178, 283: Claude Levy
Production control: Gerald Hoberman
Layout and design: Mellany Fick, Melanie Kriel, Marc Hoberman
and Stella Cohen
Editor and Indexer: Joy Clack
Assistant Editor: Lesley Frost

www.hobermancollection.com

ISBN: 978-1-919939-67-4

Stella's Sephardic Table is published by The Gerald & Marc Hoberman Collection
(Pty) Ltd Reg. No. 99/00167/07. Unit 10, Frazzitta Business Park, Freedom Way,
Milnerton 7441, Cape Town, South Africa Telephone: +27 (021) 551 0270/1/3
Fax: +27 (021) 555 1935 e-mail: office@hobermancollection.com

International marketing, corporate sales and picture library

United States of America, Canada, Asia
Hoberman Collection (USA), Inc./Una Press, Inc.
PO Box 880206, Boca Raton, FL 33488, USA
Telephone: +1 561 542 1141 e-mail: hobermanusa@gmail.com

United Kingdom, Republic of Ireland, Europe
Hoberman Collection (UK), Aston House, Cornwall Avenue, London N3 1LF
Telephone: +44(0) 208 3713021 e-mail: office@hobermancollection.com

Agents and distributors

United States of America & Canada
Perseus Distribution
387 Park Avenue South
New York NY 10016
Tel: +1 800 343 4499

South Africa
The Gerald & Marc Hoberman Collection
Unit 10 Frazzitta Business Park, Freedom Way
Milnerton, Cape Town, South Africa
Tel: +27 (0)21 551 0270
Fax: +27 (0)21 555 1935
e-mail: office@hobermancollection.com

Europe, Far East and Latin America
John Rule Sales & Marketing
40 Voltaire Road
London SW4 6DH
Tel: +44 (0)207 498 0115
email: johnrule@johnrule.co.uk

United Kingdom
DJ Segrue Ltd
7c Bourne Road
Bushey, Hertfordshire WD23 3NH
Tel: +44 (0)208 421 9521
e-mail: sales@djsegrue.co.uk

Painting in the background painted
by Stella Cohen

Printed in China

To my great grandmother, Miriam de Haham Yaacov Capouya, my great aunt Regina de Yehuda Capouya, my grandmother, Estrea de Leon Hanan, my aunt Mathilda Hanan and her baby daughter and all the women of Rhodes Island who were the keepers of knowledge, traditions & spirituality of my Sephardic culinary heritage. This book is dedicated to their memory! It encapsulates for posterity their extraordinary gastronomic skills, honed over time and tragically snuffed out by their deportation to Auschwitz in 1944.

Stella

Contents

Introduction

"Nonna! Where are the *reshikas*?"

After long hugs and warm kisses, this is one of the first questions I hear from my grandchildren on my frequent visits to New York from Zimbabwe, where I live.

This question speaks volumes as to why it was vital for me to document my favourite recipes in this book. The *reshikas* that my grandchildren yearn for are pretzel-shaped biscuits coated with either cinnamon and sugar or with sesame seeds. They are one of the many typical Sephardic confections my mother baked for me as a child and represent the extraordinary Sephardic cooking tradition that goes back generations. Sadly, the home cooking of our foremothers handed down orally in the

medieval language, Judesmo or Ladino, is fading, together with its rich heritage.

The cuisine and customs of the Jews of Spain were kept alive and evolved as the exiles migrated and dispersed from their beloved homeland, Spain, called 'Sepharad' in Hebrew, to newly adopted homes during the Spanish Inquisition of 1492. Those who settled on the Mediterranean island of Rhodes were strongly influenced by the culture of the Ottoman Empire, which ruled over the island for centuries, followed by the Italian occupation in 1912.

The Sephardic community thrived in Rhodes until the Second World War, when most perished in Nazi concentration camps. Some of those who had emigrated before the war and a handful of those who survived the Holocaust settled in southern Africa. My parents were among these *émigrés* from the east Mediterranean who met and married in the Belgian Congo and established roots in Southern Rhodesia, where I was born.

Since early childhood, I was immersed in and deeply drawn to this soulful cuisine, which celebrates life. As an adult, my passion for learning and perfecting the best versions of the *Rhodesli* food has been insatiable, leading me to one of the most rewarding journeys and culminating in this book. During my quest, I discovered the alchemy of cooking as I unearthed the mysteries of various ingredients. Food cooked with love, presence, and as a way of caring for those you treasure, makes all the difference to a dish.

The variety of food in this cuisine was enriched with the travels of my ancestors through the ages. From Spain came the love of our favourite grain, rice, and the myriad dishes using chickpeas, artichokes and aubergines in everyday fare. Moorish Spain brought an array of savoury pies and pastries. They include the crescent-shaped vegetable-filled pies known as *empanadas* and the medieval meat-filled pies called *pastels*, all served with braised hard-boiled eggs, *huevos haminados*. From the convents of Toledo came our passion for almonds ground into ivory-coloured homemade marzipan and sesame-seed and almond brittle candies.

My great grandparents, Rabbi of Rhodes Island, Yaacov and Miriam Capouya

My aunt, Mathilda Hanan, who perished in Auschwitz, 1936

Me in front of the Castellania Fountain, Rhodes Island, 75 years later

With our resettlement in the east Mediterranean, Greek and Turkish influences provided a magnificent source of produce: plump olives, tart pickled vegetables, salted fish and a splendid variety of cheeses, which became staples at the *meze* table. Nut-filled, syrupy pastries – aromatic with cloves and cinnamon – added a sumptuous touch. Exquisite rice pilafs, chargrilled skewered lamb and poultry and a variety of enticing stuffed leaves and vegetable dishes became part of our daily fare. Our immigration to Africa enhanced the cuisine with local ingredients and new tastes. The bounty of luscious tropical fruit led to the inclusion of clementines, passion fruit and mangoes in the sweet dishes. Spicy *piri-piri* chicken from

neighbouring Mozambique became a delicious addition to barbecued foods.

This book is a collection of my most-loved traditional Sephardic everyday food and festive dishes from Rhodes, together with a handful of recipes that evolved within our communities in southern Africa and from my travels in Morocco. I have endeavoured to pass on to you easy-to-follow recipes with detailed explanations for any beginner or intermediate cook to tackle with confidence. It is my hope that you and your loved ones will derive as much pleasure as I have making and savouring this wonderful cuisine.

My Enchanted Childhood, and a Blessing

I was born and raised in the city of Salisbury, in the British colony of Southern Rhodesia (present-day Harare, Zimbabwe). The hospital in which I was born had a very colonial name, the Lady Chancellor Maternity Home. This setting was a world away from the Aegean villages and towns that were the birthplaces of my parents and grandparents.

My mother, Marie Sevim, was born in 1926 in the village of Marmaris, Turkey. Her family had originally emigrated from the island of Rhodes, the largest of the Dodecanese islands in the Aegean Sea. The small Jewish community of Marmaris considered itself to be an extension of the much larger Jewish community of Rhodes. At the age of ten my mother and her family fled Turkey to escape the oppressive climate of Turkish nationalism that followed the end of the Ottoman Empire. With the assistance of a cousin, Hillel Franco, who had immigrated to Africa from Rhodes, my grandparents obtained visas for the Belgian Congo (present-day D.R. Congo). They initially settled in the town of Jadotville (present-day Likasi) and then the town of Elizabethville (present-day Lubumbashi), both of which were located in the mineral-rich Copper Belt. My mother, who was fluent only in Turkish when she arrived in the Congo, was schooled in a French-speaking convent in Elizabethville.

My father, Sam Hanan (1913–1987), was born on the island of Rhodes. He was educated in Italian and Hebrew, and also conversed in both medieval Judeo-Spanish (Ladino) and Greek. By the 1930s, economic conditions in Rhodes had become very difficult, and many members of the Jewish community, the *Rhodeslis*, left Rhodes to seek their fortunes elsewhere, including in Africa. In 1936, my father immigrated to find work in Southern Rhodesia. He sailed alone and in debt, having borrowed money to pay for his passage. It was his hope to eventually afford to pay for the relocation of his parents and his brothers and sister to Africa.

Despite his humble beginnings my father's ambition and resourcefulness would fuel his future success in business. His first job in Southern Rhodesia was as an apprentice in a butcher shop. He made sure to send his mother a portion of his meagre earnings every month. After a few years he had saved enough to open a small trading company in the mining town of Shabani (present-day Zvishavane).

The outbreak of the Second World War restricted the ability of the *Rhodeslis* to emigrate. Any hope he had of being reunited with his family was irrevocably shattered when, on 23 July 1944, the entire Jewish population was deported from this peaceful island to the Nazi extermination camps in Poland. My father's parents, siblings and most of their fellow deportees perished in the Holocaust.

Despite this devastating loss he worked harder than ever and went on to build many businesses, including furniture and clothing manufacturing, as well as property development. My father met my mother during a business trip to the Congo. His standing joke was that he went there to source timber and came back with a bride. They married in 1947 in Elizabethville and settled in Salisbury, as it was then called.

Even as a child, I could appreciate that Salisbury was a city rich in natural beauty. Plants flowered with vibrant colours that alternated from one season to another. Crimson and magenta bougainvilleas cascaded over garden walls, flamboyant trees lined the streets with clusters of bright red flowers. At the start of the summer, jacaranda trees in full bloom provided canopies of violet and their fallen velvety petals carpeted the ground in hues of lilac.

My parents' house was perched on a terraced hill. It was surrounded by indigenous msasa trees, which bore seedpods that would explode with a cracking sound in early summer afternoons. We had lemon trees and fruit trees bearing pawpaw (papaya), mulberries, guavas and mangoes. Our garden blossomed with roses, gardenias, frangipane, fuchsia-coloured geraniums and flame lilies with their distinctive slender red-and-yellow petals. At nightfall, the heady scent of jasmine and honeysuckle permeated the air around our home. At the back of the house a large vegetable patch supplied us with fresh herbs and vegetables for our salads and stews – organic by today's standards. We even had grapevines that provided tender young leaves for our stuffed vine leaf dishes.

My younger sister, Vera, and I coveted a particular tree that bore twisted black pods that would burst and scatter seeds called "lucky beans." These pretty seeds had a deep

orange colour and a small black patch. Although we were warned that they were poisonous – if one was unlucky enough to swallow them – we would secretly gather them and thread them to make necklaces. We also picked fresh leaves from a mulberry tree to feed our silkworms, which we kept inside vented shoeboxes. This was a popular hobby practiced by children and it was a constant source of puzzlement for my grandmother who lived with us. We would take these boxes to school and compare our worm collection with those of our friends. Packed alongside our worm boxes would be a lunch-pack of Sephardic snacks, which often included savoury cheese-filled pies, *bourekas*, or meat and rice pies, *pastelikos*.

Winters were cool and dry, marked by sunny days with clear blue skies and chilly evenings. The first summer rains heralded swarms of flying ants that would be drawn to the lights of the veranda. The African diet included these ants and it wasn't uncommon to see people collecting them to be fried for dinner! The *chongologos* also appeared during the summer. Despite their multitude of legs, these shiny black millipedes would move ever so slowly in the garden and sometimes miraculously make their way up the stairs and into our house. When prodded gently with a stick, they would coil up defensively until they sensed that the danger had passed.

The beauty and almost magical aspect of our natural surroundings was a perfect backdrop for our Sephardic home, which in many ways had its own mystique. Often after meals we would sit together and listen to old tales and fables recounted by my grandmother and her contemporaries. The African rites and folk beliefs of our domestic help added yet another dimension to our extraordinary childhood experiences. For example, our cook, Avram Andrea, was a respected witch doctor, *n'anga*, in our neighbourhood, and would receive visitors seeking help during his free time. Avram also insisted on making Vera and I lucky charms for our end of term school exams, kindly pressing them into our hands as we went off to school.

Our home life was imbued with unforgettable Sephardic tenderness and affection, *kerensia*, and meal times were central to bonding amongst family and friends. At home both Ladino and English were the main spoken languages, with French, Italian, Greek and Turkish sprinkled in, as well as Shona, the local African language.

School was a sharp contrast to the warmth of our home. Dressed in colonial-style school uniforms, we were immersed in a rigid environment, where a stiff upper lip was encouraged and rules were strictly enforced. This British culture was also present in other aspects of life outside our home. Red post office boxes bearing the acronym "EIIR" of Queen Elizabeth's name were scattered about the suburbs, which were policed by members of the British South Africa Police in crisp khaki uniforms. Cricket,

rugby and polo were popular sports to follow. British culture was also evident in the food. It was considered to be a special treat to go into 'town' for afternoon high tea at one of the large departmental stores. Tea, served by waiters dressed in starched uniforms and white gloves, would be accompanied by thin cucumber sandwiches and followed by scones with lashings of cream and jam.

Returning home, we would be welcomed by the aromas released from the kitchen: coffee beans roasting in the oven, simmering stews, or the scent of rose water wafting from a warm rice pudding bubbling on the stove. As we entered the kitchen we would invariably see our mother and grandmother immersed in creating rich and diverse treasures to soon be savoured.

Growing up as a young girl, I did not fully appreciate that our home cooking traced its origins to medieval Spain and the influences of the Ottoman Empire, and that the scents and flavours that we enjoyed were identical to those my parents and grandparents experienced during their childhood in the Mediterranean. When my sister and I were old enough to travel, my family embarked on annual trips to the island of Rhodes during the school holidays. As a result of these journeys we learned about our heritage, including the origins of our cuisine.

During these trips, we explored the old Jewish quarter, *Juderia*, in the ancient fortified town of Rhodes and visited the former homes of extended family. On the Sabbath we attended services at the only existing synagogue, *Kehila Shalom*, built in the 1500s, which is also the oldest one in Greece. We would wander down the crowded cobbled walkways to the main street that the Rhodeslis called the *Calle Ancha* on our way to the market near the harbour, the *Mandraki*. Here we would sit at one of the cafés and have conversations over refreshing drinks. At the market, *tsharshi*, we would buy essential ingredients to replenish the pantry back home, which included cumin and orange blossom and also floating wicks for lighting our traditional Shabbat candles with oil, *mechas*. A boat ride would take us from Rhodes to Marmaris, where we would explore the bazaars and buy smoked cod roe encased in wax, and Turkish delight.

With my father, we discovered the places he most enjoyed as a young boy. We loved visiting the Valley of Butterflies and the Acropolis of Lindos for pony rides. Urged by my mother we sometimes visited the Kallithea thermal spa, famous for its healing waters. In the afternoons we would refresh ourselves with a swim in the clear blue waters of the Aegean Sea.

Our journeys to the island of Rhodes were, however, bittersweet. My father would at times tear up as he recalled life on the island with his lost family and friends. He would find some solace in the company of his Greek orthodox former classmates and their families. While the adults

TOP LEFT: *My first birthday, with my parents.* TOP RIGHT: *My father, my sister, Vera, and me at the Hippocrates Square in the Old City, Rhodes Island.*
MIDDLE LEFT: *Vera and me in our garden at home in Salisbury (now Harare).* MIDDLE RIGHT: *My father, my sister and me reconnecting with old Greek friends in Rhodes Island.*
BOTTOM LEFT: *My family in Rhodes Island, 1960.* BOTTOM RIGHT: *Vera with our father on her wedding day, Harare, 1973.*

Top Left: *My grandmother, Estrea de Leon (second left) and her children Moshe, Mathilda and Solomon Hanan, all exterminated at Auschwitz.*
Top Right: *My father (far right) and friends on the boat from Rhodes Island to Africa, 1936.*
Centre: *My paternal grandfather, Nissim Hanan, 1930.*
Bottom Left: *My father, seated far left, in Southern Rhodesia (now Zimbabwe), 1946.*
Bottom Right: *My parents' wedding in Elizabethville, Congo, January 1947.*
Opposite Page: *My parents, Marie and Sam Hanan, on their 25th wedding anniversary, Harare, 1972.*

18

chatted, my sister and I would play with their children, in the same streets that our forebears had played in together.

These trips made my sister and I more deeply appreciate our Sephardic heritage and the important role that our cuisine at home played as a link to our parents' past. In our home three generations of our family would gather daily and bond with warm conviviality around the table to share delicious food made with love. My parents enjoyed hosting dinners and lunches, especially those that celebrated lifecycle milestones. The appreciation of food and the joy of openhearted hospitality was the essence of the Sephardic approach to life. Entertaining with the philosophy of abundance, *bolluk*, was paramount, ensuring that the guests' pleasure and satisfaction was met.

When the community was preparing to celebrate lifecycle festivities we would often see our kitchen transformed into a hive of activity. Women of different generations who were cooking experts, *las maestras*, gathered at our home to help prepare for these events. Relying on memory for recipes, some of which were closely guarded secrets, their busy hands would deftly hollow out and fill vegetables and leaves; kneading, rolling, pinching dough; or handcrafting homemade marzipan into exquisite sweet bites.

My sister and I would sit with these women and listen intently as they recalled their childhood with nostalgia. Their lively chatter was sprinkled with competitive criticism, gossip, laughter and unsolicited advice on the matters of the day. They were adept at story-telling, *kontar konsejas*, of family legends and folklore, often singing in their beloved Ladino medieval Spanish romantic ballads, *romansos*. This interaction gave all of us a sense of belonging and continuity across generations.

Cooking was my mother's ultimate joy and she was acknowledged for her gastronomic prowess by the community. I began to understand what the Ladino word *necutchera* meant. A word that signifies all that she represents: an accomplished woman with a refined sense of taste and intuitive wisdom. As a child I felt in my mother a sense of spirituality that I believe she had inherited from her grandfather, a sage and Rabbi of Rhodes, Haham Yaacov Capouya. It was only when I began my own culinary journey that I realised that my mother's instinct and passion for cooking involved not just feeding the body but also nurturing the soul.

As a child I would try to imitate her when she cooked, especially when she was baking. I could not replicate her technique as her expert, nimble fingers shaped the dough. But somehow I knew there was something more going on in her private laboratory. How else could the flour, eggs and other basic ingredients be transformed into something so wonderful, something that not only tantalized the palette but that also gave us a sense of comfort and warmth? Certainly no such miraculous transformation took place with my own experiments. So began my lifelong fascination with Sephardic cooking. I was also motivated to perfect and preserve our culinary traditions so that I could ultimately pass them on to my children, Claude and Monique Levy, and their children.

Claude and Monique left Zimbabwe in the late 1980s to further their studies in the U.S. They live there today and are blessed with children. Each of my frequent visits over the years prompted their requests for me to appease their yearning for the distinctive flavours of our Sephardic cuisine. As the food rekindled their childhood memories and reinforced their appreciation of their heritage, they urged me to document not only our Sephardic family recipes but also our vanishing customs.

Our Sephardic table has always been a sanctuary and a link to our past; it encompasses an entire way of life that has provided nurture, support and continuity for centuries. It is my hope that these recipes will enable you to experience and enjoy the same nourishment of body and soul as my family has.

Ladino is a Sephardic language rich in sayings and blessings. The saying, *benditchas manos*, is many faceted. It is a compliment and an expression of gratitude to the cook, as well as a wish that the hands that produced such wonderful food may continue to be blessed.

I wish that you be blessed with *benditchas manos*. May this book make a difference in your kitchen and in your life.

The History & Heritage of the Jews of Rhodes

By Jane S. Gerber

Tomamos la vida kon alegria

(We take life with joy)

The expulsion of approximately 150,000 Jews of Spain in 1492 marked a turning point in Jewish history. Their departure sparked the beginning of decades of wandering: one expulsion of Jews followed upon the heels of another – from Portugal, the Kingdom of Sicily, Sardinia, the Kingdom of Naples, Provence and most of the Papal States. As the hapless refugees from Europe moved eastward in search of refuge they faced a crisis of unprecedented proportions and were introspective and melancholy. Every step of resettlement was strewn with obstacles; ports were closed to the refugees, pirates seemed to be everywhere lying in wait, unscrupulous sea captains took Sephardic refugees on board their ships only to cast them adrift. As the sixteenth-century Portuguese Jewish chronicler Samuel Usque lamented, "they were cast, like victims of contagion, upon a barren beach far from human help. Babies begged for water, and mothers raised their eyes to heaven for help, while others, reduced to despair by hunger and abandonment, dug their own graves." Yet, in testimony to their vitality and resiliency, within a few decades of their brutal uprooting, the Sephardic Jews were building new and vibrant centres of Jewish civilization throughout the eastern Mediterranean and North Africa, including on the island of Rhodes. Before long, Rhodes would be known as *La Chica Yerushalayim* (The Little Jerusalem) in recognition of the learning of her many scholars.

News of the benevolence of Turkey towards the Jews had reached Europe even before the fall of the Byzantine capital of Constantinople to the Turks in 1453. One Jewish leader reportedly summoned his co-religionists to leave the persecutions of Europe and declared to them, "Brothers and teachers, friends and acquaintances: I, Isaac Zarfat...proclaim to you that Turkey is a land wherein nothing is lacking, and where, if you will, all shall yet be well with you... Here every man may dwell at peace under his own vine and fig tree."

The Sephardic Jews arrived in the East when the Ottoman Empire was at her most dynamic and expansive, offering the exiles "a place where their weary feet would find rest." As Turkey's borders expanded westward and eastward her energetic Sultans realized that the Jewish outcasts of Europe were talented, possessed a multitude of skills in the languages and crafts of Europe, knew the arts of munitions-making and, most importantly, harboured no territorial designs on Ottoman lands. Their special skills included the manufacture of textiles and woolens. Additionally, they were accustomed to taking risks in commerce and understood the prices and economic conditions in Europe and many remote places. Their merchants were linked by bonds of family and business with one another throughout Europe and beyond. In short, the Jews of Iberia could provide a valuable human supplement to Turkey's warrior and agrarian classes. Responding to the expulsion of the Jews from Spain by Ferdinand and Isabella, Sultan Bayezid II (1481–1512) allegedly declared, "You call Ferdinand a wise king, he who impoverishes his country and enriches our own?" and reportedly ordered his provincial governors to open the borders of the Empire to the Jewish refugees.

At the time of the Turkish conquest of Rhodes from the Knights of St. John in 1523, a heterogeneous Jewish population already existed on the island. Many Jews had been captured by the Knights in the Mediterranean and were held captive on the island while others were victims of a recent forced baptism. The conquering Turks favoured Jewish settlement on the island, offering special concessions to induce their entry. Before long, the Iberian newcomers culturally overwhelmed the indigenous Greek-speaking Jews and assumed the economic and cultural leadership of the Jews on the island. The island's functioning synagogue, Kahal Kadosh Gadol, was soon known as Kahal Kadosh Grande. By

LEFT: Prayer book of my grandfather, Davitchon Hanan, dated 1937, with script in Ladino.

ABOVE: My father sailing from Rhodes Island to Africa in 1936.

the 1570s a second synagogue, Kahal Kadosh Shalom, was consecrated. As a result of the Sephardic self-confidence and dynamism, Rhodes soon emerged as a lively centre of Sephardic Jewish creativity with its own distinctive culinary tastes and customs that interwove and blended Jewish, Greek, Hispanic, Turkish and other cultural threads. The Jewish population of Rhodes rose from 500 Jews at the end of the sixteenth century to a peak of approximately 4,000 souls in 1935, boasting six synagogues and a Rabbinical College.

The development of Jewish life in Rhodes mirrored that of other Ottoman Jewish communities in early modern and modern times. The Jewish newcomers were granted a wide measure of autonomy by the Turkish authorities, enabling them to shape their own lives. New centres of Jewish life emerged and older ones were revived – in Cairo, Safed, Smyrna (Izmir), Bursa, Sarajevo, Ragusa, Sofia and above all, in Salonica and Istanbul. The location of the island of Rhodes, close to the coast of Turkey and astride the sea route to the land of Israel, was advantageous for trade, also serving as a stopover for the continuous flow of pilgrims en route to the Holy Land. The Jews of Rhodes used these geographic and economic advantages wisely, building a community in touch with the wider Jewish world, especially skilled in commerce and the manufacture of textiles. By the middle of the seventeenth century about one-half of world Jewry lived under the Ottomans.

One of the most striking characteristics of the Sephardic diaspora was its determination to preserve its Hispanic cultural traditions, particularly its language, variously known as Judeo-Espanol, Ladino or Djudezmo, as well as its traditional foods. Ladino remained the linguistic patrimony of the Jews of Rhodes until the end. Use of the Ladino language helped form a virtual Sephardic nation in the Mediterranean bound by religion, language and folk traditions. For 500 years, from the sixteenth century until its annihilation by the Nazis, the Jewish community of Rhodes tenaciously maintained and nurtured the culture of their Iberian ancestors, creating a miniature Judeo-Spanish universe on the island. All the Jews spoke Judeo-Spanish or Ladino, passing on the proverbs, ballads, folk wisdom and a unique way of life that blended the legacy of medieval Spain and the culture of their adopted land of refuge. The role of the Jewish women in the preservation of this culture cannot be emphasized enough.

The rhythm of life for the Jews in Rhodes was set by the Jewish calendar. The Jews inhabited their own quarter, the *Juderia*, known as the *calle ancha*, located in the medieval section of the town of Rhodes, where they experienced intensely social lives revolving around the Jewish holidays and lifecycle events. Extended families lived a stone's throw from one another, sharing their joys, superstitions and tragedies in melody, in story and in the festive meals that marked all occasions. While the males studied in the island's *meldars* or traditional *yeshivot* and engaged in commerce and the crafts, the women were mostly confined to the home, becoming expert in domestic and culinary skills. The distinctive cuisine of the Jews, while heavily dependent upon local custom and local produce, also served as a cultural divide between the Jews and other Ottoman ethnic groups, preserving many dishes reminiscent of medieval Spain. The Sephardic women were the mainstay in preserving this unique civilization characterized by generosity and joyous celebration despite the growing poverty that overtook the Ottoman Jewish population with the passage of time. Emigres would fondly recall the *bimuelos* (deep-fried dough dipped in honey served at Hanukkah), the *biscotchos*, *pastelikos* and marzipan reminiscent of Andalusia and the *yaprakes*, *keftes* and *baklava* of their Greek and Turkish neighbours.

By the late nineteenth century modernity and westernization were making inroads on tradition everywhere in Ottoman lands, altering peoples' self-perceptions, their family relations and their personal aspirations and notions of geographic mobility. The Jews of Rhodes were not insulated from such changes. On the one hand, the Jews of the declining Ottoman Empire suffered from the increasing lawlessness of Ottoman society and its officialdom. Balkan nationalist movements strained to rid themselves of their Turkish overlords, frequently pouncing upon their defenseless local Jewish neighbours in the process. At the same time that the Ottoman Empire was disintegrating, European influences were spreading, primarily through the introduction of westernized schools. The establishment of the Alliance Israelite Universelle introduced, for the first time in Jewish life, secular and vocational subjects and the study of foreign languages as well as the revolutionary introduction of education for Jewish girls (the Alliance school for girls was established in Rhodes in 1903). These innovations brought drastic changes to traditional Jewish life. Old patterns of arranged marriages at a very young age and traditional inheritance patterns began to break down. The patriarchal society was also giving way. With the Italian occupation of Rhodes in 1912, cultural change accelerated for the Jews. Rhodes was officially annexed by Italy in 1923. Jews quickly adapted, forming a dynamic part of the political and business community. The establishment of a Rabbinical Seminary in Rhodes in 1926 provided a short-lived (1926–1935) training ground for higher Jewish education. Students from throughout the eastern Mediterranean and Italy flocked to Rhodes to train as Jewish teachers, rabbis and scholars.

Emigration from Rhodes began in earnest during the early twentieth century as Rhodian Jews scattered to North and South America, Palestine and sub-Saharan Africa. So eager were parents to prepare their children for emigration that English became the language of instruction by 1915 in the Alliance Israelite Universelle schools in Rhodes. The local Jewish population on the island did not diminish, however, during the 1920s as Jews from Izmir and elsewhere fled to Rhodes to escape the violence of the Greco-Turkish conflict. New congregations of Jews from Rhodes began to sprout everywhere – Congregation Or ve-Shalom in Atlanta (1914), Ezra Bessarot in Seattle (1914), Ahavath Achim in Portland, OR (1916), the Sephardic Hebrew Congregation (from Peace and Progress Society) in Los Angeles, as well as new Rhodesli Sephardic congregations in Brussels, Belgium; Lubumbashi, the Belgian Congo; Salisbury, Rhodesia and Cape Town, South Africa.

The story of the Rhodesli Jews in Rhodesia is not atypical of the dynamism of its diaspora. In 1931 a Sephardic community of Rhodeslis was inaugurated. A synagogue building was consecrated in 1934 and the Sephardic Hebrew Congregation began to thrive. Over the succeeding decades it erected many communal institutions – another Sephardic synagogue, Sha'are Shalom Synagogue and Rhodes Community Memorial Hall, consecrated in 1958 with the Samuel Leon Hebrew School completed in 1962. In its early years the community was led by Rabbi Dr. M. Papo (1944–1963), a survivor of Dachau. He was succeeded by Rev. S. R. Ichay (until 1967) and Rev. I. Benzaquen (until 1974). The members of this small, proud community of Rhodesia and – after independence – Zimbabwe, comprised prominent businessmen, industrialists, doctors, lawyers and teachers, which made a positive impact on the country. The community is significantly diminished in numbers today as a result of emigration over the past few decades.

The fate of those who remained in Rhodes in the 1930s was tragic. Jewish life worsened dramatically under the Italians with the introduction of the fascist racial laws against Jews in 1938. Non-Rhodesli Jews were ousted from the island, Jewish children were expelled from the schools, *shehitah* was prohibited, and one restriction after the next was introduced. But Italian persecution was merely a prelude to the deportation and destruction of the Jewish community. The Nazi occupation of the island followed the Italian capitulation in September 1943. On July 23, 1944 the dreaded deportation of the Jews of Rhodes began. Approximately 1,600 Jews were sent to Auschwitz, most perishing immediately after arrival. Only 151 Jews of Rhodes survived. Those few who returned from the concentration camps were unable to rebuild their lives on the island.

Today the main artery through the former Jewish quarter in the eastern section of the old city of Rhodes has been renamed the Street of the Jewish Martyrs, Martyron Evreon. It bears a plaque inscribed "In memory of the 1,607 martyrs of the Jewish Community of Rhodes and the island of Cos, brutally butchered by the barbaric Nazis in the concentration camps of Germany 1944–45. May their souls rest in peace." Rhodes currently contains fewer than twenty Jews. Only the Kahal Kadosh Shalom synagogue survives in the heart of what once constituted the Jewish quarter, its inscription informing the passersby of its founding in 1577. In the centre of the Square of the Martyred Jews an ancient monument with bronze seahorses still stands. A nearby Jewish Museum tells the story of the island's illustrious Jewish past. A plaque containing an alphabetical listing of the family names of all the deported Jews can be seen. Salamon Alhadeff Street is the only street in Rhodes retaining a Jewish name in the central port area of the old town where the community was once concentrated.

Although the joyous family and holiday traditions of the Jews of Rhodes are permanently stilled on the island, their customs are preserved by the Jewish women of Rhodes now scattered on many continents. The special fragrance and tastes of the unique Jewish cuisine, reminders of a rich past, are offered from *Stella's Sephardic Table* in the following pages for all readers to share and enjoy.

Jane S. Gerber is Professor of Jewish History and Director of the Institute for Sephardic Studies at the Graduate Center of the City University of New York. She is the author of numerous books and articles, including *The Jews of Spain* (Macmillan and Simon and Schuster) which won the National Jewish Book Award in 1992. Her forthcoming books are *The Sephardic Jews of the Caribbean* (Littman Library, Oxford) and *Cities of Splendour in the Shaping of Sephardic History* (Littman Library, Oxford).

My daughter, Monique, and grandson, Nico, and me in the Kehila Shalom Synagogue in Rhodes.

The interior of this synagogue.

The Holocaust Memorial in the Square of the Martyred Jews, Rhodes Island.

The Sha'are Shalom synagogue in Harare, Zimbabwe.

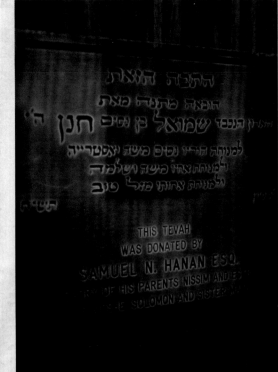

התיבה הזאת
הוצאה מתנה מאת
הנכבד שמואל בן ניסים חנן ה'
למנוחת הוריו ניסים משה ויסטרייה
ולמנוחת אחיו משה ושלמה
ולמנוחת אחותו מזל טוב
תשכ"ה

THIS TEVAH
WAS DONATED BY
SAMUEL N. HANAN ESQ.
...RY OF HIS PARENTS NISSIM AND E...
...E SOLOMON AND SISTER...

לזכר בת-אחות-דודה היקרה
וירא חנן ע"ה
ז' שבט תשל"ה
IN LOVING MEMORY OF OUR
...LOVED DAUGHTER, SISTER, AUN...
VERA HANAN
19th JANUARY 1975

Meze & Salads

Meze

Sephardic mezes not only comprise an enticing array of appetizers in the form of small dishes and finger foods, but also describes a way of eating, living and socialising. The love of sharing good food, drinks and the company of family and friends played a large role in my childhood. Most evenings I would watch the African sun set – each night exquisite in its own way – and wait for my father to come home from work. The whole family would then gather on the veranda and share stories about the day. Invariably friends would pop in for a drink, *para una bivida*, of anise flavoured ouzo, scotch or a fruit cordial. The more people that spontaneously showed up, the merrier the gathering. As the medieval Judeo-Spanish saying goes, *Ken bueno se kere en poko lugar kave*, meaning that there is always room for people who care for each other. My parents would welcome visitors with *Bouyrum!*, ("Welcome" in Turkish) or *Vengash en la buena hora*, meaning "You have come at a good time." My sister and I would sit mesmerized by the stories, rumours and gossip that were shared, while snacking on our favourite meze. In the background, Turkish or Greek folk music would play. Some nights, the backgammon sets, *tavli*, would come out for the competitive gamblers, *los komarjies*. The stage was set for the spirit of *kefi*, celebrating life wholeheartedly with the people you love, so integral to our Sephardic culture.

To supply these mini feasts, we would always have the pantry, our treasure chest, well stocked with a myriad of homemade and bought delicacies. Always at hand, was some Greek feta in brine or kashkaval cheese, an array of pickled vegetables, turnips tinged pink with beetroot and crispy chunks of cabbage. Olives were a staple, including home-cured cracked green olives and black kalamatas. My grandchildren have been hooked on black olives starting at age three!

Also plentiful at the meze table are roasted salted nuts and seeds, almonds, chickpeas and pumpkin seeds. They are known as a *passa tempo*, describing the calm paced way on which food was nibbled. We often prepare creamy spreads and dips made of aubergine, cod roe and a refreshing yoghurt, cucumber and mint dip, scooped with wedges of pita bread. Raw cured fish, marinated anchovies or sliced botarga are also common, accompanied with warm crusty bread.

The table is laden with fresh salads and cooked vegetable dishes; Turkish diced salad, a variety of cooked aubergine and roasted pepper salads, all designed to nourish, refresh and delight. Rice and fresh herb-filled vine leaves are also a real treat served cold. Assorted crispy vegetable fritters and vegetable cheese and egg gratins cut into squares are relished as an appetizer.

No meze table can be complete without the more elaborate repertoire of dainty, crisp, savoury pastries filled with meat or vegetable and cheese fillings. These were my mother's mark of excellence – family and friends alike who tasted them wanted to know her secret.

The recipes in this section serve 4–6 people as a meze or as a side dish to the main meal. For this reason I have not separated salads from mezes in the book.

Mezes are a wonderful social ritual. Taking time to share food and drinks with people you care about is just so good for the soul.

Salut! Kome kon gana or, as my grandmother would say in Turkish, *Afyet olsun*, "May it do you good."

El ke alarga la meza, alarga la vida

(Lit: The one who extends the table, lengthens their life)

The greater your hospitality, the more fulfilling your life will be

Bianca, Gemma and Nico, my beloved grandchildren, delight in being part of the Sephardic cooking tradition.

aromatic carrot salad
salata de safanorya

A wonderful way to brighten up your table is to serve this easy Moroccan-inspired carrot salad, infused with an exotic dressing that is both spicy and sweet. Resembling gold coins when sliced, it is often served on the Jewish New Year to symbolise prosperity. The carrot salad keeps well for a couple of days in the fridge, ready to serve.

1kg (2¼lb) carrots, peeled and trimmed
3 whole garlic cloves
1 tsp salt

For the dressing:
⅔ cup extra-virgin olive oil
1 tbsp cider vinegar
1 tbsp fresh lemon juice
1 tsp ground cumin
½ tsp Turkish red pepper flakes
2 tsp paprika
2 tsp honey or caster (superfine) sugar
2 tsp orange blossom water
½ tsp sea salt
2 tsp hot chilli paste (harissa) (optional)

For the garnish:
1 tbsp finely chopped fresh coriander
   (cilantro)

CUT the carrots with a sharp knife or a julienne blade into matchsticks or cut into thin slices. Bring a pan of lightly salted water to a boil and add the carrots and garlic. Cover, reduce the heat and simmer for about 10 minutes or until just tender. Drain in a colander and discard the garlic. Transfer the carrots to a bowl.

WHISK all the dressing ingredients together in a small bowl. Pour over the carrots while they are still warm. Toss until the carrots are evenly coated and leave for at least 1 hour to allow the flavours of the dressing to be absorbed. Taste and adjust the seasoning. Place the carrot salad in a wide, shallow serving bowl and garnish with coriander. Serve at room temperature.

Turkish diced salad
salata a la Turka

An excellent colourful accompaniment to a meat or fish barbecue, this refreshing crunchy salad can also be served as part of a meze with plenty of crusty bread.

3 large ripe tomatoes, seeded
1 small cucumber, peeled
1 small red onion, peeled
3 radishes
1 red bell pepper, seeded
1 cup roughly sliced rocket (arugula)
3 spring onions (scallions), thinly sliced
½ cup black olives, pitted
½ cup finely chopped flat-leaf parsley
   (use leaves and tender stems)

For the dressing:
3 tbsp extra-virgin olive oil
1 tbsp fresh lemon juice
½ tsp sea salt
a pinch freshly ground black pepper
1 garlic clove, finely grated (optional)

DICE the tomatoes, cucumber, red onion, radishes and bell pepper into 3mm (⅛in) pieces. Combine all the salad ingredients in a large bowl. Do not refrigerate.

WHISK all the dressing ingredients together in a small bowl. Taste and adjust the seasoning. Pour the dressing over the salad, toss well and serve right away.

 STELLA'S HINTS:
- *For a splash of colour, use knobbly red, yellow and green heirloom tomatoes.*
- *For a spicy flavour, add ½ tsp Turkish red pepper flakes and 1 tsp ground sumac diluted with ¼ cup chilled water to the dressing.*
- *If preparing the salad well ahead of the meal, leave the diced tomatoes over a colander to drain. Add to the salad just before serving.*

chunky aubergine spread
salata de berendjena

Chunky, garlic-flavoured roasted aubergine spread is scrumptious just freshly made and served alongside lamb patties or kebabs or simply as a dip on a wedge of pita bread as a snack.

3–4 medium aubergines (eggplants) –
    about 1kg (2¼lb)
2 garlic cloves, finely grated
2 tbsp extra-virgin olive oil
¼ cup fresh lemon juice
sea salt and freshly ground black pepper
1 ripe tomato, peeled, seeded and diced
1 tbsp each roughly chopped flat-leaf
    parsley (use leaves and tender stems)
    and fresh dill

For the garnish:
extra-virgin olive oil
a few black olives, pitted

PREHEAT the oven to 220°C (425°F).

PIERCE the aubergines with the tip of a sharp knife a few times near the stalk end. This allows the heat to penetrate the whole aubergine and stops them from bursting. Put them on a foil-lined tray and roast for about 1 hour in the oven. Turn them occasionally with tongs until they have deflated completely, the skin has blackened and the flesh is soft.

Alternatively: To flame-roast the aubergine using a gas stovetop*: Set at a medium-high heat. Roast over a naked flame, turning the aubergine with tongs, until the skin is charred all over and the flesh feels soft, about 12 minutes.

LAY the aubergines on a board when they are just cool enough to handle. Slit them open lengthways and, using a spoon, scrape out the flesh, avoiding the blackened skin. Discard the skin.

DRAIN the warm pulp in a colander and press the aubergine to squeeze out excess liquid.

COMBINE half of the pulp in a food processor together with the garlic, olive oil, lemon juice and salt and pepper and pulse a few times until it forms a creamy texture.

ROUGHLY chop the remaining pulp and fold into the purée mixture. Taste and adjust for lemon, salt and pepper. Transfer to a shallow bowl and stir in the diced tomato, parsley and dill. Drizzle with olive oil, scatter over the olives and serve at once.

 STELLA'S HINTS:

♦ **To protect your cooker from staining: Remove the hob heads, line the base with foil and place the heads back on the hob.*
♦ *When scooping out the aubergine flesh, remove any large seeds as they are bitter and unpleasant in texture.*
♦ *If making this ahead of time, refrigerate in an airtight container. Return to room temperature before serving.*

 TWIST ON TRADITION:

♦ *2 medium-sized red bell peppers, roasted, peeled and diced, or good quality store-bought roasted peppers, can be added to the aubergine spread.*

El oro fino arrelumbra

(Lit: Fine gold shines)

A person of good character reveals his true worth

borlotti beans simmered in a tomato sauce
barbunyas kon salsa di tomat

Pink-mottled borlotti beans, simmered with a bed of vegetables in a fresh tomato sauce, become creamy textured and delicious. This is a versatile dish that can be part of a meze or served alongside grilled food and a white rice pilaf (p168).

1 cup (175g/6oz) dried borlotti beans,
    soaked overnight in twice their volume
    of cold water, drained and rinsed
2 dried bay leaves
1 small whole onion, peeled

For the tomato sauce:
¼ cup extra-virgin olive oil
2 red onions, finely sliced lengthways
2 young tender celery stalks with some
    leaves, finely sliced
1 fennel bulb, finely diced
2 leeks, white part only, finely chopped
1 tsp paprika
a pinch Turkish red pepper flakes
3 garlic cloves, finely grated
2 cups peeled, seeded and chopped ripe
    tomatoes or canned chopped tomatoes
1 tsp sugar
1 tbsp dried Greek oregano
1 tbsp roughly chopped fresh dill
2 tbsp roughly chopped flat-leaf parsley
    (use leaves and tender stems)
sea salt and freshly ground black pepper

For serving:
1 tbsp roughly chopped fresh dill
1 tbsp flat-leaf parsley (use leaves and
    tender stems)
extra-virgin olive oil

Cook the beans: Put the beans in a pan with enough cold water to cover by 2.5cm (1in). Add bay leaves and onion. Bring to a boil. Cover, reduce the heat and simmer for about 1½ hours or until tender but not mushy. The cooking time depends on the quality and age of the beans. Check frequently as they cook, adding a little water as necessary. Drain in a colander and rinse well under cold running water. Discard the onion and bay leaves.

Make the sauce: Heat the oil in a large, shallow, heavy-based pan over a medium-high heat. Add the onions, celery, fennel, leeks, paprika and red pepper flakes. Cook, stirring occasionally, for 8 minutes, until softened. Add the garlic and cook for 1 minute. Stir in the tomatoes, sugar and the cooked beans. Pour in 2 cups hot water. Cover, reduce the heat and simmer for 20 minutes until the vegetables are tender and the beans are soft. As the beans simmer, maintain the liquid a little under the level of the borlotti beans, adding hot water as needed.

STIR in the oregano, dill and parsley and season with salt and pepper. Simmer for a further 20 minutes, or until the sauce has thickened. Sprinkle with dill and parsley and a drizzle of olive oil. Serve warm or at room temperature.

 STELLA'S HINT:
♦ *You can substitute 2 × 400g (14oz) cans borlotti beans, drained and rinsed for the dried beans and cook for 20 minutes in the thickened sauce with the herbs.*

El gameyo no veyi su korkova, veyi la defrente
(Lit: The camel does not see his own hump, he sees the one in front of him)

We are often unaware of our shortcomings

aubergine, bell pepper and tomato salad

salata de berendjena frita kon piminton i tomat

Aubergines, bell peppers and tomatoes are lightly sautéed and marinated in a garlic-flavoured dressing. This popular salad features frequently at the Sephardic table and works wonderfully with grills and roasts or as an appetizer.

3–4 medium aubergines (eggplants) – about 1kg (2¼lb)
1 tbsp kosher or coarse salt
1 tsp fresh lemon juice
1 green or red bell pepper, seeded and cut into wide strips
1 large ripe tomato, thickly sliced

For the dressing:
¼ cup fresh lemon juice
3 tbsp white wine vinegar
¼ cup cold water
1 tsp sugar
3 garlic cloves, finely grated
1½ tsp sea salt
freshly ground black pepper

For shallow-frying:
vegetable or grape-seed oil

For the garnish:
1 tbsp roughly chopped flat-leaf parsley (use leaves and tender stems)

Prepare the aubergines: Cut the stems off the aubergines. Using a very sharp knife, peel 1.25cm (½in) strips at intervals along the length of the aubergines, leaving it striped with some peel. Cut each aubergine into slices about 1.25cm (½in) thick. In a large bowl, dissolve the coarse salt in 2.4lt (5pt) water and add the lemon juice. Immerse the aubergine slices and place a weighted plate on top to keep them submerged. Soak for 45 minutes. Rinse under cold running water and drain. Pat dry with paper towels.

WHISK all the dressing ingredients together in a small bowl. Taste and adjust the seasoning and pour into a shallow serving dish.

Cook the aubergines: Heat enough oil for shallow-frying in a large frying pan over a medium-high heat. Cook the aubergine slices in the sizzling oil, in batches, for 3–5 minutes on each side, until fork-tender and lightly golden. Replenish the oil as necessary. Lift out with a slotted spoon and drain on paper towels. Cover with paper towels, pressing lightly to soak up excess oil and immediately immerse the aubergine slices in the serving dish containing the dressing to soak up the flavours. The lemon will keep the colour light.

FRY the bell pepper strips briefly in the same pan, followed by the tomato slices and arrange on top of the aubergines. Spoon some of the dressing over the cooked vegetables to ensure that they are well coated. Cover with plastic wrap and marinate for 1 hour at room temperature. Sprinkle with parsley and serve.

 STELLA'S HINT:
♦ *The salad can be kept chilled, covered. Return to room temperature before serving.*

La limpieza es media rikeza

(Lit: Cleanliness is half one's wealth)

The importance of being fastidious amongst the Sephardim

aubergines with tomato and onion topping

salata de berendjena kon salsa de tomat i sevoya

Tender slices of cooked aubergine are baked with a tomato, onion and fresh herb topping, making a spectacular platter as a starter or as a vegetarian entrée. I prefer to serve it hot, but it is just as delicious at room temperature with plenty of crusty bread.

3 medium elongated aubergines
  (eggplants) – about 1kg (2¼lb)
1 tbsp kosher or coarse salt
1 tsp fresh lemon juice

For the tomato and onion topping:
2 tbsp extra-virgin olive oil
1 large onion, finely chopped
2 garlic cloves, finely grated
2 cups peeled, seeded and chopped ripe
  tomatoes or canned chopped tomatoes
1 tsp sugar
1 tsp dried Greek oregano
sea salt and freshly ground black pepper
½ cup finely chopped flat-leaf parsley
  (use leaves and tender stems)
1 tbsp red wine vinegar

For shallow-frying:
vegetable or grape-seed oil

For the sauce:
1 tbsp tomato paste and 1 tsp sugar
  diluted in ¼ cup hot water
1 tbsp extra-virgin olive oil

For the garnish:
1 tbsp finely chopped flat-leaf parsley
  (use leaves and tender stems)

Prepare the aubergines: Cut the stems off the aubergines. Using a very sharp knife, peel 1.25cm (½in) strips at intervals along the length of the aubergines, leaving it striped with some peel. Cut each aubergine into slices about 1.25cm (½in) thick. In a large bowl dissolve the coarse salt in 2.4lt (5pt) water and add the lemon juice. Immerse the aubergine slices and place a weighted plate on top to keep them submerged. Soak for 45 minutes. Rinse under cold running water and drain. Pat dry with paper towels.

Prepare the topping: Heat the oil in a small pan over a medium-high heat. Add the onion and cook for 5 minutes, stirring frequently, until softened. Add the garlic and tomatoes. Stir in the sugar and oregano and season with salt and pepper. Reduce the heat and simmer, uncovered, for 15 minutes, or until the tomato and onion mixture thickens. Stir in the parsley and vinegar. Taste and adjust the seasoning.

Cook the aubergines: Heat enough oil for shallow-frying in a large frying pan over a medium-high heat. Cook the aubergine slices in the sizzling oil, in batches, for 3–5 minutes on each side, until fork-tender and lightly golden. Replenish and adjust the temperature of the oil as necessary. Lift out with a slotted spoon and drain on a plate lined with paper towels. Press lightly with paper towels to soak up excess oil.

PREHEAT the oven to 190°C (375°F).

TRANSFER the aubergine slices into a large, shallow, ovenproof dish and place in a single layer, slightly overlapping. Spoon the tomato and onion mixture over the centre of each aubergine slice.

MIX the sauce ingredients together in a small bowl and carefully pour into the dish – not over the aubergine. Cover the dish with tented aluminium foil and bake for 20 minutes. There should be little liquid left. Sprinkle with parsley and serve hot or at room temperature.

Kada suvida tiene su abashada

(Lit: Every step up has a step down)

Every upside has a downside

black-eyed bean salad
salata de fijones

While still hot, black-eyed beans are doused in vinaigrette and topped with chopped hard-boiled eggs. On the island of Rhodes and in Egypt the Sephardic custom was to serve black-eyed beans for the Sabbath and New Year, representing new life and abundance. The combination of textures and flavours makes this a delicious and substantial salad that can be served alongside grilled meat, chicken or fish or even as part of a meze.

For the beans:
1 cup (175g/6oz) dried black-eyed beans, soaked for 2 hours in cold water to cover, drained and rinsed
1 whole small onion, peeled
2 dried bay leaves
1 carrot, cut into chunks
sea salt

For the dressing:
5 tbsp extra-virgin olive oil
3 tbsp red wine vinegar
⅛ tsp ground cumin
1 garlic clove, finely grated
1 tsp sea salt
freshly ground black pepper

For the salad:
1 medium red onion, thinly sliced lengthways
3 tbsp roughly chopped flat-leaf parsley (use leaves and tender stems)
2 tbsp roughly chopped fresh dill

For the garnish:
2 hard-boiled eggs
a handful pitted oil-cured black olives
6 bottled or canned anchovy fillets

Cook the beans: Put the beans in a large pan with enough cold water to cover by 2.5cm (1in). Add the onion, bay leaves and carrot and bring to a boil. Cover, reduce the heat and simmer for about 1¼ hours or until the beans are soft to the bite but not mushy. Check frequently as they cook, adding more boiling water as necessary. Add the salt in the last 10 minutes of cooking.

MEANWHILE whisk all the dressing ingredients together in a small bowl.

WHEN the beans are cooked, drain well and discard the onion, bay leaves and carrot. While the beans are still warm, tip into a serving bowl with the sliced onion, parsley and dill.

POUR the dressing immediately over the beans to absorb the flavours. Toss well to combine.

JUST before serving, taste and adjust the seasoning. Garnish with finely chopped or quartered eggs, pitted olives and anchovy fillets and serve.

 STELLA'S HINT:
- *You can substitute a 450g (16oz) can of black-eyed beans, drained and rinsed, or any canned legume (pulse) of your choice, for the dried beans. Warm the canned beans in their liquid, drain and then pour in the prepared dressing to better absorb the flavours.*

 TWIST ON TRADITION:
- *You can add ½ cup chopped pickled cucumbers and 2 diced ripe plum tomatoes. Toss in just before serving.*

Amostrami ken son tus amigos te dire ken sos

(Lit: Show me who your friends are and I will tell you who you are)

cabbage salad with fresh herbs
salata de kol blanka

Shredded raw cabbage, fragrant with fresh herbs, is tossed in a fresh lemon dressing. This refreshing salad offers lively flavours alongside grilled piri-piri chicken, kebabs or when served with a succulent roasted joint of lamb.

1 small Savoy or baby green cabbage
½ tsp sea salt
1 small cucumber, halved lengthways
    and thinly sliced
1 red onion, thinly sliced lengthways,
    half again crossways
½ cup roughly chopped flat-leaf parsley
    (use leaves and tender stems)
½ cup roughly chopped fresh dill

For the dressing:
1½ tbsp fresh lemon juice
1 tbsp white wine vinegar
½ tsp sea salt
3 tbsp extra-virgin olive oil
a pinch freshly ground black pepper
1 garlic clove, finely grated (optional)

CUT the cabbage in quarters, discard the outer leaves and trim off any thick, hard stems as well as the hard base. Lie each quarter on its side and shred the cabbage as finely as possible with a very sharp knife or a mandolin, until you reach the central core, which should be discarded. Place the shredded cabbage in a bowl and season lightly with salt. Stir the remaining salad ingredients into the cabbage.

WHISK the lemon juice, vinegar and salt together in a small bowl. Gradually whisk in the oil and season with pepper. Add the garlic (if using). Taste and adjust the seasoning. Pour over the salad and toss until the ingredients are well coated. Let stand for 20–30 minutes (but not longer) to absorb the flavours.

 STELLA'S HINT:

♦ *Select a head of cabbage that is firm and heavy for its size, not one that is pale or discoloured.*

 TWIST ON TRADITION:

♦ *To bring a splash of colour to the table, mix in some shredded ruby red cabbage. Add 1 fennel bulb, shaved into very thin slices, for an aniseed flavour.*

roasted baby beetroot salad
salata di pandjar kon ajada

In this Greek-inspired recipe the beetroot has a more intense and pure flavour than the pickled version and is customarily served with garlic and potato dip (p46).

2 bunches red or golden baby beetroot
    (beets) – about 1kg (2¼lb)*
1 tbsp olive oil
sea salt
¼ cup water

PREHEAT the oven to 180°C (350°F).

RINSE the beetroot well under cold running water to remove any grit.

LINE a roasting pan with a large sheet of aluminium foil, shiny side down, and place the beetroot in the centre. Drizzle a little olive oil over them, sprinkle lightly with salt and pour the water over the beetroot. Fold over the edges of the foil to enclose the beetroot completely. Bake for 2–3 hours or until they can be easily pierced with a small sharp knife. Carefully unwrap the foil and when the beetroot is cool enough to handle slip off the skins and either slice or cut into wedges. (Do not rinse the beetroot.)

 STELLA'S HINT:

♦ *When trimming the beetroot, cut off the green tops, leaving stems of 2.5cm (1in) attached. Do not pierce the skin and leave the root intact as this prevents the maroon colour from bleeding.*

fragrant herb and bulgur salad

salata de bulgur

A variety of rustic bulgur salads are popular in the east Mediterranean. My family enjoys this earthy salad laden with fragrant herbs, juicy diced tomatoes, scooped up with crunchy Cos lettuce leaves at barbecues. Add this to your favourite foods for summer entertaining.

½ cup fine grain bulgur (cracked wheat), rinsed and drained

1 cup boiling water

3 tbsp extra-virgin olive oil

¼ cup fresh lemon juice

¼ tsp ground cumin

½ tsp sea salt

1 tsp Turkish red pepper flakes

½ cup finely chopped spring onions (scallions), trimmed with white part and some of the light green part

2 cups diced (6mm/¼in) ripe, firm tomatoes

1½ cups finely chopped flat-leaf parsley (use leaves and tender stems)

½ cup finely chopped fresh mint leaves

For serving:
tender Cos (Romaine) lettuce leaves

PLACE the bulgur in a wide bowl and pour in the boiling water. Give it a quick stir. Allow to soak, uncovered, for 30 minutes or until the grain is tender. Drain in a fine mesh sieve and squeeze out any excess liquid. Add the oil, lemon juice, cumin, salt and red pepper flakes and use a fork to fluff up the bulgur. Add the spring onions, tomatoes and chopped fresh herbs. Toss well, taste and adjust the seasoning. Serve immediately with tender lettuce leaves to scoop up this delicious salad.

 STELLA'S HINT:

♦ *Chop the mint just before serving to preserve the flavour and prevent the leaves from darkening.*

El haragan I el selozo, nunka no tienen repozo

(Lit: The lazy and the envious ones never have peace)

garlic and potato dip
ajada

Inspired by the Greek skordalia *this garlic dip is blended with both bread and potatoes, tart with fresh lemon juice and fruity extra-virgin olive oil. This addictive dip is a hit served with crudités, fried fish (p95), roasted beetroot (p42) or alongside crispy vegetable fritters (p119). I like to keep some on hand as it stores well in the fridge, in an airtight container, for 5 days, retaining its robust flavours.*

1 medium potato, unpeeled
6 garlic cloves
1 tsp sea salt
3 × 2.5cm (1in) thick slices of white
    bread, crusts removed
5 tbsp water
⅓ cup extra-virgin olive oil
3 tbsp fresh lemon juice

PUT the potato in a pan with cold salted water to cover by 5cm (2in) and bring to a boil over a medium-high heat. Reduce the heat and simmer for 25 minutes or until the potato is very tender when pierced with a knife. Drain and when cool enough to handle peel off the skin and put through a ricer. Set aside.

PULSE the garlic and salt in a food processor until smooth. Use a silicone spatula to scrape down the sides of the bowl a few times.

IN a bowl, soak the bread in the water and squeeze to remove most of the moisture. Transfer to the food processor and pulse to combine evenly with the garlic and salt. With the motor running, drizzle in the oil in a slow, steady stream and process until the mixture thickens.

SCRAPE the mixture into a medium-sized bowl and fold in the potato and lemon juice. (Do not use a food processor for this, as the potato will become gummy.) You should have a smooth and thick dip. Cover and refrigerate for at least 1 hour before serving.

 STELLA'S HINTS:
- *I like to use the brand Wonder bread in the U.S.*
- *If the mixture becomes too stiff, stir in 1–2 tbsp hot water.*
- *For best flavour make sure that you have the freshest crunchy garlic for this recipe.*

 TWISTS ON TRADITION:
- *For a crunchy bite, add ½ cup roughly ground blanched almonds to the dip.*
- *Adding ¼ cup of capers, preferably salt-packed, rinsed and drained, will give a tart dimension to the dip. As capers are salty, add salt sparingly.*

Ken se kema en la tshorba ashupla en el yogourt

(Lit: Whoever gets burnt with hot soup blows on yoghurt)

Once bitten, twice shy

cod roe dip
taramosalata

This delicate, creamy salmon-pink spread is irresistible scooped up with warm wedges of pita bread, served with drinks. It can be kept chilled in an airtight container for a few days, on stand-by, ready to serve as a tasty snack.

8 slices white bread, crusts removed
1 cup milk
¾ cup good-quality smoked cod's roe
¼ cup olive oil and ½ cup vegetable oil, mixed
2–3 tbsp water, as needed
1–2 tbsp fresh lemon juice

For the garnish:
a few black olives

IN a large bowl, soak the bread in the milk and squeeze to remove most of the moisture. Combine the bread and half the roe with an electric stand mixer fitted with a whisk attachment, and beat until the roe is broken down and blended with the bread. With the motor running, slowly drizzle in the mixed oils and water alternately, until the mixture becomes emulsified and creamy. Fold in the remaining cod's roe. Gradually add the lemon juice and taste for tartness to suit your palate. Transfer into a small serving bowl and garnish with olives. Cover with plastic wrap and refrigerate for 1 hour to make the dip firm.

 STELLA'S HINTS:

- *I like to use the brand Wonder bread in the U.S.*
- *A food processor can be used by pulsing on and off until smooth. However, it does not give as light a consistency as using an electric mixer.*
- *If the mixture is too thick, add a little water.*
- *Smoked cod's roe can be found in Greek speciality stores. I like the Krinos brand.*

yoghurt, garlic, cucumber and herb dip
'tzatziki' in Greece and 'cacik' in Turkey

Fresh tasting, thick, creamy yoghurt and cucumber dip, redolent with garlic and fresh herbs, makes a refreshing complement to the meze table, served with crusty bread. Irresistible spooned over vegetable fritters (p114, 115, 119).

1 small young cucumber
1 tbsp finely chopped fresh dill or mint
1 tbsp extra-virgin olive oil
450g (1lb) natural thick Greek yoghurt
2 garlic cloves, finely grated
1 tsp white wine vinegar
1 tsp sea salt

For the garnish:
a drizzle of extra-virgin olive oil
sprigs of fresh dill or mint

COARSELY grate the cucumber and place in a colander. Sprinkle with salt and toss to combine. Set aside to drain for 10 minutes. Rinse and pile the cucumber into a clean tea towel and squeeze to remove excess liquid.

PLACE the cucumber, dill or mint and oil into a bowl and mix to combine with the yoghurt. Stir in the garlic and vinegar. Cover and chill for at least 30 minutes or until required.

STIR in the salt just before serving. Transfer to a small serving bowl. Drizzle with olive oil and garnish with a few sprigs of fresh dill or mint. This dip is best eaten the day it is made.

 STELLA'S HINT:

- *Choose a thin-skinned, young, crisp Lebanese cucumber, leaving the skin intact or ½ English cucumber, peeled, halved lengthways, seeds scraped out and grated.*

Greek country salad
salata a la horiatiki

This salad is packed with juicy sun-drenched tomatoes, sweet red onion and crunchy cucumber (olives and feta are mandatory). Other ingredients depends on one's preference and availability of fresh pickings. I love choosing colourful heirloom tomatoes in New York and serve this salad as a starter or with grills and roasts.

1kg (2¼lb) vine-ripe or heirloom tomatoes
1 cup sliced radishes
1 medium red onion, cut in half lengthways
   and sliced paper-thin
2 crisp young cucumbers, peeled and sliced
   thickly on the diagonal
½ cup roughly chopped flat-leaf parsley
   (use leaves and tender stems)
1 cup brined or oil-cured black olives, pitted
120g (4oz) feta cheese
1 tsp dried Greek oregano

For the dressing:
3 tbsp extra-virgin olive oil
1 tbsp red wine vinegar
½ tsp sea salt
a pinch freshly ground black pepper

CUT the tomatoes into quarters, then cut each quarter lengthways and drain in a colander.

PLACE the radishes, onion, cucumbers, parsley and olives into a large, wide salad bowl. Just before serving stir in the tomatoes.

WHISK the dressing ingredients together in a small bowl. Taste and adjust the seasoning. Pour over the salad and toss well.

BREAK the feta cheese into large chunks and scatter over the salad with the oregano. Serve with crusty bread to dunk in the dressing!

 STELLA'S HINT:
♦ *Mixed colourful heirloom tomatoes make a wonderful touch and are usually found at selected greengrocers or markets. Small Persian or Lebanese cucumbers are best for this salad.*

 TWIST ON TRADITION:
♦ ***Add to the salad:*** *1 iceberg lettuce, thinly sliced; ½ cup roughly chopped fresh dill; 10 whole caper berries; 6 bottled or canned anchovy fillets; 1 fennel bulb, trimmed and thinly sliced crossways.*

green spring salad
salata de lechuga

Whatever fresh greens are in season are combined for a leafy salad – using both the mild and bitter leaves, coated with a fresh tasting lemon dressing. Lettuce was one of the giveaways of secretly practicing Jews as lettuce salads were an important part of their food at the time of the trials of the 1492 Spanish Inquisition. This green salad is a perfect palate cleanser served with braised one-pan meals and a rice pilaf.

a handful of young rocket (arugula) leaves
1 large Cos (Romaine) lettuce, outer leaves
   discarded
1 red endive (red chicory), leaves separated
²/₃ cup spring onions (scallions)
2 tbsp each of roughly chopped flat-leaf
   parsley and fresh dill

For the dressing:
¼ cup fresh lemon juice and 1 tbsp cold water
1 tsp Dijon mustard
1 garlic clove, finely grated
½ tsp sea salt and freshly ground black pepper
1 tsp honey and ½ cup extra-virgin olive oil

WASH the greens well in cold water and dry in batches in a salad spinner. Wrap in paper towels. Stack lettuce leaves together and, using a sharp knife, slice in ribbons crossways, 5mm (¼in) thick.

PLACE the leaves, spring onions, parsley and dill in a large salad bowl. Chill.

WHISK the lemon juice, water, mustard, garlic, salt, a grinding of pepper and honey, in a small bowl. Drizzle in the oil, whisking constantly. Taste and adjust the seasoning. Just before serving pour over the salad and toss gently.

 TWIST ON TRADITION:
♦ *Add a handful of purslane leaves; 1 fennel bulb, trimmed and thinly sliced lengthways; 4 Belgian endives, cut crossways; and a radicchio, finely sliced with a handful of toasted pine nuts scattered over the salad.*

pickles

salamura

Sephardic pickles are very similar to those of varied cuisines in the east Mediterranean. Vegetables used should be picked young and fresh in order to retain their flavour and crunch. They are brined with vinegar, water and salt to preserve a crisp texture and are often flavoured with garlic, celery and bell peppers.
If you like a fiery bite, add 1 or 2 dried red chillies to the brine. I vividly recall these jewel-like pickles giving a gorgeous splash of colour displayed on my mother's kitchen counter.

 STELLA'S HINTS:

- You will need wide-mouthed pickling jars with tight-fitting lids.
- **To sterilise the jars:** Bring a large pan of water to a boil. Submerge the jar, ring and lid and boil for 10 minutes. Do this immediately before you are ready to fill the jar with pickles to have it as sterile as possible.
- When taking out pickles from the jar, be sure to use a clean utensil and reseal tightly.
- Use kosher or additive-free coarse sea salt to avoid cloudiness.
- If possible use filtered or spring water.
- Allow to mature in a cool dark place for 5–6 days before eating.
- Vegetable pickles will keep for up to 2 weeks, if unopened, either refrigerated or stored in a cool dark place.

baby beetroot pickle
salamura di panjar

Ruby-red or golden yellow baby beetroot, boiled and pickled in sugared vinegar brine with sliced onion is served at regular meals, meze, and at the festivals of Sukkot, Passover and the New Year.

2–3 bunches red or golden yellow baby
    beetroot (beets) – about 1kg (2¼lb)*
2 large onions, halved and thinly sliced
    lengthways

For the brine:
1 cup red wine vinegar
1 cup water
1–2 tbsp sugar
1 dried bay leaf
1 tsp kosher or coarse salt

You will need:
a 1.4lt (3pt) pickling jar

RINSE the beetroot well under cold running water to remove any grit. Place the beetroot in a large pan, cover with cold water and bring to a boil. Cook for 1 hour, until just tender or it can be easily pierced with a small sharp knife.

WHILE the beets are cooking, combine the pickling ingredients in a stainless steel small pan and boil for 2 minutes over a high heat.

DRAIN the beetroot and cool briefly in iced water. Slip off the skins and either slice or cut into wedges and place the beetroot and onion slices in the jar. Immediately pour over the pickling brine. Leave to cool, cover and refrigerate.

 STELLA'S HINT:
- **When trimming the beetroot, cut off the green tops, leaving stems of 2.5cm (1in) attached. Do not pierce the skin and leave the root intact as this prevents the maroon colour from bleeding.*

black olives in brine
azetúnas pretas en salamura

3 cups black or kalamata olives

For the brine:
2 cups water
1 cup red wine vinegar
½ cup vegetable oil

You will need:
a 1.4lt (3pt) pickling jar

RINSE the olives in cold water. Soak for 30 minutes in hot water. Drain. Pour the olives into a wide-mouth sterilised pickling jar. Combine the brine ingredients, fill the jar and seal.

vine leaves in brine
ojas de parra en salamura

100 young vine leaves (grape leaves)

For the brine:
1 heaped tbsp kosher or coarse salt
3 cups cold water

You will need:
a 1.4lt (3pt) pickling jar

WASH the leaves and trim the stalks, leaving about 1.25cm (½in) near the stem end. Place the leaves flat with the stalk ends together and roll in bundles of 10. Pack tightly into the pickling jar.

DISSOLVE the salt in the water and cover the leaves with brine. Seal the jar and refrigerate. The leaves should be ready in 5–6 days.

Alternatively: Rinse the leaves in boiling water and drain. When cool, cover in plastic wrap, then in foil. Freeze until required for making stuffed vine leaves.

home-cured green cracked olives
azetúnas tzakistes

If you can find freshly picked green olives, I thoroughly recommend you try this recipe. Living in Zimbabwe, my dedicated mother would ask her brother Jacques to select the best ones, when they were in season, and have them air-freighted from Cape Town. These olives are cured in a water and salt solution to leach most of the bitterness, then steeped in brine and flavoured with aromatics. As in ancient times, olives are a mainstay at mealtime. I even serve them with sesame biscuits or sweet bread rolls for tea or coffee, often with a wedge of kashkaval or feta cheese.

450g (1lb) green olives, freshly picked
   and unbruised

For soaking:
4 cups water
1 cup kosher or coarse salt

For the brine:
3 cups water
1 cup fresh lemon juice
½ cup vegetable oil
1 heaped tbsp kosher or coarse salt

For pickling:
1 green bell pepper, halved
1 lemon, quartered
2–3 dried red chillies
3 garlic cloves
a few sprigs of fresh thyme
strips of lemon zest

You will need:
a 1.2lt (2½pt) pickling jar

RINSE the olives with water and slit down one side, or crack with a heavy stone.

SOAK the olives in a large glass or pottery container with sufficient water to cover. Sprinkle with salt and place a plate with a weight on top of the olives to ensure they are completely submerged. Soak for 7–8 days, changing the water daily until most of the bitterness is leached out from the olives. When the olives are no longer too bitter and the taste is as desired, drain the salt water and rinse with fresh water.

Make the brine: Combine the brine ingredients.

PUT the olives into the jar together with the pickling ingredients. Pour the brine over the olives, seal and refrigerate.

 STELLA'S HINT:
- *Fresh olives are usually available at Farmer's Markets or at speciality food stores, when in season.*

pickled cucumbers
pepino en salamura (trushi)

For the brine:
3 cups water
½ cup white wine vinegar
1 heaped tbsp kosher or coarse salt

1.75kg (3½lb) firm, small, equal-sized
   baby cucumbers
3 garlic cloves, halved
4 sprigs fresh dill
4 fresh vine (grape) leaves (optional)
1 thick slice stale white bread

You will need:
a 1.2lt (2½pt) pickling jar

Make the brine: Combine the water, vinegar and salt in a bowl.

CUT the ends off the cucumbers and place them vertically close together in the jar. Add the garlic and dill and a few vine leaves (if using). Completely submerge with enough brine, leaving a space of about 2.5cm (1in) between the pickles and the top of the jar. Top with the slice of bread (this should prevent any mould from forming). Seal the jar and shake well.

WHEN ready to use remove the bread with tongs. Taste and add more salt if necessary.

pickled aubergine parcels

berendjena reynada en salamura

These unusual and appetizing pickles my mother makes consist of baby aubergines stuffed with a celery, chilli and garlic filling and wrapped in tender celery stalks.

1kg (2¼lb) fresh baby aubergines
  (eggplants) – 8–9cm (3–3½in) long

For the stuffing:
4 tender celery stalks, very finely chopped
6 garlic cloves, finely grated
2 heaped tsp salt
1 tsp dried chilli flakes

For wrapping:
a few tender inner celery stalks
1 red bell pepper

For the brine:
4 cups water
2 cups red wine vinegar
1 tbsp kosher or coarse salt

You will need: a 1.4lt (3pt) pickling jar

WASH and trim the stalk end of the aubergines.

PLACE the aubergines in a pan and cover with water. Bring to a boil. Reduce the heat and simmer, uncovered, for 10 minutes or until just tender. Drain and immediately immerse in cold water. Then drain again. Carefully cut a slit lengthways down the centre of each aubergine but not right through, leaving the ends intact to form a pocket for stuffing. When cool, squeeze the aubergines gently to get rid of excess water.

Make the stuffing: Combine the chopped celery, garlic, salt and chilli flakes in a small bowl. Carefully stuff 1 tsp of the stuffing into the pocket of the aubergine. Press the two halves back together. Press in any protruding stuffing. Repeat with the remaining aubergines.

CUT the celery stalks lengthways into thin ribbons and blanch briefly in boiling water. Cut the bell pepper into 4cm (1½in) strips. Place a piece of bell pepper over the stuffing and wrap the celery around the aubergine parcels, securing them tightly with a knot.

Make the brine: Combine the water, vinegar and salt in a bowl.

PACK the stuffed aubergines tightly into the jar. Pour the brine over the aubergines. Seal the jar and refrigerate. When matured, in about 5 days, cut into chunks with a serrated knife and serve.

pickled cabbage

kol en salamura

1 large firm green cabbage
2 celery stalks, cut into chunks
4 garlic cloves
2 green bell peppers, halved
3 red dried chillies (optional)

For the brine:
6 cups water
2 cups white wine vinegar
½ cup kosher or coarse salt

You will need: a 2.4lt (5pt) pickling jar

CUT the cabbage into eight wedges and place in a jar with the remaining ingredients. Pour in enough brine to ensure the vegetables are covered. If necessary increase the brine in the same proportions.

 TWIST ON TRADITION:
◆ *Substitute the cabbage with 1kg (2¼lb) small green tomatoes, stemmed, rinsed and halved or 1 large cauliflower, cut into florets, or firm green bell peppers, quartered and seeds discarded.*

pickled turnips

shalgan en salamura

These crisp white turnips are stained bright pink with beetroot, giving them a colourful hue.

For the brine:
3 cups water
1 cup white wine vinegar
3 tbsp kosher or coarse salt
1 tbsp caster (superfine) sugar

1kg (2¼lb) small, firm turnips, peeled
  and quartered
few celery leaves
1 beetroot, peeled and sliced

Make the brine: Combine the water, vinegar, salt and sugar in a bowl.

PACK the turnips into pickling jars with the beetroot pieces and celery leaves amongst them. Pour the brine over the turnips, filling the jar to the top. If necessary increase the brine in the same proportions. Seal the jars tightly.

potato, egg, olives and fresh herb salad
salata di patata kon huevos

This tasty citrusy-flavoured potato salad, redolent with fragrant herbs and tossed with black olives, capers and quartered hard-boiled eggs, makes a fabulous accompaniment to grills or roasts.

1kg (2¼lb) baby potatoes, scrubbed

2 tsp salt

2 hard-boiled eggs, quartered

1 small red onion, thinly sliced
    lengthways

1 cup caper berries, drained or 1 tsp
    capers, preferably salt-packed, and
    rinsed

½ cup brined or oil-cured black olives,
    pitted

½ cup roughly chopped flat-leaf parsley
    (use leaves and tender stems)

¼ cup roughly chopped fresh dill

For the dressing:

½ cup extra-virgin olive oil

½ cup fresh lemon juice or white wine
    vinegar

½ tsp sugar

1 tsp Dijon mustard

sea salt

a pinch freshly ground black pepper

PUT the unpeeled potatoes in a large pan and cover them with water. Add the salt and bring to a boil over a medium-high heat. Reduce the heat and simmer until knife tender, 20–25 minutes. Drain the potatoes and peel when cool enough to handle (or leave the skins on if you prefer) and cut them in half. Transfer to a salad bowl.

WHISK all the dressing ingredients together in a small bowl.

POUR the dressing over the potatoes while they are still warm. Add the eggs, onion, capers, olives and herbs, and toss through gently until the potatoes are evenly coated with the dressing. Cover with plastic wrap and let stand for about an hour to absorb the flavours. Taste for salt. Serve at room temperature.

 STELLA'S HINT:

- *The salad can be kept overnight in the fridge. Return to room temperature before serving. Near serving time, drizzle a little extra-virgin olive oil over the salad if the potatoes have soaked up too much dressing. Taste and adjust the seasoning.*

La aluenga mata mas muncha djente ke la espada
(Lit: The tongue kills more people than the sword)

Negative speech and gossip is more harmful than any weapon

roasted pepper salad
pimintones asados

Plump, succulent, roasted bell peppers doused in a vinaigrette are topped with anchovies, capers and crunchy pine nuts. Easy to make, this colourful salad partners grilled foods perfectly.

2 large red and 2 large yellow bell
    peppers

For the dressing:
3 tbsp extra-virgin olive oil
1 tbsp red wine vinegar
1 tsp sea salt
½ tsp sugar

For the garnish:
2 tbsp capers, rinsed in hot water and
    drained
1 tbsp pine nuts, toasted (p287)
4 anchovies in oil, cut into pieces

PREHEAT the grill/broiler.

LAY the peppers on a foil-lined baking tray and place under the grill. Keep turning the peppers until the skin is blistered and evenly charred on all sides and the flesh is soft.

Alternatively: For a smoky flavour, use a gas flame from a stovetop burner. With tongs or a long fork, hold the pepper in the flame and char the peppers, turning, until the skin is thoroughly blackened and blistered and the peppers have softened.

TRANSFER the peppers to a bowl and cover with plastic wrap for 5 minutes to steam. When cool enough to handle, slit the still hot peppers in half, lengthways. Using a paring knife, carefully scrape off the blackened skin. To retain the flavour avoid using water to peel the peppers. As you peel collect and reserve any of the flavourful juice. Remove the seeds, ribs and stems. Slice the peppers into wide pieces and layer them in a shallow dish.

WHISK all the dressing ingredients together with the reserved juices in a small bowl. Taste and adjust the seasoning. Pour over the peppers and toss well. Cover and refrigerate for a day to absorb the flavours. Return to room temperature before serving.

SCATTER over the capers and toasted pine nuts along with the anchovies. Serve with chunks of fresh pita bread to soak up the delicious combination of flavours. The peppers keep well in a sealed container for up to 1 week.

TWISTS ON TRADITION:
- *The peel of ½ preserved lemon, rinsed and diced into small pieces can be added as part of the garnish. Preserved lemon peel can be purchased at Middle Eastern stores.*
- *For a quick and easy cheat salad you can use store-bought flame-roasted peppers from a jar, packed in brine or olive oil. Make sure they are a good quality. Simply drain and toss with the dressing, garnish and serve.*

La pera alavada sale guzanada
(Lit: The most prized pear is sometimes worm-eaten)

Do not simply rely on appearances

rustic country salad
fattoush

This colourful Lebanese-inspired salad combines fresh salad pickings scattered with toasted pita bread and jewel-like pomegranate seeds, which gives an added crunch. It is flavoured with a lemon dressing and sumac, providing a delicious tartness. Fattoush is a versatile salad perfect for a lazy summer outdoor lunch or at an elegant dinner party.

1 medium-sized pita bread
1 tbsp ground sumac
2 tbsp extra-virgin olive oil
1 Cos (Romaine) lettuce, outer leaves
    discarded
1 pomegranate
1 cup finely sliced spring onions (scallions),
    including light green parts
1 cup thinly sliced radishes
2 crisp, young cucumbers, diced into 6mm
    (¼in) pieces
1 cup roughly chopped purslane (optional)
handful roughly chopped rocket (arugula),
    stems removed
3 tbsp roughly chopped flat-leaf parsley
    (use leaves and tender stems)
2 tbsp roughly chopped mint leaves
1½ cups firm, ripe, diced tomatoes
    (6mm/¼in)

For the dressing:
3 tbsp extra-virgin olive oil
1 tbsp fresh lemon juice or to taste
1 garlic clove, finely grated
½ tsp sea salt
a pinch freshly ground black pepper

CUT around the seam of the pita and flatten it out. Toast the pita briefly under a grill until crisp and golden. Break into small bite-sized pieces, sprinkle with sumac and toss in olive oil, coating the bread on all sides.

SHRED the lettuce into 1.25cm (½in) ribbons.

HALVE the pomegranate and scoop out the seeds, removing coarse attached pieces of membrane. Combine the lettuce, spring onions, radishes, cucumbers, purslane (if using), rocket, parsley and mint in a large salad bowl.

ADD the tomatoes, pita bread and pomegranate seeds to the salad 10 minutes before serving.

WHISK all the dressing ingredients together in a small bowl. Taste and adjust the seasoning. Pour over the salad, toss well and serve.

 STELLA'S HINTS:
- *Sumac is a ground spice made from burgundy-red berries, giving a refreshing citrus flavour. Available at Middle Eastern delicatessens.*
- *The small Persian or Lebanese cucumbers are best.*

La ija kon la madre komo la unya en la karne

(Lit: The daughter with the mother like the nail in the flesh)

Profound relationship between mother and daughter

salt preserved fish
palamida / lakerda

Raw salted fish, cured in olive oil, makes an unusual and delicious meze. Since it's not easy to find in Zimbabwe, when I do find fresh bonito at the fishmonger I salt several portions and store in the freezer.

1kg (2¼lb) of 10cm (4in) fresh bonito
  steaks, with bone intact
kosher or coarse salt

For serving:
fresh lemon or orange juice to taste
olive oil

RINSE the fish and pat dry with paper towels. Place the fish steaks in a glass container, salting each layer generously. Place a plate on top of the fish and weigh it down with a can of food or a large stone. Leave the fish to salt in the fridge for 4–5 days. Drain the water that accumulates daily and add more salt each time before returning to the fridge. On the fourth or fifth day pack each portion individually in foil and freeze. When ready to use, slice the fish thinly with a sharp knife whilst still frozen. Remove the bone. When thawed, pour over lemon or orange juice and drizzle with olive oil.

Bottarga: Another prized, dried salted fish eaten in our home is the roe of tuna or grey mullet. The roe eggs are left intact in their membrane and salted, dried and then coated in wax. Remove the wax and thinly slice. Served with crusty bread and a squeeze of lemon juice, it is considered a delicacy that most Mediterranean Sephardim treasure.

marinated anchovies
anchúgas en salamura

Marinated anchovies – which couldn't be simpler to prepare – make an exquisite meze, served with crusty bread. Once prepared they keep for 2–3 weeks in the fridge.

450g (1lb) salt-packed anchovies

For the marinade:
1 tsp red wine vinegar
1 tsp fresh lemon juice
4 garlic cloves, thinly sliced
1 cup finely chopped flat-leaf parsley
  (use leaves and tender stems)
1 red chilli, finely sliced
extra-virgin olive oil

WASH the anchovies thoroughly under running water to rid them of salt and pat dry with paper towels. Lay the anchovies in a shallow glass dish. Thoroughly combine all the marinade ingredients, except the olive oil, and pour over the anchovies. Cover with olive oil and refrigerate. It's ready!

 STELLA'S HINT:

◆ *The salted anchovies often come packed in a 1kg (2¼lb) can. Remove what you need and transfer remaining contents to a glass container with a tight-fitting lid.*

El peshkado fieyde de la kavesa

(Lit: A fish stinks from the head)

The rot starts at the top

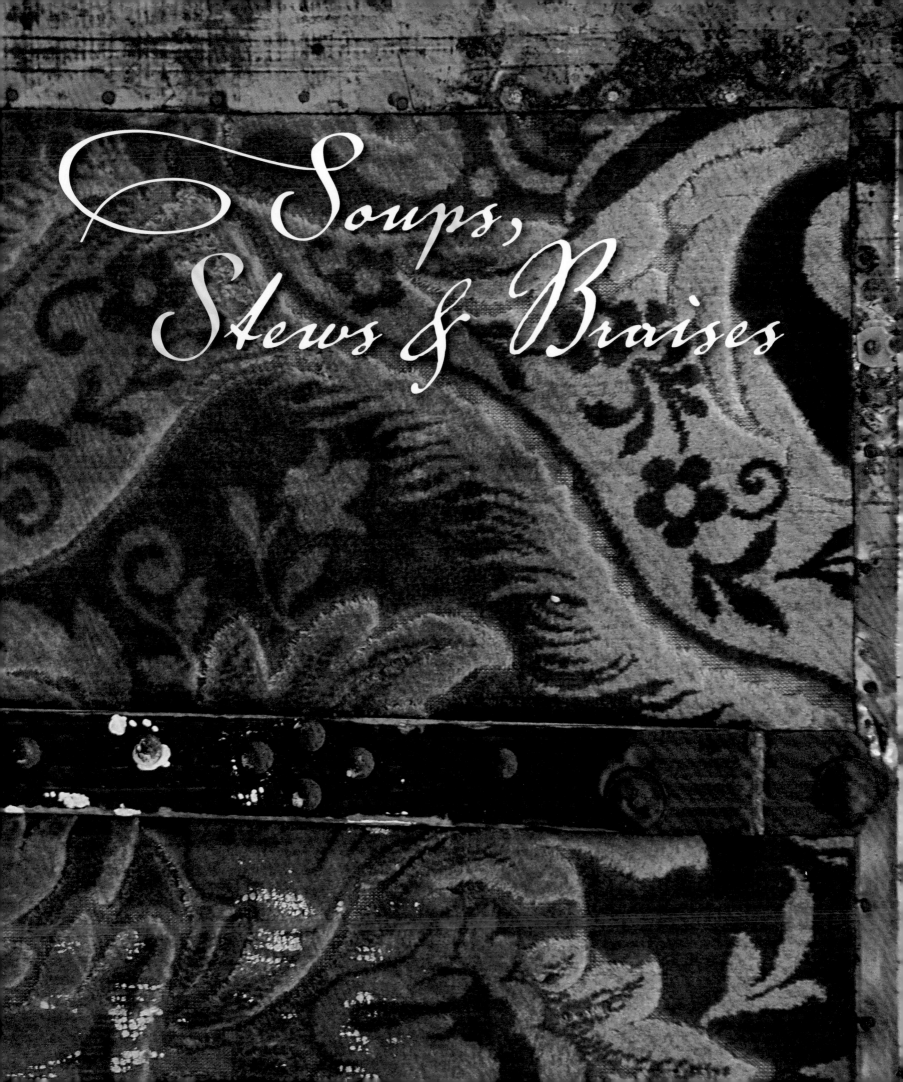

Soups, Stews & Braises

Soups, Stews & Braises

Soups, stews and one-pan meals – which are collectively referred to as *komidas* – are the cornerstone of Sephardic every day food. Historically stews and braises allowed Sephardim to make use of typically inexpensive but tougher cuts of meat which were combined together with seasonal vegetables, beans or chickpeas, to make complete, balanced and economical meals. While these one-pan meals slow-cook for an hour or two, making the meat succulent and meltingly tender, they are also simple to prepare and can be put together in stages – perfect for multi-taskers. Another advantage is they are best prepared a day ahead, allowing the flavours to deepen and develop. My daughter, for instance, often makes a *komida* on a Sunday making Monday dinner much easier. Stews should be accompanied with a rice pilaf that you feel complements the dish. These recipes should serve 4–6 people.

Komidas epitomise rustic satisfying mid-week dining with friends and at family gatherings. This more relaxed manner of cooking is not exacting and reflects the traditional Sephardic way of life – taking pleasure and time to cook and savour the food.

Braises and stews have a few common steps and hints:

- A good braising pan is required (p290).
- To cook the meat, pat the meat or poultry dry with paper towels. The oil must be hot enough for the meat to caramelise when browning. Brown the meat in batches as if you pack too much meat or poultry in the pan the temperature of the oil drops preventing the meat from browning well. When the meat no longer sticks to the pan turn the pieces over with tongs. Transfer the browned batches of meat to a heatproof dish.
- After the onions and garlic are softened in the oil return the meat or poultry and any collected juices to the pan.
- Choose a light chicken or vegetable stock that is low in salt and either in cubes or a paste.

For me, *komidas* represent comfort food – not only nourishing the body but also nurturing the soul. The aromas alone, drifting through the house, are calming and grounding, evoking memories of home and feelings of belonging. *Komidas* are love in a pot.

El ke tiene amigos es riko

(Lit: The one who has friends is wealthy)

chicken and rice soup
supa de gayina

The heart-warming aroma of chicken and rice soup simmering on the stovetop lifts the spirits. As early as the 13th century, Maimonides, the Judeo-Spanish philosopher and physician, advocated the healing properties of this broth. This flavourful, nutritious broth thickened with rice is warming and soothing – a must for kids when they're under the weather.

a 1.5kg (3¼lb) whole free-range chicken
1 large onion, peeled and quartered
6 spring onions (scallions), roughly chopped
1 fennel bulb, quartered
6 tender celery stalks, with leaves, roughly chopped
3 leeks, washed, trimmed and roughly chopped
3 medium carrots, cut into chunks
2 garlic cloves, halved
2 dried bay leaves
3 whole black peppercorns
6 flat-leaf parsley stalks and leaves
4 sprigs fresh thyme
4 dill stalks and leaves
sea salt
½ cup basmati rice
1 tbsp fresh lemon juice

For the garnish:
2 tbsp finely chopped dill

RINSE the chicken. Place in a large, heavy-based pan with enough cold water to cover. Bring to a boil. Reduce the heat to medium and cook for 30 minutes. Skim off any scum that rises to the surface.

ADD the vegetables, garlic, bay leaves, peppercorns and half the parsley, thyme and dill. Cover, reduce the heat and simmer for 40 minutes or until the chicken is cooked through. Towards the end of cooking add the salt. Taste and adjust the seasoning. Set aside to cool a little.

STRAIN the stock into a clean pan. Discard the vegetables, peppercorns and fresh herbs. Remove the skin from the chicken and discard. Debone and shred the chicken into strands with a fork.

RETURN the shredded chicken to the broth. Add the rice and the remaining fresh herbs to the soup and boil for a further 10–15 minutes or until the rice is tender. Add the lemon juice. Taste and adjust the seasoning. Ladle the piping hot soup into bowls, garnish with dill and serve.

 STELLA'S HINTS:
* *If you will not be serving the soup immediately, cook the rice separately and add before serving. The soup, without the rice, can be kept in the fridge for 2 days. Cover the cooled soup and place in the fridge as soon as possible to prevent souring. Skim off the fat that accumulates on top if desired.*
* *To freeze: The soup can be frozen without the rice being added.*

TWIST ON TRADITION:
* *Chicken soup with egg and lemon sauce (avogolemono/sopa de huevos i limon): In a medium bowl, lightly beat 2 eggs. Gradually whisk in ¼ cup fresh lemon juice. While continuing to whisk, gradually ladle 1 cup of hot soup into the egg mixture. As a last step, slowly pour the egg mixture back into the simmering soup, stirring constantly. Immediately remove the pan from the heat and serve at once. Do not boil.*

La para es redondo, por esto no keda en un lugar

(Lit: Coins are round so they never stay in the same place)

Everyone has their chance

Moroccan chickpea and lentil soup

harira

Harira is a hearty soup made from lamb, pulses and vegetables, aromatic with exotic spices and fresh herbs. This ancient recipe is believed to have originated from the Berbers, who used it during the cold winters of the Atlas Mountains in North Africa. This soup has been widely adopted by the Sephardim in Morocco.
On chilly nights, I serve it as a main course in rustic earthenware bowls with crusty bread and a red chilli paste, harissa (p158), for those who enjoy a fiery bite to their soup.

1 cup dried chickpeas, soaked overnight
   in twice their volume of cold water,
   drained and rinsed
1 cup brown lentils
3 tbsp olive oil
3 medium red onions, finely chopped
3 tender celery stalks with leaves, finely
   chopped
500g (1lb 2oz) boneless lean lamb, finely
   cubed
2 marrowbones, washed
7 cups hot chicken stock or water
2 cups canned chopped tomatoes
1 tbsp tomato paste
sea salt and freshly ground black pepper
¼ tsp saffron threads
¼ tsp ground ginger
1 tsp turmeric
¼ tsp ground cinnamon
1 cup roughly chopped flat-leaf parsley
   (use leaves and tender stems)
1 cup roughly chopped fresh coriander
   (cilantro)
¼ cup small pasta (orzo)
2 tbsp fresh lemon juice

For serving:
2 lemons, cut into wedges
a small bowl of plump Medjool dates

Cook the chickpeas: Put the chickpeas in a large pan with enough cold water to cover by 2.5cm (1in). Bring to a boil. Cover, reduce the heat and simmer for 1½–2 hours or until the chickpeas are tender but not mushy. The cooking time depends on the quality and age of the chickpeas. Check frequently as they cook, adding more hot water as necessary. When the chickpeas are tender, drain in a colander.

PLACE the lentils on a tray and pick through them, discarding any shrivelled lentils or bits of grit. Rinse and soak for 1 hour in warm water. Drain and set aside.

HEAT the oil in a large, heavy-based pan over a medium-high heat. Add the onions and celery and cook for about 3 minutes, stirring occasionally, until softened. Add the lamb and marrowbones. Cover with the hot stock or water. Bring to a boil. Cover, reduce the heat and simmer for about 1¼ hours or until the lamb is very tender.

ADD the cooked chickpeas, lentils, tomatoes, tomato paste, salt, pepper, saffron, ginger, turmeric, cinnamon and ½ cup each parsley and coriander. Cook for a further 45 minutes or until the lentils are tender. The soup will thicken as the pulses release their starch. Stir in the pasta, cover and simmer for 20 minutes. Discard the marrowbones. Five minutes before serving, add the lemon juice and remaining parsley and coriander. Stir well. *Harira* should not be too thick – add hot water if necessary. Taste and adjust the seasoning.

SERVE piping hot with lemon wedges and dates.

 STELLA'S HINT:
- *400g (14oz) canned chickpeas, rinsed and drained, can be substituted for the dried chickpeas. Add canned chickpeas at the same time as the pasta.*

 TWIST ON TRADITION:
- *For a vegetarian version, omit the lamb and marrowbones and use vegetable stock.*

Todo si va aser koulay i liviano

(Lit: Everything will become easy and light)

It will all work out fine in the end

cauliflower florets stew
karnabit frita

Crisp, fried cauliflower florets are simmered on a bed of chopped vegetables, creating an irresistible vegetarian entrée. The florets can be dipped in matza meal in place of flour to make this dish suitable for Passover. I like to serve it with grilled foods and a Spanish fried rice pilaf (p169).

1 large cauliflower – about 1kg (2¼lb)

For coating:
½ cup plain (all-purpose) flour
3 eggs, lightly beaten

For shallow-frying:
vegetable or grape-seed oil

For the vegetable base:
¼ cup olive oil
1 large onion, roughly chopped
reserved cauliflower leaves and stalks
1 large carrot, diced
1 large potato, diced
4 spring onions (scallions), sliced
1 cup peeled, seeded and chopped ripe
   tomatoes or canned chopped tomatoes
½ tsp sugar
sea salt and finely ground white pepper
1 cup hot chicken or vegetable stock
2 tbsp fresh lemon juice
½ cup hot water

Prepare the cauliflower: Cut off the green leaves and stalks from the cauliflower, slice them and reserve for the vegetable base. Break the cauliflower florets off the stem and clean thoroughly by soaking in cold salted water for 15 minutes. Rinse well and drain. Steam the florets over boiling salted water for about 7 minutes or until just tender. Be careful not to overcook the cauliflower. Refresh with cold water and drain in a colander.

HEAT 2.5cm (1in) oil in a deep frying pan over a medium-high heat. Coat the florets with flour and then with beaten egg, a few at a time. Cook the florets in batches until they are crisp and golden on all sides. Lift out with a slotted spoon and drain on paper towels.

Make the vegetable base: Heat the oil in a large, shallow, oven-to-table casserole over a medium heat. Toss in the onion, reserved cauliflower leaves and stalks, carrot, potato and spring onions and cook for 5 minutes, stirring. Stir in the tomatoes, sugar, salt and pepper and pour in the hot stock. Bring to a boil. Cover, reduce the heat and simmer for 30 minutes, stirring occasionally. Pour in the lemon juice and hot water. Taste and adjust the seasoning.

ARRANGE the cauliflower on top of the vegetable base. Cover and continue to simmer for 10 minutes.

To serve: Preheat the oven to 180°C (350°F). Bake, uncovered, for 15 minutes or until the cauliflower floret tops are crisp and golden brown. Serve piping hot.

Si mi esuegra era mi madre,
otro gayo mi cantara!

(Lit: If my mother-in-law was my mother, another rooster would be singing!)

If my mother-in-law was my mother, that would be another story!

celery and cannellini beans stewed with veal

apio kon avas

Tender celery stalks are stewed with veal and cannellini beans, making this a hearty midweek meal when accompanied by a white rice pilaf (p168).

For the beans:

1 cup (200g/7oz) dried cannellini or haricot (navy) beans, soaked overnight in twice their volume of cold water, drained and rinsed

1 small onion, peeled

2 dried bay leaves

3 sage leaves

1 tsp sea salt

For the veal:

4 tbsp olive oil

1kg (2¼lb) veal shanks, cut at 5cm (2in) intervals, or shoulder of veal, cut into 3.5cm (1½in) chunks

1 large onion, finely chopped

2 cups hot chicken stock

500g (1lb 2oz) tender celery stalks, trimmed and sliced into 1.75cm (¾in) pieces

1 cup peeled, seeded and chopped ripe tomatoes or canned chopped tomatoes

½ tsp sugar

sea salt and finely ground white pepper

1 tbsp fresh lemon juice

Cook the beans: Put the beans in a large pan with enough cold water to cover by 2.5cm (1in). Add the onion, bay and sage leaves. Bring to a boil. Cover, reduce the heat and simmer for 1½ hours or until the beans are tender, but not mushy. The cooking time depends on the quality and age of the beans. Check frequently as they cook, adding more water as necessary. Add the salt in the last 10 minutes of cooking. When the beans are tender drain in a colander and discard the onion and herbs.

HEAT the oil in a large, heavy-based pan over a medium-high heat. Add the veal and cook in batches until lightly browned. Remove the veal with tongs and keep in a heatproof dish.

ADD the onion to the pan and cook for 3 minutes, stirring frequently, until softened. Return the browned meat to the pan and pour in the hot stock. Bring to a boil. Cover, reduce the heat and simmer for 1½–2 hours or until the veal is very tender. Add hot water as necessary.

STIR in the beans, celery, tomatoes, sugar and salt and pepper. Bring to a boil. Cover, reduce the heat and simmer for 30 minutes. Add the lemon juice 10 minutes before serving. Taste and adjust the seasoning. Serve hot.

 TWISTS ON TRADITION:

♦ *2 × 400g (14oz) cans cannellini beans, drained and rinsed, can be substituted for the dried beans. Add the canned beans to the stew 10 minutes before serving.*

♦ *Chicken legs and thighs may be used instead of veal, with 2 potatoes, peeled and quartered, instead of beans.*

Para kada oya, ay su tapedera

(Lit: Each pot has its lid)

For everything there is a solution

chicken and aubergine stew

yuvetch de gayina kon berendjenas

This is an easy-to-prepare and delicious stew, especially for aubergine lovers. Chicken is simmered on the stovetop with tomatoes and lightly sautéed thick, succulent aubergine slices. It goes very well with Spanish fried rice pilaf (p169) and a cabbage salad (p42).

3–4 firm aubergines (eggplants) –
  about 1.5kg (3¼lb)
1 tbsp kosher or coarse salt
1 tsp fresh lemon juice
1kg (2¼lb) free-range chicken thighs
3 tbsp olive oil
1 large onion, finely sliced lengthways
2 garlic cloves, finely grated
1 cup canned chopped tomatoes
½ tsp sugar
½ tsp dried Greek oregano
¼ tsp Turkish red pepper flakes
1 tsp sea salt
½ tsp finely ground white pepper
1 tbsp fresh lemon juice
1 cup hot water

For shallow-frying:
vegetable or grape-seed oil

For the garnish:
2 tbsp roughly chopped flat-leaf parsley
  (use leaves and tender stems)

Prepare the aubergines: Cut the stems off the aubergines. Using a very sharp knife, peel 1.25cm (½in) strips at intervals along the length of the aubergines, leaving it striped with some peel. Cut each aubergine into slices about 1.25cm (½in) thick. In a large bowl, dissolve the coarse salt in 2.4lt (5pt) water and add the 1 tsp lemon juice. Immerse the aubergine slices and place a weighted plate on top to keep them submerged. Soak for 45 minutes. Rinse under cold running water and drain. Pat dry with paper towels.

RINSE the chicken portions, trim off the excess fat and pat dry.

HEAT the oil in a large, shallow, heavy-based pan over a medium-high heat. Add the chicken pieces and cook in batches until golden brown. Remove the chicken with tongs and keep in a heatproof dish.

ADD the onion to the pan and cook for 5 minutes, stirring frequently, until softened. Add the garlic and cook for 1 minute. Return the chicken to the pan, skin side up. Add the tomatoes, sugar, oregano, red pepper flakes and season with salt and pepper. Pour in enough hot water to come midway up the chicken. Bring to a boil. Cover and simmer for 30 minutes or until the chicken is tender.

Cook the aubergines: Heat enough oil for shallow frying in a large frying pan over a medium-high heat. Cook the aubergine slices in the sizzling oil, in batches, for 3–5 minutes on each side, until fork tender and lightly golden. Replenish the oil as necessary. Lift out with a slotted spoon and drain on paper towels. Cover with paper towels and press lightly to soak up excess oil.

ARRANGE the aubergine slices in the pan between the browned chicken portions. Add 1 tbsp lemon juice with 1 cup hot water and ladle the cooking liquid over the aubergines to absorb the flavour. Cover and simmer for 20 minutes, shaking the pan occasionally. Taste and adjust the seasoning.

GARNISH with parsley and serve hot.

 STELLA'S HINT:
♦ *400g (14oz) canned chickpeas, drained and rinsed, can be added and heated through 10 minutes before serving.*

Uno mano lava la otra i dos lavan la kara

(Lit: One hand washes the other and together they wash the face)

Emphasises the importance of teamwork

chicken stewed in tomatoes with potatoes
kapama di gayina kon tomat i patata

A rustic one-pan chicken and potato stew is a simple light meal, traditionally eaten on the evening meal preceding the Fast, accompanied with vermicelli.

1kg (2¼lb) free-range chicken thighs
¼ cup olive oil
1 large onion, finely chopped
1 cup peeled, seeded and chopped ripe
    tomatoes or canned chopped tomatoes
2 tender celery stalks with leaves, cut
    into chunks
½ tsp sugar
1 tsp sea salt
2 cups hot chicken stock or water
3 medium potatoes, quartered
2 tbsp fresh lemon juice

For the garnish:
1 tbsp roughly chopped flat-leaf parsley
    (use leaves and tender stems)

RINSE the chicken portions, trim off the excess fat and pat dry.

HEAT the oil in a large, shallow, heavy-based pan over a medium-high heat. Add the chicken pieces and cook in batches until golden brown. Remove the chicken with tongs and keep in a heatproof dish.

ADD the onion to the pan and cook for 3 minutes, stirring frequently, until softened. Return the chicken to the pan, skin side up. Stir in the tomatoes, celery, sugar and salt. Pour in enough hot stock or water to come midway up the chicken. Bring to a boil. Cover, reduce the heat and simmer for about 30 minutes or until the chicken is tender. Add the potatoes and cook for a further 20 minutes. Add the lemon juice, taste and adjust the seasoning. Sprinkle with parsley and serve immediately with vermicelli.

 TWIST ON TRADITION:

◆ *My mother prepares this variation: Add 1 can (400g/14oz) artichoke hearts, rinsed and drained or a 275g (10oz) packet frozen artichoke hearts, thawed, along with the potatoes and 1 tbsp of roughly chopped fresh dill.*

Ritar avas meter garvansos!

(Lit: Replace beans with chickpeas!)

This phrase was muttered frequently by the poor who could only sustain

themselves with these nutritious, affordable legumes

ox tongue simmered in a tomato sauce
aluenga kon salsa de tomat

Sliced tongue braised in an aromatic garlic and tomato sauce has always drawn my family to the table. I recommend you try this easy, prepare-ahead meal, partnered with a white rice pilaf (p168) and a green salad (p48). You may have to order the salted tongue from your friendly butcher.

1 salted ox or veal tongue –
   about 1kg (2¼lb)
1 carrot, halved
1 onion, halved
2 tender celery stalks with leaves,
   cut into chunks
4–5 whole black peppercorns
2 dried bay leaves
3 tbsp plain (all-purpose) flour
2 tbsp white wine vinegar

For the tomato sauce:
3 tbsp olive oil
2–3 garlic cloves, finely sliced
1 stalk celery with leaves, roughly sliced
2 cups canned chopped tomatoes, puréed
1 tsp sugar
finely ground white pepper
1 cup hot water
1 tsp fresh lemon juice
a pinch sea salt

RINSE the tongue well under cold water. Put in a large pan, cover with cold water and bring to a boil. After 5 minutes tip into a colander and drain. Rinse the pan and put the carrot, onion, celery, peppercorns and bay leaves into the pan together with the tongue and cover with cold water. Bring to a boil.

MIX the flour with the vinegar into a paste, add to the pan and whisk in. It will make the water appear cloudy but it will help to keep the colour and bring out the flavour of the tongue. Cover, reduce the heat and simmer for 2½ hours or until the tongue is tender. Add more hot water as necessary. When cooked remove the tongue from the pan. Cut away the gristle and fat at the thick end and peel the skin off the tongue while still warm. Return to the pan with the cooking liquid and refrigerate until ready to use.

Make the tomato sauce: Heat the oil in a large, shallow, heavy-based pan over a medium-high heat. Add the garlic and celery and cook for 1 minute. Stir in the tomatoes, sugar and pepper.

REMOVE the tongue from the fridge and discard the cooking liquid. Cut into 7.5mm (1/3in) slices and arrange on top of the tomato sauce. Pour in 1 cup of hot water and simmer for about 30 minutes for the tongue to absorb the sauce. Add the lemon juice. Taste and add a little salt if needed. If the sauce thickens too much add a little hot water. Serve hot.

Esto esta fuego sin flama

(Lit: This is a fire without a flame)

This is too expensive

courgettes braised with veal

kuartikos di kalavasa kon karne

A delicate tasting veal and courgette stew, fragrant with fresh herbs and partnered with a vermicelli rice pilaf (p177), brings a comforting, mellow flavour to a wintry table.

1.5kg (3¼lb) young courgettes (zucchini), peeled
3 tbsp olive oil
1kg (2¼lb) veal shank, cut into 5cm (2in) intervals, or shoulder of veal, cut into 3.5cm (1½in) chunks
1 large onion, finely chopped
1 garlic clove, thinly sliced
1½ cups hot chicken stock
1 cup canned chopped tomatoes
½ tsp sugar
sea salt and freshly ground black pepper
2 tbsp roughly chopped fresh dill

For the garnish:
2 tbsp each roughly chopped flat-leaf parsley (use leaves and tender stems) and fresh dill

CUT the courgettes on the diagonal into 3–4 pieces. Place in a colander and lightly coat with salt on all sides. Set the colander over a bowl and leave to stand for 1 hour to drain excess moisture. Rinse, drain and set aside.

HEAT the oil in a large, shallow, heavy-based pan over a medium-high heat. Add the veal and cook in batches until lightly browned. Remove the veal with tongs and keep in a heatproof dish.

ADD the onion and cook for 3 minutes, stirring frequently, until softened. Add the garlic and cook for 1 minute. Return the browned meat to the pan and pour in the hot stock. Bring to a boil. Cover, reduce the heat and simmer for 1½–2 hours or until the veal is very tender. Add water as necessary.

STIR in the tomatoes, sugar, salt and pepper and simmer for a further 30 minutes.

ADD the courgettes and dill to the stew and pour in a little hot water as necessary. Cover and simmer for 15 minutes or until the courgettes are tender, shaking the pan occasionally to prevent the stew from sticking. Do not stir.

SERVE hot, sprinkled with chopped parsley and dill.

 TWISTS ON TRADITION:
- *For a vegetarian dish, omit the meat and use vegetable stock.*
- *1.25kg (2¾lb) canned artichoke hearts, drained and rinsed, can be substituted for the courgettes.*

Mas deguele la palavra del amigo, ke la kuchiyada del enemigo

(Lit: A harsh word from a friend is more painful than a stab from an enemy)

fresh broad bean and veal stew

avas freska kon karne

Fresh, bright green broad beans are used to make this delicious and unusual stew. Always choose small, young and tender pods. Broad beans are often eaten over Passover. In fact, historians claim that they were a staple food amongst Israelites while enslaved in Egypt.

1kg (2¼lb) fresh, tender broad (fava) beans, unshelled

2 tbsp fresh lemon juice

3 tbsp olive oil

1kg (2¼lb) veal shank, cut at 5cm (2in) intervals, or shoulder of veal, cut into 3.5cm (1½in) chunks

1 large onion, finely chopped

2 cups hot chicken stock or water

sea salt and freshly ground black pepper

For the garnish:

1 tbsp roughly chopped fresh dill

SHELL the beans and cut the pods into 5cm (2in) lengths. Soak the beans and pods in water with 1 tbsp of the lemon juice to prevent discolouration.

HEAT the oil in a large, shallow, heavy-based pan over a medium-high heat. Add the veal and cook in batches until lightly browned. Remove the veal with tongs and keep in a heatproof dish.

ADD the onion to the pan and cook for 3 minutes, stirring frequently, until softened. Return the browned meat to the pan. Pour in the hot stock or water and season with salt and pepper. Bring to a boil. Cover, reduce the heat and simmer for 1½–2 hours or until the veal is very tender. Add more hot water as necessary.

ADD the beans and pod pieces. Cover and simmer until the beans are very tender, stirring occasionally. Add more hot water as necessary. Five minutes before serving add the remaining lemon juice and taste and adjust the seasoning.

GARNISH with chopped dill and serve with a white rice pilaf (p168) and a Turkish diced salad (p32).

 STELLA'S HINT:

♦ *2 × 275g (10oz) packets of frozen broad beans can be substituted for the fresh beans.*

Mira kon ojos quatros

(Lit: Look with four eyes)

Be alert, look with eyes at the back of your head

green beans braised with carrots and potatoes
fasùlya kon safanorya i patata

Fasùlya is a simple vegetarian dish made with young green beans. The secret with this stew is to let the beans, carrots and potatoes braise slowly in the fresh tomato and olive oil sauce, allowing the beans to become very tender. Spanish fried rice pilaf (p169) complements this stew best. In Turkey, fasùlya is served as part of a meze at room temperature, with crusty bread.

3 tbsp olive oil

1 large onion, roughly chopped

2 garlic cloves, sliced

2 cups peeled, seeded and finely chopped ripe tomatoes or canned chopped tomatoes

1 tender celery stalk with leaves, cut into chunks

sea salt and freshly ground black pepper

1 tsp sugar

1 tbsp fresh lemon juice

500g (1lb 2oz) stringless green (runner) beans, trimmed and cut into 3 pieces

2 medium carrots, cut into chunks

1 medium potato, quartered

1 cup hot vegetable stock or water

2 tbsp roughly chopped fresh dill

For the garnish:

1 tbsp roughly chopped fresh dill

1 tbsp extra-virgin olive oil

HEAT the oil in a large, shallow, heavy-based pan over a medium-high heat. Add the onion and cook for 4 minutes, stirring frequently, until softened. Add the garlic and cook for 1 minute.

ADD the remaining ingredients. Bring to a boil. Cover, reduce the heat and simmer for 40–50 minutes until the beans are very tender and the sauce is reduced. Stir occasionally to ensure the beans are well immersed in the sauce. Add more hot water as necessary. Taste and adjust the seasoning.

SERVE warm sprinkled with dill and drizzled with olive oil.

 STELLA'S HINTS:

* *Tender green string beans or the delicate yellow wax beans, known as* hanum fasùlya, *can be used instead of runner beans.*
* *This stew can be refrigerated for up to 2 days if covered. You'll notice the flavours meld and improve.*

 TWISTS ON TRADITION:

* *Fasùlya kon grano: Beans were commonly cooked with rice in Rhodes, making a substantial one-pan meal. When the vegetables are cooked make a hollow in the centre of the stew with a wooden spoon. Add ½ cup of washed, soaked and drained long-grain rice. Pour in 1 cup hot water with ½ tsp salt. Cover and simmer for 15 minutes or until the rice is cooked and has absorbed the liquid.*
* *This stew can be made with 1kg (2¼lb) free-range chicken thighs. Heat the oil in a large, shallow, heavy-based pan. Add the chicken and cook in batches until lightly browned. Lift out the chicken and keep in a heatproof dish. Add the onion to the pan and cook for 3 minutes, stirring frequently, until softened. Add the garlic and cook for 1 minute. Return the chicken to the pan. Pour in enough hot stock or water to come midway up the chicken. Bring to a boil. Cover, reduce the heat and simmer for 30 minutes or until the chicken is tender. Add more hot water as needed. Add the tomatoes, vegetables and seasoning and continue as above.*

Ovras son amores

(Lit: Deeds express love)

Actions speak louder than words

leeks and cannellini beans braised with veal
prasa kon avikas i karne

The combination of leeks, cannellini beans and tender veal in this stew is exquisite; each time I make it I marvel at how the raw leeks slowly transform into delicate, buttery morsels. Accompanied with Spanish fried rice pilaf (p169) and a green spring salad (p48) this stew is another wonderful meal, but it can also be cooked without veal to create a vegetable side dish for grilled foods.

For the beans:

1 cup (200g/7oz) dried cannellini or haricot (navy) beans, soaked overnight in twice their volume of cold water, drained and rinsed

1 small onion, peeled

1 bay leaf

3 sage leaves

1 tsp salt

500g (1lb 2oz) young slender leeks, not more than 2.5cm (1in) in diameter

¼ cup olive oil

500g (1lb 2oz) veal shank, cut into 5cm (2in) intervals, or shoulder of veal, cut into 3.5cm (1½in) chunks

1 large onion, finely chopped

2 cups hot chicken stock or water

1½ cups canned chopped tomatoes

½ tsp sugar

salt and freshly ground black pepper

1 tbsp fresh lemon juice

For the garnish:

2 tbsp each roughly chopped flat-leaf parsley (use leaves and tender stems) and fresh dill

1 lemon, cut into wedges

Cook the beans: Put the beans in a large pan with enough cold water to cover by 2.5cm (1in). Add the onion and bay and sage leaves. Bring to a boil. Cover, reduce the heat and simmer for 1½ hours or until the beans are tender but not mushy. The cooking time depends on the quality and age of the beans. Check frequently as they cook, adding more hot water as necessary. Add the salt in the last 10 minutes of cooking. When the beans are tender, drain in a colander and discard the onion and herbs.

PEEL away the tough outer leaves of the leeks and trim off the root and dark green tops. Slit through the tops of the leeks lengthways with a sharp knife. Fan them out to separate the leaves and rinse out any dirt under cold running water. Drain well. Cut the leeks crossways, into 2.5cm (1in) chunks.

HEAT the oil in a large, heavy-based pan over a medium-high heat. Add the veal and cook in batches until lightly browned. Remove the veal with tongs and keep in a heatproof dish.

ADD the chopped onion to the pan and cook for 3 minutes, stirring frequently, until softened. Return the browned meat to the pan and pour in the hot stock or water. Bring to a boil. Cover, reduce the heat and simmer for 1½–2 hours or until the veal is very tender.

STIR in the leeks, beans, tomatoes, sugar and season with salt and pepper. Bring to a boil. Cover, reduce the heat and simmer for 20 minutes or until the leeks are tender and the sauce has reduced. Add more hot water as necessary. Add the lemon juice 5 minutes before serving. Taste and adjust the seasoning.

GARNISH with parsley and dill. Serve hot with lemon wedges.

STELLA'S HINT:

♦ *2 × 400g (14oz) cans cannellini or haricot beans, drained and rinsed, may be substituted for the dried beans.*

Avas sin arroz es komo boda sin tanyedores

(Lit: Beans without rice are like a wedding without musicians)

Swiss chard and chickpeas braised with veal
pazi kon garvansos

If you like the idea of eating Swiss chard but aren't sure how to prepare it then this is the stew for you. In this dish the contrasting flavours of golden chickpeas and dark green, velvety Swiss chard are combined in a rich tomato sauce. Both Swiss chard and chickpeas were introduced to Spain by the Moors during the Middle Ages and are now common in Sephardic, Greek and Turkish cuisine. It is often a New Year dish, the round chickpeas symbolic of fullness and hope and the Swiss chard representing newness. With this stew I prefer a white rice pilaf (p168), garlic and potato dip (p46) and, of course, lemon wedges.

For the chickpeas:

1 cup (250g/9oz) dried chickpeas, soaked overnight in twice their volume of cold water, drained and rinsed

1 small onion, peeled

2 dried bay leaves

3 fresh sage leaves

5 tbsp olive oil

1kg (2¼lb) veal shanks, cut at 5cm (2in) intervals, or shoulder of veal, cut into 3.5cm (1½in) chunks

2 large onions, finely chopped

1¾ cups hot chicken stock

1 cup canned chopped tomatoes

1 tsp sugar

sea salt and freshly ground black pepper

1kg (2¼lb) fresh Swiss chard (silver beet), rinsed, dried, stalks removed and shredded into 1.25cm (½in) ribbons

1 tbsp roughly chopped fresh dill

2 tbsp fresh lemon juice

Cook the chickpeas: Put the chickpeas in a large pan with enough cold water to cover by 2.5cm (1in). Add the onion, bay and sage leaves. Bring to a boil. Cover, reduce the heat and simmer for 1½–2 hours or until the chickpeas are tender but not mushy. Check frequently as they cook, adding more hot water as necessary. When the chickpeas are tender, drain and discard the onion and herbs.

HEAT 4 tbsp oil in a large, shallow, heavy-based pan over a medium-high heat. Add the veal and cook in batches until lightly browned. Remove the veal with tongs and keep in a heatproof dish.

ADD the chopped onions to the pan and cook for 3 minutes, stirring frequently, until softened. Return the browned meat to the pan and pour in the hot stock. Bring to a boil. Cover, reduce the heat and simmer for 1½–2 hours or until the veal is very tender. Add hot water as necessary.

STIR in the chickpeas, tomatoes, sugar and season with salt and pepper. Simmer, uncovered, for 10 minutes until the tomatoes have reduced. Pile about two-thirds of the Swiss chard on top of the chickpeas and tomatoes. Cover and continue cooking for about 6 minutes or until the Swiss chard has cooked down. Stir in the remaining Swiss chard with 1 tbsp olive oil, dill and lemon juice. Cover and simmer for 10 minutes. Shake the pan to distribute the ingredients evenly but do not stir. Taste and adjust the seasoning. Serve hot.

 STELLA'S HINT:

♦ *2 × 400g (14oz) cans chickpeas, rinsed and drained, may be substituted for the dried chickpeas. Add at the same time as the second batch of Swiss chard.*

 TWIST ON TRADITION:

♦ *Swiss chard with rice (pazi kon grano): Swiss chard and chickpeas cooked with rice becomes a complete one-pan meal. When all the Swiss chard and chickpeas are cooked, make a hollow in the centre of the stew with a wooden spoon. Add ½ cup of washed, soaked and drained long-grain rice. Pour in 1 cup hot water with ½ tsp salt. Cover and simmer for 15 minutes or until the rice is cooked and has absorbed the liquid.*

Al ijo komo lo kriates, al marido komo lo ambezates

(Lit: The son becomes the way you brought him up, the husband the way you trained him)

No need to elaborate on this one!

lentils braised with veal

lentejas kon karne

The Italians occupied Rhodes and the Dodecanese islands for 50 years towards the end of the 19th century. One of their influences on Sephardic cuisine was the cooking of legumes and pasta together – this dish being a perfect example. In Rhodes, lentil dishes were traditionally served on Thursday night as the evening meal before the Sabbath and also eaten the evening before the Fast of Tisha b'Av. I like to serve the lentils with a white rice pilaf (p168) and a green spring salad (p48).

For the lentils:

1 cup (250g/9oz) dried brown or green lentils, picked over and rinsed under cold running water in a fine mesh sieve

1 small onion, peeled

2 dried bay leaves

1 carrot, cut into chunks

1 celery stalk, cut into chunks

¼ cup olive oil

500g (1lb 2oz) veal shin, cut at 5cm (2in) intervals, or shoulder of veal, cut into 3.5cm (1½in) chunks

1 large onion, finely chopped

1–2 garlic cloves, grated

a few fresh sage leaves

1 celery stalk with leaves, cut into chunks

2 cups hot water

1 cup canned chopped tomatoes

½ tsp sugar

sea salt and finely ground white pepper

½ cup crushed vermicelli

For the garnish:

1 tbsp extra-virgin olive oil

1 lemon, cut into wedges

Cook the lentils: Put the lentils in a large pan with enough cold water to cover by 2.5cm (1in). Add the onion, bay leaves, carrot and celery. Bring to a boil. Cover, reduce the heat and simmer for 25 minutes or until the lentils are just tender but not mushy. Check frequently as they cook, adding more boiling water as necessary. Drain in a sieve over a jug, reserving 1 cup of the cooking liquid. Discard the onion, bay leaves, carrot and celery.

HEAT the oil in a large, heavy-based pan over a medium-high heat. Add the veal and cook in batches until lightly browned. Remove the veal with tongs and keep in a heatproof dish.

ADD the chopped onion to the pan and cook for 3 minutes, stirring frequently, until softened. Add the garlic, sage and celery and cook for 1 minute. Return the browned meat to the pan and pour in the hot water. Bring to a boil. Cover, reduce the heat and simmer for 1½–2 hours or until the veal is very tender.

TIP the lentils into the pan with the reserved cooking liquid and add the tomatoes and sugar. Add enough water to make sure the lentils are covered. Season with salt and pepper. Bring to a boil. Cover, reduce the heat and simmer for 15 minutes or until the lentils are soft to the bite. Stir gently from time to time to prevent the lentils from sticking to the base of the pan.

INCREASE the heat to high. Once the stew comes to a boil add the vermicelli. Cover, reduce the heat and simmer for 8 minutes or until the pasta is tender but not mushy, adding more hot water as necessary. Taste and adjust the seasoning. Serve hot in a deep plate with a drizzle of extra-virgin olive oil and lemon wedges.

 STELLA'S HINT:

♦ *The stew tends to thicken so if you prepare it ahead of time, add a little hot water before reheating.*

Tiene la kara de Tisha b'Av

(Lit: Someone who has a long face)

The Fast of Tisha b'Av is to commemorate the destruction of the two temples in Jerusalem. However, to describe someone with a happy countenance would be 'kara de Pourim', relating to the joyous festival of Purim

okra stewed with fresh tomatoes
bamia kon tomat

In this stew, fresh young okra or 'ladies fingers' are slow-cooked in a fresh tomato, onion and garlic sauce. The sticky texture of okra gives the stew its succulent and velvety body. The vegetable originated in Africa and is very popular in Zimbabwe where it is called dererere *and is eaten with* sadza, *which is a local corn-based staple food (it looks a bit like polenta). I offer the okra served hot as a side dish with grilled foods or as a vegetarian entrée with chickpea rice pilaf (p169). It is also delicious prepared a day in advance and refrigerated where the flavours have time to develop further. You can also serve it at room temperature as part of a meze.*

750g (1½lb) fresh small okra, about 6cm (2½in) long
½ cup white wine vinegar
1 tbsp kosher or coarse salt
2 tbsp vegetable oil
3 tbsp olive oil
2 large onions, cut in half lengthways, thinly sliced
½ tsp Turkish red pepper flakes
2 garlic cloves, finely sliced
1 cup peeled, seeded and chopped ripe tomatoes or canned chopped tomatoes
1 tbsp tomato paste
1 tsp sugar
1 tsp sea salt
½ tsp finely ground white pepper
2 tbsp fresh lemon juice
1 cup hot water or as needed

Prepare the okra: Trim the tips and pare the conical caps of the okra pods with a paring knife, being careful not to expose the seeds and sticky juices inside. This technique takes practice. Place the okra in a flat glass dish and sprinkle with the vinegar and salt. Let the okra soak for 30 minutes. Rinse well, drain and pat dry with paper towels. Heat the vegetable oil in a large frying pan over a medium-high heat. Stir-fry the okra in batches until they are bright green and crisp. Remove with a slotted spoon and place in a colander, allowing the sticky residue to drain. This helps retain the okra's shape and enhances the flavour.

Cook the okra: Heat the olive oil in a medium, shallow pan over a high heat. Add the onions and red pepper flakes and cook for 5 minutes, stirring occasionally, until softened. Add the garlic and cook for 1 minute. Stir in the tomatoes, tomato paste and sugar and season with salt and pepper. Cook for 5 minutes. Scatter the okra over the tomato sauce, add the lemon juice and pour in enough hot water to just cover the okra. Bring to a boil. Cover, reduce the heat and simmer for 40 minutes or until the okra is tender. Gently shake the pan from side to side occasionally to distribute the tomato sauce. Do not stir so as not to break the okra. Add more hot water as necessary. Taste and adjust the seasoning. Serve hot.

 STELLA'S HINTS:

♦ *If fresh okra is hard to find, speciality food stores usually have tiny Egyptian frozen okra. Allow the tomato sauce to thicken for 15 minutes. Then add the okra with the lemon juice and simmer for about 10 minutes or until the okra is tender.*

♦ *Alternatively canned okra is easy to use. Allow the tomato sauce to thicken for 15 minutes. Drain and rinse the canned okra and add with the lemon juice and simmer for 5 minutes.*

 TWIST ON TRADITION:

♦ *The Rhodeslis would bake the cooked okra in a preheated oven at 180°C (350°F) for 20 minutes to lightly brown the okra.*

Ande se arapa el guerko

(Lit: Where the devil shaved)

Someone or something is so far away, or to 'hell and gone'

Ottoman-style braised meat with cannellini beans
karne kon avikas

This nutritious one-pan meal unlocks the wintry flavours of slow-cooked meat and cannellini beans. Popular in Judeo-Spanish households in Rhodes, Salonica, Turkey and the Balkans, it was often served on Friday night for the Sabbath dinner and leftovers kept simmering on a hot plate for the Sabbath lunch. Like many stews, this one improves on the second day. If you prepare ahead, refrigerate overnight but bring back to room temperature before reheating and serving. Add a little hot water, as braised beans tend to thicken as they sit. My son likes this dish especially served with a white rice pilaf (p168), raw sliced red onions, lemon wedges (lots of them!) and a crispy green salad (p48).

For the beans:
2 cups (400g/14oz) dried cannellini or
    haricot (navy) beans, soaked overnight
    in twice their volume of cold water,
    drained and rinsed
1 small onion, peeled
2 dried bay leaves
3 fresh sage leaves
1 tsp sea salt

For the meat:
4 tbsp olive oil
2kg (4½lb) lamb neck with bone, or beef
    short ribs
5 beef marrow bones, washed
1 large onion, finely chopped
1 leek, white part only, halved
    lengthways and then sliced crossways
1 tender celery stalk with leaves, sliced
1 bay leaf
2 sprigs fresh parsley
4 cups hot chicken stock
2 cups peeled, seeded and chopped ripe
    tomatoes or canned chopped tomatoes
½ tsp sugar
2 sprigs fresh thyme
½ tsp Turkish red pepper flakes
freshly ground black pepper
2 tsp sea salt
1 tbsp fresh lemon juice

For serving:
1 tbsp extra-virgin olive oil
2 lemons, cut into wedges
1 large red onion, thickly sliced

Cook the beans: Put the beans in a large pan with enough cold water to cover by 2.5cm (1in). Add the onion, bay and sage leaves. Bring to a boil. Cover, reduce the heat and simmer for 1½ hours or until the beans are tender but not mushy. The cooking time depends on the quality and age of the beans. Check frequently as they cook, adding more hot water as necessary. Add the salt in the last 10 minutes of cooking. When the beans are tender drain in a colander and discard the onion and herbs.

HEAT the oil in a large, heavy-based pan over a medium-high heat. Add the meat and marrow bones and cook in batches until lightly browned. Remove the meat with tongs and keep in a heatproof dish. Add the onion, leek, celery, bay leaf and parsley sprigs. Cook for 8 minutes, stirring occasionally, until softened. Return the browned meat to the pan. Pour in 2 cups hot stock. Bring to a boil. Cover, reduce the heat and simmer for 1½–2 hours or until the meat is very tender. Add hot water as necessary.

STIR in the beans, tomatoes, sugar, thyme sprigs, red pepper flakes and pepper. Pour in the remaining 2 cups hot stock. Bring to a boil. Cover, reduce the heat and simmer for about 30 minutes or until the beans are fully cooked. Add more hot water as necessary. Ten minutes before the end of cooking time add the salt and lemon juice. Taste and adjust the seasoning. Discard the herbs.

SPOON into a deep serving dish and drizzle with olive oil. Serve with lemon wedges and sliced red onion.

 STELLA'S HINT:
- *3 × 400g (14oz) cans cannellini beans, drained and rinsed, can be substituted for the dried beans. Add the beans 10 minutes before serving.*

peas, potato, carrot and chicken stew
biselyas kon patata, safanorya i gayina

This stew is remarkably flavourful, despite such simple ingredients. I recently discovered in Rhodes a wonderful variation to this stew with artichokes, which enhances the overall taste and texture. I encourage you to try it both ways.

1kg (2¼lb) free-range chicken thighs
3 tbsp olive oil
1 small onion, finely chopped
1 cup canned chopped tomatoes
2½ cups hot chicken stock or water
1kg (2¼lb) fresh young peas in pods,
    shelled – about 500g (1lb 2oz) shelled
    peas
1 medium carrot, diced
1 medium potato, diced
2 tbsp roughly chopped fresh dill
1 tsp sugar
1 tsp sea salt

For the garnish:
1 tbsp roughly chopped fresh dill

RINSE the chicken portions, trim off the excess fat and pat dry.

HEAT the oil in a large, shallow, heavy-based pan over a medium-high heat. Add the chicken pieces and cook in batches on all sides until golden brown. Lift out the meat and keep in a heatproof dish.

ADD the onion to the pan and cook for 3 minutes, stirring frequently, until softened. Return the chicken to the pan, skin side up. Stir in the tomatoes. Pour in enough hot stock or water to come midway up the chicken. Bring to a boil. Cover, reduce the heat and simmer for 15 minutes. Add the peas, carrot, potato, dill, sugar and salt. Cover and simmer for a further 15 minutes or until the vegetables are tender and the chicken is cooked. Taste and adjust the seasoning. If the tomato sauce is too watery, increase the heat and boil, uncovered, until slightly reduced.

GARNISH with chopped dill and serve hot with vermicelli rice pilaf (p177).

 STELLA'S HINTS:
- *2 × 275g (10oz) packets of frozen green peas can be substituted for the fresh peas. They will only require cooking for 4–5 minutes.*
- *If using artichokes, simply add 2 cups canned and drained or frozen artichoke hearts, cut in half lengthways, to the vegetables.*

No te araskes ande no te kome

(Lit: Don't scratch if it doesn't itch)

If it ain't broke, don't fix it

fish

fish cakes
keftes de peshkado

As children we loved to tuck into crispy fish keftes *or* frikadelles *as they are called in South Africa, with potato chips (French fries) and a dollop of homemade mayonnaise, which we made pink using a drop of ketchup. Beetroot salad (p42) and garlic and potato dip (p46) are ideal with these* keftes. *This recipe makes enough for 4–6 people. I like to make double the quantity and freeze a batch for an impromptu meal.*

1 tender stalk of celery with some leaves, cut into chunks

½ carrot, cut into chunks

1½ tbsp fresh lemon juice

3 black peppercorns

1 tsp sea salt

a handful of parsley stalks

500g (1lb 2oz) firm fish fillets (a mixture of hake, cod or salmon)

150g (5oz) potatoes, peeled and cut into chunks

a few fresh dill stalks

1 tbsp olive oil

1 egg, lightly beaten

1 tbsp finely chopped spring onions (scallions)

1½ tbsp finely chopped flat-leaf parsley (use leaves and tender stems)

1 tbsp finely chopped fresh dill

½ tsp sea salt

a pinch finely ground white pepper

For coating:
prepare in separate bowls:

½ cup plain (all-purpose) flour

1–2 eggs, beaten

½ cup dried breadcrumbs or matza meal

For frying:
olive oil and 1 tbsp butter

Cook the fish: Put the celery, carrot, lemon juice, peppercorns, salt and parsley stalks in a pan of boiling water. Reduce to a simmer. Add the fish and cook for 15 minutes or until the fish flakes easily when tested with a fork. Drain in a colander and discard the celery, parsley stalks and peppercorns. Retain the carrot and chop finely. Flake the fish with your fingers into small pieces, discarding any bones, and allow to cool.

SIMMER the potatoes with dill stalks in salted water until they are tender when pierced with a knife. Drain and remove the dill stalks. While still hot, mash with a potato masher or for a smoother and fluffier result use a potato ricer. Mix in the olive oil.

GENTLY combine the flaked fish, potato, carrot, egg, spring onions, parsley, dill and salt and pepper in a bowl.

Shape the fish cakes: With your hands, form the mixture into balls about the size of an egg and flatten them slightly into patties. Dredge the fish cakes in flour and tap off the excess. Then dip in the egg and finally coat with breadcrumbs or matza meal. Transfer the fish cakes onto a tray lined with plastic wrap and chill in the fridge until ready to cook.

Cook the fish cakes: Heat 2–3cm (1in) oil in a large frying pan together with the butter over a medium-high heat. Fry the fish cakes, in batches, for 3 minutes on each side, until crisp and golden. Remove with a slotted spoon and drain on a plate lined with paper towels. Serve immediately.

STELLA'S HINTS:

- *I like to use a 4½cm (1¾in) ice cream scoop to form firmly packed, evenly sized fish cakes.*
- **To freeze:** *Open-freeze the crumbed uncooked fish cakes on a plastic wrap-lined tray until completely solid (about 1 hour). Place in layers between baking paper in an airtight container and freeze. For a speedy meal, fry the frozen fish cakes in hot oil and butter until piping hot all the way through.*

Del viejo el konsejo i del riko el remedio

(Lit: Take advice from the elderly but solutions from the wealthy)

grilled fish

peshkado asado

Fish can be very simply barbecued over charcoal or in a stovetop griddle pan. In Rhodes, as elsewhere in the Mediterranean, large fish like bonito are cut into steaks or smaller fish, like snapper and sea bass, are left whole. The grilled fish is drizzled with a lemon dressing and accompanied with a tomato rice pilaf (p172). Steamed greens or a bean salad (p41) will also highlight the flavours of the fish.

1kg (2¼lb) skinned firm fish fillets or 2.5cm (1in) thick steaks (bonito, swordfish, or halibut) or 4 snapper or sea bass (about 450g/1lb each), scaled and gutted
sea salt and freshly ground black pepper
olive oil

For the dressing:
2 tbsp fresh lemon juice
sea salt
¼ cup extra-virgin olive oil
freshly ground black pepper

For serving:
1 tsp dried Greek oregano, crumbled

RINSE the fish and pat dry with paper towels. Season the fish with salt and pepper. If the fish are thick, score diagonal slits on each side of the fish with a small sharp knife to ensure it cooks evenly. Rub the fish with oil on all sides.

Make the dressing: Whisk the lemon juice and salt together in a small bowl and slowly add the oil to emulsify. Add the pepper.

HEAT the barbecue or place the griddle on the stovetop over the highest setting. Brush the grill with oil and grill the fish on both sides, brushing the fish with a little oil, until cooked through. The cooking time will depend on the thickness of the fish. To see if the fish is ready, remove a piece from the heat and gently part the flesh – it should be barely opaque right through. Sprinkle with crumbled oregano and serve immediately with the dressing poured over the fish.

 STELLA'S HINT:
♦ *If grilling whole fish, preferably use a hinged wire grill basket brushed with oil.*

Passado sea i olvidado

(Lit: May it be a thing of the past and forgotten)

fish sauces
salsas de peshkado

Sephardim of the Levant make these popular sauces to serve with fried or grilled fish or vegetable fritters. These tasty sauces are simple to prepare and add a beautiful layer of flavour and texture to any fish dish. You should try all of them at some stage!

egg–lemon sauce
agristada

This thick lemon-flavoured egg-base sauce was widespread in Jewish cuisine in medieval Spain. The citrusy fresh taste of the sauce goes perfectly with cold or warm fried fish prepared with matza cake flour, often served on the Sabbath and over Passover.

3 tbsp olive oil or vegetable oil

3 heaped tbsp plain (all-purpose) flour or matza cake flour

2 cups hot water

3 tbsp fresh lemon juice

1 tsp sea salt

3 eggs, well beaten, in a bowl

 STELLA'S HINT:

♦ *If the sauce becomes lumpy, pass through a fine sieve.*

HEAT the oil in a small, heavy-based pan over a medium-high heat. Add the flour a tablespoon at a time, stirring constantly for 2 minutes with a small balloon whisk until smooth and blended. Reduce to a low heat.

DRIZZLE in the hot water, lemon juice and salt, still whisking constantly, and continue cooking, adjusting the heat as necessary to keep at a gentle simmer. Add the beaten eggs gradually into the hot sauce, stirring constantly with a silicone spatula or a whisk until the consistency of a thick smooth cream. Do not let the sauce boil as the eggs could curdle.

TO prevent a skin from forming as it cools, press a piece of plastic wrap directly against the surface of the sauce or alternatively, as my mother does, heat 1 tbsp oil and pour it over the sauce and gently smooth the oil over the surface. The sauce will thicken as it cools.

To serve: Heat through gently just before serving.

fresh dill, parsley and garlic sauce
salsa a la maneko

3½ heaped tbsp plain (all-purpose) flour

2 cups cold water

3 tbsp olive oil

2–3 garlic cloves, finely grated

3 tbsp fresh lemon juice

1 tsp sea salt

2 tbsp finely chopped flat-leaf parsley (use leaves and tender stems)

1 tbsp finely chopped fresh dill

BLEND the flour and water with a small balloon whisk in a small, heavy-based pan over a medium-high heat. Add the oil, garlic, lemon juice and salt. Stir continuously over a medium-low heat for 8 minutes or until the sauce thickens. Toss in the fresh herbs and serve hot or warm.

tomato sweet-and-sour sauce
salsa de vinagre

3 tbsp olive oil

3–4 garlic cloves, finely grated

1¼ cups canned chopped tomatoes

2 tbsp each of finely chopped tender celery leaves and flat-leaf parsley

1 heaped tbsp plain (all-purpose) flour

½ cup red wine vinegar

1 tsp sea salt and 1½ tbsp honey

1 cup water

HEAT the oil in a small, heavy-based pan over a medium-high heat and cook the garlic until aromatic. Reduce to a low heat, add the tomatoes and celery and simmer.

IN a small bowl, mix the flour, vinegar, salt, honey and water together with a small balloon whisk. Still whisking constantly, stir the flour mixture into the simmering garlic and tomato sauce and cook for 15–20 minutes or until the sauce thickens. Toss in the parsley and remove from the heat. Serve at room temperature.

fried fish
peshkado frito

Seasoned fish fillets are dredged in flour and then dipped in beaten egg, coating the moist fish in a light crisp-textured batter. The art of shallow-frying fish dates back to medieval Spain and spread throughout the Sephardic communities in the east Mediterranean. Fried fish is a favourite of the Iberian Jews, especially on the Sabbath, served with a tomato rice pilaf (p172) or potato chips (French fries). Sephardic Jews from Holland brought this dish to Britain – the iconic 'Fish 'n Chips'.

1kg (2¼lb) skinned firm fish fillets (red snapper, sea bass, cod, flounder or halibut), cut into about 60g (2oz) even pieces
salt and finely ground white pepper

For shallow-frying:
vegetable or grape-seed oil

For dredging:
¾ cup plain (all-purpose) flour and ¼ cup cornflour (cornstarch) or matza meal
2–3 eggs, lightly beaten in a shallow dish

RINSE the fish and pat dry with paper towels. Season the fish with salt and pepper.

HEAT 2.5cm (1in) oil in a large, deep, heavy-based frying pan over a medium-high heat.

DREDGE four pieces of fish lightly in flour and shake off the excess. Slide the fish into the beaten eggs. Using tongs, lift the pieces gently one-by-one and lower the fish carefully into the hot oil. Use a splatter screen if you have one. Fry, without moving the fish, until golden brown on the bottom, about 3 minutes. Carefully turn the fillets over once to cook for a further 2 minutes. The cooking time will depend on the thickness of the fish. Reduce the heat to medium if the oil is getting too hot. While the first batch is frying, flour and coat with egg the next four pieces. To test if the fish is ready, remove a piece from the heat and gently part the flesh – it should be barely opaque right through.

LIFT out the fried fish with a wire skimmer and drain in a heatproof dish lined with paper towels. Keep warm in a 95°C (200°F) oven until all the fish is fried. Serve immediately or at room temperature with one of the delicious fish sauces (p94).

 STELLA'S HINT:
♦ *The fish will absorb less oil and keep its juices sealed in when the oil is at the right temperature – it should be sizzling, but not so hot that the coating quickly burns. Keep an eye on the oil and adjust the heat as needed.*

La roza en su tiempo se avre

(Lit: The rose blooms in its own time)

All things happen in their own good time

fish stewed in a fresh tomato sauce
peshkado abafado (ahilado) kon salsa de tomat

Fish gently cooked in a flavoursome tomato sauce with sliced potatoes, makes a simple, healthful, homely one-pan dish. I like to cook this dish in a colourful, shallow, cast-iron pan and take this pan directly to the table. This subtle-tasting dish makes a light meal, which is often served at the meal preceding the Fast of Tisha b'Av.

1kg (2¼lb) firm fish fillets or steaks
(snapper, sea bass, cod or grouper)
cut into 2.5cm (1in) steaks
salt and finely ground white pepper
3 tbsp olive oil
1 large onion, thinly sliced lengthways
2 garlic cloves, thinly sliced
2 cups peeled, seeded and roughly
chopped ripe tomatoes or canned
chopped tomatoes
½ tsp sugar
5 black peppercorns
1 stalk flat-leaf parsley with leaves
2 dried bay leaves
sea salt
2 medium potatoes, peeled, boiled and
thickly sliced
¼ cup boiling water
½ tbsp fresh lemon juice

For dredging:
¼ cup plain (all-purpose) flour

For the garnish:
1 tbsp roughly chopped flat-leaf parsley
(use leaves and tender stems)

RINSE the fish and pat dry with paper towels. Season with salt and pepper.

HEAT the oil in a shallow, heavy-based pan over a medium-high heat. Add the onion and cook for 5 minutes, stirring frequently, until softened. Add the garlic and cook for 1 minute. Add the tomatoes, sugar, peppercorns, parsley stalk, bay leaves and salt. Simmer, uncovered, stirring occasionally, for 10 minutes or until the sauce thickens slightly. Reserve ½ cup of the sauce and set aside.

LAY the potato slices over the tomato sauce.

DREDGE the fish lightly in flour and shake off the excess. Slip the fish in between the potatoes, add the boiling water and lemon juice and spoon the reserved tomato sauce over the fish. Cover and simmer for 10–12 minutes, depending on the thickness of the fish. The fish should be opaque in the centre but still juicy and flake easily when tested with a fork. Shake the pan occasionally to prevent sticking. Discard the peppercorns, parsley stalk and bay leaves.

SPRINKLE with chopped parsley and serve at once in the pan, accompanied with white rice pilaf (p168) or toasted noodles (p174) and a green spring salad (p48).

 TWISTS ON TRADITION:
* *Scatter 1 cup lightly toasted pine nuts and a handful of halved black pitted olives, such as Kalamata, on top with the chopped parsley.*
* *For a mildly spicy version, add ½ tsp ground cumin (typical of Rhodian cuisine) and a pinch of Turkish red pepper flakes with the tomatoes.*

Bushkar kon kandela

(Lit: To search with a candle)

Not easy to come by

fried marinated fish
peshkado frito a la rozetta

Pan-fried fish fillets, marinated in a lemon, garlic and fresh herb sauce, is an easy dish that can be made hours or even a day ahead. Chill in the fridge to allow the flavours to meld and return to room temperature before serving. I like to prepare this on a Friday, ready to be served for the Saturday Sabbath lunch with a potato salad (p54).

1kg (2¼lb) firm sole or plaice fish
    fillets, skinned and cut into 7.5cm
    (3in) pieces
salt and finely ground white pepper

For shallow-frying:
olive oil

For dredging:
2 tbsp plain (all-purpose) flour

For the marinade:
¼ cup extra-virgin olive oil
3–4 large garlic cloves, crushed
1 tsp sea salt
½ tsp sugar
2 tbsp fresh lemon juice
2 tbsp water
3 tbsp roughly chopped flat-leaf parsley
    (use leaves and tender stems)
1 tbsp roughly chopped fresh dill

RINSE the fish and pat dry with paper towels. Season with salt and pepper.

HEAT 1.25cm (½in) oil in a wide, shallow frying pan over a medium-high heat.

DREDGE the fish lightly in seasoned flour and shake off the excess. When the oil is hot lay the fish carefully into the pan. Fry in batches until golden and crisp on one side, 2–3 minutes, or longer depending on the thickness of the fish. Gently flip with a fish slice and cook on the other side for a further 2 minutes. Remove the fillets from the pan with a wire skimmer and drain on paper towels. Lay the fried fish in a single layer in a large heatproof serving dish.

Make the marinade: When the fish is cooked, pour off the oil and wipe the pan clean. Return the pan to the stove. Heat the olive oil, add the garlic and stir for 1 minute. Stir in the remaining marinade ingredients.

POUR the heated marinade evenly over the fish and leave to cool completely. Cover with plastic wrap and refrigerate for 2–3 hours or overnight. Bring the fish up to room temperature when ready to eat.

 TWIST ON TRADITION:
* *For an alternative marinade: Combine ¼ cup extra-virgin olive oil; 3 large garlic cloves, crushed; 2 tbsp red wine vinegar; ½ cup water; 1 tsp chopped fresh rosemary; 1 tsp sea salt; ½ tsp sugar; and 2 tbsp of the hot oil the fish has been fried in and proceed as above.*

El peshkado esta ayinda en la mar,
tu ya estas frieyendo el'azeite

(*Lit: The fish are still in the water, you are already heating the oil*)

Don't count your chickens before they are hatched

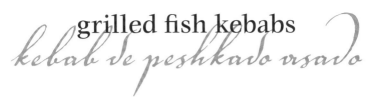

grilled fish kebabs
kebab de peshkado asado

Chunks of marinated fish are speared on skewers and interspersed with bay leaf, tomato and onion to impart a delicate flavour. These grilled or barbecued fish kebabs make a quick, easy and light entrée, and are also ideal for a weekend lunch with a tomato rice pilaf (p172) and Greek country salad (p48).

1kg (2¼lb) thick, firm fish fillets, skinned (sea bass, cod or grouper)

For the marinade:
2 garlic cloves, finely grated
1 tsp sea salt
2 tbsp fresh lemon juice
½ cup extra-virgin olive oil
½ tsp dried Greek oregano

For the vegetables:
24 whole cherry tomatoes
1 large red onion, cut into 2.5cm (1in) chunks
12 fresh bay leaves, torn in half

For basting:
1–2 tbsp olive oil

For the dressing:
2 tbsp fresh lemon juice
3 tbsp extra-virgin olive oil
½ tsp sugar
3 tbsp roughly chopped flat-leaf parsley (use leaves and tender stems) or fresh dill
sea salt to taste

You will need:
12 small metal skewers

RINSE the fish, pat dry with paper towels and cut into 2.5cm (1in) pieces. Arrange the fish chunks in a single layer in a wide, shallow earthenware dish.

Make the marinade: Combine all the ingredients in a small bowl and pour over the fish. Cover and chill in the fridge for 20 minutes.

Prepare the kebabs: When ready to cook, thread the fish chunks onto the skewers, alternating the fish with a cherry tomato, a piece of onion and an occasional bay leaf. Discard the marinade.

HEAT the barbecue or place a griddle on the stovetop over the highest setting. Brush the grill with oil.

BASTE the kebabs generously with olive oil and grill for about 4 minutes on each side until cooked through. Check frequently to avoid overcooking.

COMBINE all the dressing ingredients together in a small bowl. Pour the dressing over the kebabs and serve immediately.

Ijos de mis ijos, dos veses mis ijos

(Lit: Sons of my sons, twice my sons)

Expressing how special grandchildren are

red snapper roasted on a bed of baby potatoes

kapama de peshkado kon tomat, patata i sevoya

During a recent visit to the island of Rhodes, especially for this book, I made this dish at my friend Thanos Stavrianakis' restaurant, The Archipelagos. Thanos' father and mine grew up as best friends in Rhodes and stayed in touch even when my father moved to Zimbabwe. During summer vacations, families met up and the 'kids' got to know each other. Thanos allowed me to use his wonderful kitchen where his sous chef and I roasted a freshly caught whole red snapper over a bed of potatoes, topped with Mediterranean vegetables. I like to serve this impressive fish dish as part of a buffet, or family style with tomato rice pilaf (p172) and a green spring salad (p48).

1.5kg (3¼lb) whole red snapper or striped
    sea bass, cleaned, with head intact
¼ cup olive oil, plus extra for brushing
sea salt and freshly ground black pepper
2 tsp fresh thyme leaves, stripped from
    the stem
6 whole garlic cloves
450g (1lb) new baby potatoes
1 large fennel bulb, trimmed
1 large red onion, thinly sliced
    lengthways
5 ripe plum tomatoes, quartered
1 red bell pepper, cored and cut into strips
1 tbsp tomato paste
1 tsp dried Greek oregano
a handful black olives, pitted (stoned)
1 tbsp capers, rinsed and drained
2 tbsp fresh lemon juice
1 cup dry white wine

For serving:
1 lemon, cut into wedges

PREHEAT the oven to 220°C (425°F). Oil a shallow roasting pan, large enough to lay the fish in whole.

RINSE the fish and pat dry with paper towels. Score diagonal slits on each side of the fish with a small sharp knife to ensure that it cooks evenly. Rub the fish well with oil and sprinkle both inside and outside with salt and pepper. Stuff the cavity with 1 tsp thyme leaves and 3 garlic cloves and refrigerate.

PUT the unpeeled potatoes in a pan of salted water. Bring to a boil, cover and cook over a medium heat for about 20 minutes, or until knife tender. Drain and cut the potatoes in half. Lay the potatoes in the prepared pan. Season with salt and pepper and drizzle with 1 tbsp olive oil.

CUT the fennel bulb lengthways and cut into 4mm (¼in) thick slices. Blanch in hot water for 1 minute.

COMBINE the onion, tomatoes, fennel, bell pepper strips, tomato paste, oregano, remaining garlic and thyme leaves and salt and pepper in a bowl. Spread half the mixture over the potatoes. Remove the fish from the fridge and lay on top of the vegetables. Scatter the remaining vegetables, olives and capers over the fish. Combine the remaining 3 tbsp olive oil, lemon juice and wine and pour around the fish.

COVER the pan with foil, sealing well, and bake for 20 minutes, basting 3 or 4 times with the pan juices, until the vegetables are cooked through and the fish is opaque throughout when cut along the spine. Remove the foil and bake for a further 20 minutes. Top up with hot water if the fish and vegetables start to dry out.

DRIZZLE with olive oil and serve straight from the roasting pan with lemon wedges.

Vijita de yerno, komo el sol de l'envierno,
sale tadre i se va presto!

(Lit: A son-in-law's visit is like the winter sun, he comes late and leaves early!)

Gratins, Fritters & Egg Dishes

Passover bakes and fritters

beef matza bake
guajado de karne kon matza

4 tbsp olive oil, plus extra for brushing
¾ cup finely chopped spring onions
    (scallions)
1kg (2¼lb) minced (ground) beef or veal
1 cup hot chicken stock
2 tomatoes, grated and seeds removed
sea salt and finely ground white pepper
3 tbsp roughly chopped flat-leaf parsley
    (use leaves and tender stems)
2 tbsp roughly chopped fresh dill
4 sheets matza
8 eggs, separated

 STELLA'S HINT:
- *The bake can be made a day ahead. To reheat, warm through in a 180°C (350°F) preheated oven.*

PREHEAT the oven to 180°C (350°F). Brush a 35 × 25cm (14 × 10in) ovenproof dish lightly with oil.

HEAT the oil in a large, heavy-based pan over a medium-high heat and glaze the spring onions until a little translucent. Add the meat, making sure the meat is covering the base of the pan. Leave for 2–3 minutes so that the meat seals underneath before you start stirring. Crumble the meat with a fork to break up the meat as it colours, about 10 minutes. Pour in the hot stock, add the tomatoes and season with salt and pepper. Reduce the heat and simmer, uncovered, for 20 minutes until reduced. Toss in the parsley and dill. Transfer to a large bowl and let cool.

SOAK the matza in a bowl of boiling water for 1 minute or until semi-soft. Drain in a colander, pressing and squeezing out excess water.

PLACE the prepared ovenproof dish in the preheated oven for 5 minutes.

BEAT the egg yolks in a large bowl until creamy. Stir in the meat mixture. In a separate large bowl, whip the egg whites with an electric mixer until stiff. Gently fold the egg whites and matza into the meat mixture and combine well. Spread the mixture into the heated dish and bake for about 40 minutes or until the top is golden and crusty.

To serve: Cut the bake into squares and serve hot or at room temperature with *huevos haminados* (p113).

potato, cheese and matza fritters
fritadikas de matza, patata i kezo

These delicious savoury fritters are a simple and easy stand-by, especially over Passover.

6 medium potatoes, unpeeled
3 sheets matza
3 eggs, beaten
1½ cups grated kefalotiri or Parmesan
    cheese
½ cup grated feta cheese
salt and finely ground white pepper

For shallow-frying:
vegetable or grape-seed oil

PUT the potatoes in a pan with enough cold salted water to just cover. Bring to a boil. Cover, reduce the heat and simmer for 30–40 minutes or until tender when pierced with a knife. Drain and, whilst still hot (using a fork to hold the potato steady and tongs to peel off the skin), peel and return to the pan for about 1 minute to dry off any excess moisture. Put through a potato ricer.

SOAK the matza in a bowl of boiling water for 1 minute or until semi-soft. Drain in a colander, pressing and squeezing out excess water.

COMBINE all the ingredients in a large bowl. Pinch off walnut-sized pieces and shape into patties.

HEAT enough oil for shallow-frying in a frying pan over a medium-high heat. When the oil is hot but not smoking, gently drop 4–5 patties at a time in the oil, turning over once, until golden and crispy. If the fritters are browning too quickly lower the heat slightly.

REMOVE with a slotted spoon and drain on paper towels. Serve immediately.

chicken matza bake
guajado de gayina kon matza

This dish is traditionally served over Passover with a green spring salad (p48).

For pot-roasting the chicken:
4 tbsp olive oil
1kg (2¼lb) free-range chicken
sea salt and finely ground white pepper
1 large carrot, peeled and cut into chunks
1 large onion, thickly sliced
1 celery stalk, cut into chunks
2 garlic cloves, crushed
3 sprigs fresh thyme
2 dried bay leaves

For the bake:
3 tbsp olive oil
¾ cup finely chopped spring onions
   (scallions)
1 tbsp fresh lemon juice
1½ cups hot chicken stock, including
   reserved roasting juices
3 tbsp roughly chopped flat-leaf parsley
   (use leaves and tender stems)
2 tbsp roughly chopped fresh dill
4 sheets matza
8 eggs, lightly beaten
sea salt and freshly ground black pepper

PREHEAT the oven to 200°C (400°F).

HEAT 2 tbsp olive oil in a deep roasting pan. Rub the chicken with salt, pepper and remaining 2 tbsp olive oil. Arrange the vegetables and herbs in the roasting pan and place the chicken on top. Roast the chicken for about 1½ hours or until tender and golden and the juices run clear.

REMOVE the chicken from the pan and allow to rest.

POUR the roasting juices and vegetables from the pan into a fine-mesh sieve set over a bowl. With the back of a spoon, press out as much juice as you can from the vegetables. Skim off and discard any excess fat from the surface of the juices and reserve these juices for the chicken bake.

WHEN the chicken has cooled enough to handle remove the skin and debone the chicken. Finely chop the chicken pieces by hand or in a food processor.

PREHEAT the oven to 190°C (375°F). Oil an ovenproof rectangular dish 33 × 23cm (13 × 9in) with 1 tbsp olive oil and place in the oven until hot.

HEAT remaining olive oil in a frying pan over a medium heat and glaze the spring onions until a little translucent.

IN a medium-sized bowl combine chopped chicken, spring onions, lemon juice, stock and herbs.

SOAK the matza in a bowl of boiling water for 1 minute or until semi-soft. Drain in a colander, pressing and squeezing out excess water.

COMBINE the matza and chicken mixture. Then fold in the beaten eggs, season with salt and pepper and mix well.

POUR the mixture into the heated dish and bake for 40 minutes or until golden and crusty.

To serve: Cut the bake into squares and serve hot or at room temperature with *huevos haminados* (p113).

 STELLA'S HINT:
- *The bake can be made a day ahead. To reheat, warm through in a 190°C (375°F) preheated oven.*

Va onde te arrogan, i no onde te arrojan

(Lit: Go where you are begged for and not where you are kicked out)

Only go where you are welcome

fried matza fritters

resha frita (bimuelos de matza)

These crispy fried fritters are made from soaked matza dipped in egg, much like French toast, and served for breakfast on Passover. Resha frita are so scrumptious my family likes to eat these topped with honey and cinnamon for breakfast throughout the year. Some like to eat it with sweet preserves or Greek-style yoghurt or as a savoury option with fresh cheese and olives.

6 sheets matza
about 4 cups warm water or whole milk
4 eggs, lightly beaten

For shallow-frying:
vegetable or grape-seed oil

For serving:
honey, maple or raisin syrup (p227) and
    ground cinnamon

SOAK the matza in warm water or milk for 1 minute, until soft but not mushy. Drain in a colander, pressing and squeezing out excess water. Take 2 tbsp of the moistened matza, shape into patty-like mounds and place on a plate.

HEAT enough oil for shallow-frying in a pan over a medium-high heat.

GENEROUSLY coat the matza patties in the beaten egg and gently slip 4–5 pieces at a time into the hot oil. Fry for 2 minutes on each side until golden brown. Remove with a slotted spoon and drain on paper towels.

SERVE immediately, drizzled with honey, maple or raisin syrup and sprinkled with cinnamon.

Negro kon bueno, no si yama negro

(Lit: Bad with good is not called bad)

Look on the bright side of things

braised hard-boiled eggs
huevos haminados

Huevos haminados is one of the most ancient and characteristic foods in the Judeo-Spanish repertoire. In a Sephardic kitchen red and brown onion skins are always saved and stored ready to make these beautiful eggs. Although the recipe is straightforward, the result is quite spectacular. Eggs, in their shells, are slowly braised for 6 hours in water in which a little oil and red and brown onion skins have been added. Ground coffee can also be stirred in, imparting a unique flavour and colour. The porous eggshells become tinged with distinctive rich shades of golden brown, russet and maroon. Do not worry if the shells cracks when simmering as the egg whites can become marbled with patterns in similar colours, encasing creamy yolks. Huevos haminados are served alongside savoury pies, gratins and fritters and at the Sabbath brunch. They also feature throughout Passover.

red or brown dried outer skins from
    10 onions (about 4 cups)
8 eggs in their shells, at room temperature
water to cover
2 tbsp vegetable oil
1 tbsp ground Turkish coffee (optional)
1 tbsp red wine vinegar
1 tsp sea salt
½ tsp freshly ground black pepper

For sprinkling:
sea salt and freshly ground black pepper
    or cumin

ARRANGE the onion skins to line the base of a large, deep, stainless steel pan. Cradle the eggs on top of the onion skins and pour over enough cold water to cover the eggs by 7.5cm (3in). Add the oil, coffee (if using), vinegar and salt and pepper. Cover with a tight-fitting lid and bring to a slow boil. Cover, reduce the heat and simmer for at least 6 hours, checking the water level occasionally.

SCOOP out the eggs with a slotted spoon and run them under cold water until they are just cool enough to handle. Roll the eggs to crack the shells and then slip off the shells.

CUT the eggs in half and sprinkle with salt and pepper or cumin. Serve warm or at room temperature.

 STELLA'S HINT:
- *The hard-boiled eggs can be refrigerated in their shells with the cooking liquid for up to a day. Before serving return to room temperature first and then bring the cooking liquid to a slow boil. Reduce the heat and simmer for 15 minutes.*

El huevo de mi vizina tiene dos yemas

(Lit: The neighbour's eggs seem to have two egg yolks)

The grass is always greener on the other side

courgette fritters with herbs and cheese
keftes de kalavasa i keso

On the island of Rhodes, vegetable patties were made from the abundant seasonal greens or courgettes combined with fresh herbs and spring onions and sharpened with tangy cheese. These scrumptious, crisp fritters can be enjoyed as part of a meze or brunch served with yoghurt and garlic and potato dip (p46).

750g (1½lb) small, firm courgettes
(zucchini)

1 tsp sea salt

1 cup finely chopped spring onions
(scallions), **green and white parts**

2 tbsp roughly chopped flat-leaf parsley
(use leaves and tender stems)

1 heaped tbsp roughly chopped fresh dill

1 heaped tbsp finely chopped fresh mint

½ cup crumbled feta cheese

½ cup grated kefalotiri or Parmesan
cheese

2 eggs, lightly beaten

½ tsp paprika

freshly ground black pepper

1 heaped tbsp cornflour (cornstarch)
mixed with 1 tsp baking powder

For shallow-frying:
vegetable or grape-seed oil

TRIM and coarsely grate the courgettes with the skin. Transfer into a colander set over a bowl. Sprinkle lightly with salt and let drain for 45 minutes. Place in a tea towel and twist the tea towel tightly, squeezing out excess liquid.

COMBINE the courgettes, spring onions, parsley, dill, mint, feta, cheese, eggs, paprika and pepper in a bowl. Blend in the cornflour with the baking powder. Should the mixture not hold its shape, add a little more cornflour.

SHAPE heaped tablespoons of mixture into patties and place on a tray lined with plastic wrap.

HEAT 1.25cm (½in) oil in a large frying pan over a medium-high heat. When the oil is hot, but not smoking, gently drop 4–5 fritters in the oil to prevent crowding. Fry for about 5 minutes or until they are golden brown and crispy on both sides, turning over once. Lower the heat if they are browning too quickly, adding more oil as necessary. Scoop out with a slotted spoon and drain on paper towels. Serve hot with yoghurt and garlic dip.

Al eskarso ni repozo, ni deskanso

(Lit: The miser knows neither peace nor rest)

leek, potato and meat fritters

keftes de prasa karne

Leek and meat fritters are creamy and delicious partnered with a Turkish diced salad (p32), a vermicelli rice pilaf (p177) and a fresh tomato sauce (p148). They make a light yet satisfying meal, perfect for a summery lunch.

500g (1lb 2oz) young leeks, ends trimmed
    and dark green tops discarded
280g (10oz) potatoes, peeled and quartered
500g (1lb 2oz) minced (ground) beef
1 egg, lightly beaten
2 tbsp finely chopped flat-leaf parsley
    (use leaves and tender stems)
1 tbsp finely chopped fresh dill
1 ripe tomato, halved and coarsely grated
    (about 1 tbsp)
sea salt and finely ground white pepper

For shallow-frying:
vegetable or grape-seed oil

For dredging:
½ cup flour
2 eggs, lightly beaten

REMOVE the outer layer of the leeks, cut in half lengthways and across into chunks. Wash thoroughly.

PUT the leeks and potatoes in a large pan of generously salted water. Bring to a boil. Cover, reduce the heat and simmer for 20–30 minutes or until tender. Drain in a colander and let the vegetables cool. Place in a tea towel and twist the tea towel tightly, squeezing out excess liquid.

BLITZ the leeks and potatoes in a food processor, pulsing a few times until combined, while still retaining some texture. Do not purée. In a large bowl, combine the leek-potato mixture with the meat, egg, parsley, dill and tomato. Season with salt and pepper. Cover with plastic wrap and chill in the fridge for 30 minutes.

Shape the patties: With a small bowl of water nearby, dampen your hands and shape the mixture into round patties, about 5cm (2in) wide and 1.25cm (½in) thick. Place on a tray lined with plastic wrap.

HEAT 1.25cm (½in) oil in a large frying pan over a medium-high heat. When the oil is hot but not smoking, dredge 4–5 patties lightly with flour and dip in beaten egg. Gently drop the fritters in the oil and fry for 3–5 minutes on each side. Lower the heat if they are browning too quickly so that they cook through but do not burn. Add more oil as necessary. Scoop out with a slotted spoon and drain on paper towels. In between each batch discard any bits of batter that may be floating in the oil.

SERVE hot or at room temperature.

 STELLA'S HINT:
* *The fritters can be fried ahead of time and kept warm in a 120°C (250°F) oven for about 20 minutes.*

Ijo kreser, es fierro al mashkar

(Lit: To bring up children is like chewing iron)

Raising children is tough going!

eggs poached with tomatoes
huevos kon tomat

Huevos kon tomat is an easy and fast stand-by that consists of eggs poached in a fresh, thick tomato sauce and served hot in the same frying pan in which it is cooked. Be sure to have lots of warm flat bread to mop up the tasty sauce. This appetizing meal is a favourite with my family for brunch or as a Sunday dinner.

For the tomato sauce:

5 tbsp olive oil

1 small red onion, sliced lengthways

2 cups ripe, peeled and chopped tomatoes
   or canned chopped tomatoes

1 tbsp tomato paste

1 tsp sea salt

1 tsp sugar

½ tsp paprika

6–8 eggs

½ cup cubed feta or kashkaval cheese

2 tbsp roughly chopped flat-leaf parsley
   (use leaves and tender stems)

For serving:

1 tbsp roughly chopped flat-leaf parsley
   (use leaves and tender stems)

a handful marinated black olives

Make the tomato sauce: Heat the oil in a large frying pan over a medium-high heat. Cook the onion for 3–4 minutes, stirring frequently, until softened. Stir in the tomatoes, tomato paste, salt, sugar and paprika. Simmer for about 7 minutes over a low heat until thickened and well reduced. Taste and ensure you adjust the seasoning at this stage as the sauce cannot be stirred or seasoned once the eggs are in*.

MAKE small indentations in the surface of the sauce. Carefully crack an egg and one by one slide into each hollow. Stir the whites gently with a fork so they are thinly spread over the tomatoes. Partly cover with a lid and simmer over a low heat for 4–5 minutes. Scatter over the cheese and sprinkle with parsley. Cook until the eggs are just set but both the whites and the yolks are still soft. Cover briefly with a lid if you prefer your eggs well done.

To serve: Sprinkle with parsley, toss in some black olives and serve hot in the pan with warm flat bread.

 STELLA'S HINT:

◆ *The tomato sauce may be prepared ahead. Refrigerate until ready to use.*

 TWIST ON TRADITION:

◆ *To add a bite to the sauce, stir in 1 tsp Turkish red pepper flakes with the onion.*

En la kaza yena, presto si giza la sena

(Lit: In a well-stocked home it is easy to cook the dinner)

leek, potato and fresh herb fritters
keftes de prasa i patata

These scrumptious fritters are often served on the New Year and on Passover using matza cake meal. They also make a tasty meze or can be served as a side dish with an entrée. My mother would usually make a large quantity and serve some hot at the table, keeping leftovers as a snack.

500g (1lb 2oz) young leeks, ends trimmed and dark green tops discarded

1 medium onion, peeled

300g (10½oz) potatoes, peeled and quartered

2 eggs, lightly beaten

3 tbsp finely chopped flat-leaf parsley (use leaves and tender stems)

1 tbsp finely chopped tender celery leaves

1 tbsp finely chopped fresh dill

sea salt and finely ground white pepper

2 tbsp dried breadcrumbs or matza cake meal

For shallow-frying:
vegetable or grape-seed oil

REMOVE the outer layer of the leeks, cut in half lengthways and across into chunks. Wash thoroughly.

PUT the leeks, whole onion and potatoes in a pan of generously salted cold water. Bring to a boil. Cover, reduce the heat and simmer for 30 minutes or until tender. Drain in a colander and let the vegetables cool. Place in a tea towel and twist the tea towel tightly, squeezing out excess liquid.

BLITZ the leeks, onion and potatoes in a food processor, pulsing a few times until combined, while still retaining some texture. Do not purée. In a large bowl, combine the leek-potato mixture with the eggs, parsley, celery leaves and dill. Season with salt and pepper. Stir in as much breadcrumbs or matza meal as necessary to make a mixture that holds its shape. Cover with plastic wrap and chill in the fridge for 30 minutes.

Shape the patties: With a small bowl of water nearby, dampen your hands and shape the mixture into round patties, about 5cm (2in) wide and 1.25cm (½in) thick. Place on a tray lined with plastic wrap.

HEAT 1.25cm (½in) oil in a large frying pan over a medium-high heat. When the oil is hot, but not smoking, gently drop 4–5 fritters in the oil and fry for 3–4 minutes on each side. Lower the heat if they are browning too quickly so that they cook through but do not burn. Add more oil as necessary. Scoop out with a slotted spoon and drain on paper towels.

SERVE hot or at room temperature with a fresh tomato sauce (p148) or garlic dip (p46).

 STELLA'S HINT:

♦ *The fritters can be fried ahead of time and kept warm in a 120°C (250°F) oven for about 20 minutes.*

Pensando la vijes, piedras la manseves

(Lit: Thinking of your old age you lose your youth)

You waste your youth by worrying about old age

macaroni and meat bake
macaron reynado de karne

This appetizing Sephardic version of the Greek meat bake pastitsio is baked in an earthenware ovenproof dish and brought straight to the table. It makes an excellent meal eaten hot or at room temperature for brunches, mezes, picnics and children's packed lunches. This bake is delicious with a tasty homemade tomato sauce (p148) and a green spring salad (p48).

3 tbsp olive oil, plus more for brushing
6 spring onions (scallions), finely sliced
500g (1lb 2oz) minced (ground) beef or
    veal
1 tsp salt
½ tsp finely ground white pepper
1½ cups hot chicken stock
½ cup canned chopped tomatoes
2 tbsp roughly chopped flat-leaf parsley
    (use leaves and tender stems)
1 tbsp roughly chopped fresh dill
500g (1lb 2oz) macaroni, tubular pasta or
    pasta shells
9 eggs, well beaten

BRUSH a 35 × 25cm (14 × 10in) and 6.25cm (2½in) deep earthenware ovenproof dish lightly with olive oil.

HEAT the oil in a large, heavy-based pan over a medium-high heat. Add the spring onions and cook for 2 minutes, stirring frequently, until softened. Add the meat and salt and pepper and stir for 5 minutes. Crushing the meat with a fork, stir until it changes to a light brown colour.

ADD 1 cup hot chicken stock and the tomatoes. Bring to a boil. Reduce the heat and simmer, uncovered, until the sauce has reduced but the mixture is still moist. Taste and adjust the seasoning. Toss in the parsley and dill and transfer to a large bowl.

BRING a large pot of generously salted water to a boil. Add the pasta and stir frequently as the water returns to a boil. Cook the pasta according to packet instructions until just tender but retaining some bite. Drain well.

PREHEAT the oven to 200°C (400°F) and heat the oiled dish in the oven for 5 minutes.

ADD the pasta to the meat mixture and pour in the beaten eggs. Mix well.

REMOVE the heated dish from the oven and immediately pour the mixture into it, evenly distributing the meat and pasta. Smooth the surface with the back of a spoon. Bake in the centre of the oven for 30 minutes or until the top is crusty and golden. Switch off the oven. Pour the remaining ½ cup of hot chicken stock over the baked pasta and return to the still warm oven until the stock has been absorbed.

CUT into squares and serve hot or at room temperature.

Esti esta en sus treje

(Lit: He is in his 13)

He won't budge

The source of this saying goes back to the Spanish Inquisition in 1492 when the Jews resisted forced conversion to Catholicism. Priests would utter these words, meaning 'Jews refuse to change their belief in the 13 Fundamental Principles of Faith in Judaism.'

pasta and cheese bake
fideos kon kezo i leche al orno

Pasta baked with a luscious creamy blend of Mediterranean cheeses and eggs is topped with breadcrumbs and grated cheese for a burnished crusty top. This pasta and cheese bake is so simple to make my young granddaughters prepare it themselves. It is ideal as a scrumptious family dish for brunch and any leftovers are perfect for school lunches.

1 tbsp olive oil, plus extra for brushing
1 tbsp dried breadcrumbs
500g (1lb 2oz) egg noodle wide pasta
    (pappardelle or tagliatelli)
½ cup heavy cream
6 eggs, lightly beaten
1 cup grated kefalotiri, Parmesan or
    kashkaval cheese
1 cup cubed mozzarella or crumbled
    feta cheese
1 cup ricotta or cream cheese
½ tsp sea salt
½ tsp finely ground white pepper

For the topping:
2 tbsp grated kefalotiri, Parmesan or
    kashkaval cheese
1 tbsp dried breadcrumbs
a few knobs unsalted butter

BRUSH a 35 × 25cm (14 × 10in) earthenware ovenproof dish lightly with oil and sprinkle breadcrumbs around the dish.

BRING a large pan of generously salted water to a boil. Cook the pasta according to packet instructions until just tender but retaining some bite.

DRAIN the pasta and toss it in a large bowl with the remaining olive oil. Set aside.

PREHEAT the oven to 160°C (325°F) and heat the oiled dish in the oven for 5 minutes.

IN a bowl, combine the cream and eggs and mix in all the cheeses. Season with salt and pepper. Pour the mixture over the pasta and fold in well.

REMOVE the heated dish from the oven and immediately pour in the pasta mixture. Smooth the surface with the back of a spoon. Top with the grated cheese, breadcrumbs and a few knobs of butter. Bake for 45 minutes until the top is golden brown and crisp. Serve hot.

tomato bake
fritada de tomat

2 tbsp olive oil, plus extra for brushing
4 × 400g (14oz) cans good-quality Italian
    tomatoes, whizzed in a processor
1 tsp sugar
sea salt and finely ground white pepper
200g (7oz) cream crackers, made into
    crumbs in a food processor
½ cup chopped flat-leaf parsley (use leaves
    and tender stems)
1 cup grated kefalotiri or Parmesan cheese
8 eggs, well beaten

BRUSH a 35 × 25cm (14 × 10in) ovenproof dish lightly with olive oil.

HEAT the oil in a large, heavy-based pan over a medium heat. Add the tomatoes and cook, uncovered, for 25–30 minutes or until the tomatoes are reduced to a thick consistency. Add the sugar, salt and pepper. Remove from the heat. Adjust the seasoning and if it tastes acidic add a pinch more sugar.

PREHEAT the oven to 210°C (410°F) and heat the oiled dish in the oven for 5 minutes.

PUT the cream cracker crumbs, parsley and cheese in a large bowl. Add the tomato pulp, mixing thoroughly, and then stir in the eggs.

REMOVE the heated dish from the oven and immediately pour in the mixture. Smooth the surface with the back of a spoon. Bake for 30–35 minutes or until firm on top. Cut into squares and serve at room temperature.

Swiss chard, potato and cheese gratin
guajado di pasi kon patata i keso (sfongo)

Swiss chard gratin of Turkish origin is characterised by small mounds of mashed potato and cheese mixture interspersed in a bed of Swiss chard, egg, cheese and potato. It is traditionally served during the Passover week, on the New Year and the festival of Shavuot. Served piping hot, this makes a wholesome light family meal.

500g (1lb 2oz) Swiss chard (silverbeet), stalks removed, washed and finely shredded
500g (1lb 2oz) potatoes, unpeeled
7 eggs, lightly beaten
1½ cups freshly grated kashkaval or Parmesan cheese mixed with ½ cup crumbled feta
sea salt and finely ground white pepper
2 eggs, lightly beaten
1 tbsp milk

For the topping:
⅓ cup grated kashkaval or Parmesan cheese
1 tbsp unsalted butter

BRUSH a 35 × 25cm (14 × 10in) earthenware ovenproof dish with oil.

DRY the Swiss chard in batches in a salad spinner. Spread out the shredded chard on paper towels and pat gently ensuring that it is thoroughly dry. I like to do this step the night before so the leaves dry thoroughly.

PUT the potatoes in a pan with enough cold salted water to just cover. Bring to a boil. Cover, reduce the heat and simmer for 30–40 minutes or until tender when pierced with a knife. Drain and, whilst still hot (using a fork to hold the potato steady and tongs to peel off the skin), peel and return to the pan for about 1 minute to dry off any excess moisture. Put through a potato ricer. Divide the potato mixture into two-thirds and set aside the remaining third.

PREHEAT the oven to 180°C (350°F) and heat the oiled dish in the oven for 5 minutes.

IN a very large bowl, and using your hands, mix the Swiss chard with two-thirds of the mashed potato and 1½ cups of grated mixed cheese, salt and pepper. When evenly incorporated add the 7 beaten eggs and combine well.

IN another bowl combine the remaining third of the mashed potato with 2 beaten eggs, the remaining ½ cup mixed cheeses and the milk. Season with salt and pepper. Mix well.

REMOVE the heated dish from the oven and spread the Swiss chard and potato mixture evenly into the dish.

WITH a spoon, scoop out golf ball-sized hollows in the layer of the Swiss chard and potato mixture spacing them evenly in rows about 2.5cm (1in) apart. Fill with teaspoonfuls of the potato and cheese mixture, forming small mounds.

SPRINKLE the gratin with cheese and dot with a few small knobs of butter. Bake for 50 minutes or until the top is crusty and golden brown. Serve directly from the dish, hot or cold, cut into squares.

 STELLA'S HINTS:
- *Use ricotta or fresh goat's cheese instead of feta for a blander taste.*
- *The volume of the trimmed Swiss chard seems large but it reduces significantly when cooked.*

El pan de mi vizina, es melizina
(Lit: The neighbour's bread is like medicine)

A good neighbour brings good cheer

veal, egg and herb-filled potato croquettes
rollos de karne i patata

These are excellent meat-filled crisp potato croquettes, scrumptious to eat but not so easy to prepare for beginners. This is my mother's recipe, inspired by her Turkish roots. It is a superb alternative to the traditional matza bake at Passover. I like to freeze these, uncooked, as a fabulous stand-by, especially when the grandchildren are around. I simply fry the frozen croquettes in hot oil and serve with a salad.

For the meat filling:
3 tbsp olive oil
¾ cup finely chopped spring onions
    (scallions)
500g (1lb 2oz) minced (ground) veal
¼ cup hot chicken stock
2 eggs, hard-boiled and coarsely chopped
2 tbsp pine nuts
3 tbsp finely chopped flat-leaf parsley
    (use leaves and tender stems)
1 tsp sea salt
pinch of finely ground white pepper

For the potato mixture:
1kg (2¼lb) potatoes, unpeeled
2 eggs, lightly beaten
1 tsp sea salt
finely ground white pepper
¼ cup fresh breadcrumbs or matza meal

For breading:
1 cup plain (all-purpose) flour
2 eggs, lightly beaten with 1 tbsp olive oil
1½ cups dried breadcrumbs or matza
    cake flour

For deep-frying:
vegetable or grape-seed oil

Prepare the filling: Heat the oil in a large, heavy-based pan over a medium-high heat. Add the spring onions and cook, stirring frequently, for 2 minutes, until softened. Add the meat, making sure the meat is covering the base of the pan. Leave for 2–3 minutes so that the meat seals underneath before you start stirring. Crumble the meat with a fork to break up the meat as it colours, about 10 minutes. Pour in the hot chicken stock and simmer, uncovered, until the liquid has reduced. Transfer to a bowl and let cool. Stir in the eggs, pine nuts, parsley, salt and pepper.

PUT the potatoes in a pan with enough cold salted water to just cover. Bring to a boil. Cover, reduce the heat and simmer for 30–40 minutes or until tender when pierced with a knife. Drain and whilst still hot (using a fork to hold the potato steady and tongs to peel off the skin), peel and return to the pan for about 1 minute to dry off any excess moisture. Put through a potato ricer. Mix well with the beaten eggs, salt, pepper and breadcrumbs or matza meal.

Shape the croquettes: With a small bowl of water nearby, dampen your hands and break off a portion of the potato mixture the size of an egg and shape into a ball. Hold the ball in the cup of your left hand using your right thumb to flatten the potato so that it takes the shape of your palm. Put 1 heaped tsp of the meat filling in the centre of the potato mixture and press the edges together to seal over the filling and roll between your hands to shape into a smooth oval. Repeat with the remaining potato and meat mixtures. (The croquettes can be prepared ahead to this point and stored in the fridge for up to 1 day.)

Bread the croquettes: Dredge lightly in the flour, then dip into the beaten egg mixture, ensuring all sides are well-coated, and roll in the breadcrumbs. Place on a tray lined with baking paper to 'set'.

To fry: Heat 5cm (2in) oil in a medium-sized pan on a high heat. Fry the croquettes in small batches for about 4 minutes, turning once, until golden brown all over. Scoop out with a slotted spoon and drain on paper towels. Serve immediately or keep warm in an oven on low heat.

 STELLA'S HINTS:

* *Use a 4½cm (1¾in) ice-cream scoop to form firmly packed, evenly sized potato balls.*
* *For Passover, substitute the breadcrumbs with matza meal and plain flour with matza cake flour.*
* *Open-freeze the crumbed uncooked croquettes in a single layer until solid (about 1 hour). Then stack between layers of baking paper in an airtight container and freeze for up to 1 month. When required, place the frozen croquettes in hot oil and fry as above.*

Stuffed Vegetables

cabbage leaves stuffed with meat, rice and herbs
yaprakes de kol kon karne

This tasty meat, rice and fresh herb-filled leaf dish uses one of the oldest known and humblest of vegetables – the cabbage. It is delicious accompanied with an egg-lemon sauce (p94) and a chickpea rice pilaf (p169).

1 tbsp salt
1 large cabbage, outer leaves removed

For the filling:
2 tbsp olive oil
½ cup finely chopped onion
1 cup finely chopped spring onions
    (scallions)
500g (1lb 2oz) lean ground (minced) lamb
⅔ cup medium-grain rice, soaked in
    hot water for 10 minutes, rinsed and
    drained
½ cup canned chopped tomatoes
¼ cup water
½ cup finely chopped flat-leaf parsley
    (use leaves and tender stems)
2 tbsp finely chopped fresh dill
¼ tsp ground allspice
1 tsp sea salt
½ tsp finely ground white pepper

For the vegetable base:
2 tbsp olive oil
1 cup roughly chopped cabbage stalks
1 cup peeled and diced carrots
1 small potato, peeled and diced
1 cup canned chopped tomatoes
1 cup roughly sliced spring onions
2 tender celery stalks with leaves, chopped
1 tbsp tomato paste diluted in ¼ cup water
sea salt and finely ground white pepper

For cooking:
3 garlic cloves
2 cups hot chicken stock
1 tbsp cornflour (cornstarch)
½ cup fresh lemon juice

For serving:
2 lemons, cut into wedges

Prepare the leaves: Bring a large pan of water to the boil over a high heat and add 1 tbsp salt. Cut out and discard the core of the cabbage. Put the whole cabbage into the boiling water. When the water returns to the boil, cook, uncovered, for 8–10 minutes, until the cabbage is tender and pliable enough to separate the leaves but not cooked all the way through. Briefly place the cabbage into a large bowl of iced water and drain well in a colander. Carefully pull the outer leaves off, keeping them intact as far as possible – take care as they break easily. Reserve 1 cup roughly chopped inner cabbage stalks for the vegetable base.

Make the filling: Heat the oil in a heavy-based frying pan over a medium-high heat and cook the onion and spring onions for 3 minutes, stirring frequently, until softened. Place all the remaining ingredients for the filling in a medium-size bowl together with the cooked onions.

Make the vegetable base: Heat the oil in a shallow, large, heavy-based pan over a medium-high heat. Add the chopped vegetables and cook for 4 minutes, stirring occasionally. Stir in the diluted tomato paste and salt and pepper. Bring to a boil. Cover, reduce the heat and simmer for 20 minutes or until the vegetables have cooked. Add hot water as necessary. Set aside.

Stuff the leaves: Lay a few cabbage leaves at a time on a work surface, outer side of the leaves facing down. Cut large leaves in half along the central rib, discarding the rib. With smaller leaves cut away the thick stem end at the base of the leaf. Place a tablespoon of the filling in the centre of the cut end. Fold both sides inward over the filling and roll up snugly into a cigar shape. Repeat with remaining leaves until all the filling is used.

To cook: Arrange the stuffed leaves side-by-side, seam side down, over the vegetable base, packing them tightly in concentric circles. Slip the garlic cloves in between the parcels. Weigh the stuffed cabbage leaves down with an inverted heatproof plate large enough to fit the pan to keep the *yaprakes* from unravelling during cooking. Pour the hot stock down the inside of the pan just enough to cover the *yaprakes*. Bring to a boil. Cover, reduce the heat and simmer for about 1 hour or until the cabbage leaves have cooked. Shake the pan from time to time to prevent the vegetables from catching. Add hot water as necessary. Test one stuffed leaf to ensure the leaves have softened and the filling is cooked. Stir the cornflour into a little of the hot liquid and pour in with the lemon juice. Continue to simmer for a further 5 minutes.

To serve: Remove the plate and serve hot from the pan with lemon wedges.

Swiss chard leaves stuffed with meat and rice
yaprakes de pasi

Swiss chard leaves, enveloping a meat and rice filling, are gently cooked on a bed of chopped vegetables. This flavoursome meal, accompanied with a white rice pilaf (p168), lemon wedges and a garlic and potato dip (p46), is an ideal make-ahead dish that can be refrigerated overnight and warmed through with the flavours heightened. The tender Swiss chard leaves give their own unique flavour and texture to this dish, perfect for a summery al fresco lunch.

1kg (2¼lb) large Swiss chard (silver beet) leaves

For the filling:
500g (1lb 2oz) minced (ground) lamb or beef
⅔ cup finely chopped spring onions (scallions)
½ cup finely chopped flat-leaf parsley (use leaves and tender stems)
¼ cup finely chopped fresh dill
⅔ cup medium-grain rice, soaked in hot water for 10 minutes, rinsed and drained
¼ tsp ground cumin
½ cup canned chopped tomatoes
1 tbsp olive oil
1 tsp sea salt
½ tsp finely ground white pepper

For the vegetable base:
3 tbsp olive oil
1 large onion, roughly chopped
4 spring onions, roughly chopped
1 large potato, peeled and chopped
2 cups roughly chopped Swiss chard stalks
1½ cups canned chopped tomatoes
½ tsp sugar
sea salt and finely ground white pepper

For cooking:
1 cup hot chicken stock
2 tbsp fresh lemon juice

For serving:
2 lemons, cut into wedges

Prepare the leaves: Cut off the central stalk with a sharp knife and reserve for the vegetable base. Blanch the Swiss chard leaves in batches in a large pan of boiling water for about 5 seconds and refresh in a bowl of cold water for 1 minute. Drain in a colander and gently press out the excess liquid with the back of a spoon.

Make the filling: Combine all the ingredients in a large bowl.

Make the vegetable base: Heat the oil in a large, shallow, heavy-based pan over a medium-high heat. Add the chopped vegetables and cook for 4 minutes, stirring occasionally. Add the tomatoes and sugar and season with salt and pepper. Bring to a boil. Cover, reduce the heat and simmer for 20 minutes or until the vegetables are tender. Add hot water as necessary.

Stuff the leaves: Lay a few Swiss chard leaves at a time on a work surface, shiny side down. If the leaves are very large they may be trimmed to about 12.5cm (5in) irregular rectangles. Place a heaped tablespoon of filling in the centre at the bottom end. Fold both sides inward over the filling and roll up snugly into a cigar shape. Repeat with the remaining leaves until all the filling is used.

To cook: Arrange the stuffed leaves side-by-side, seam side down, over the vegetable base, packing them tightly in concentric circles. Weigh the stuffed chard leaves down with an inverted heatproof plate large enough to fit the pan to keep the *yaprakes* from unravelling during cooking. Pour the hot stock down the inside of the pan just enough to cover the *yaprakes*. Bring to a boil. Cover, reduce the heat and simmer for about 45 minutes or until the filling has cooked. Shake the pan from time to time to prevent the vegetables from catching. Add hot water as necessary. Test one stuffed leaf to ensure the leaves have softened and the filling is cooked.

To serve: Remove the plate, then add the lemon juice and swirl the pan gently to combine it with the cooking liquid. Taste for salt and lemon juice. Serve hot from the pan with lemon wedges.

El palo verde se enderacha

(Lit: A green sapling can straighten itself out)

If you catch a problem early it is easier to correct

meat and rice-stuffed vine leaves stewed with beans
yaprakes de oja de parra kon avas

Vine leaves stuffed with meat, rice and fresh herbs and stewed with beans is perhaps the most well-loved and treasured dish characteristic of Sephardic home-cooking from Rhodes. Yaprakes, *derived from the Turkish word* yaprak *or leaf, is a version of the Greek* dolmas. *Although this recipe may seem challenging at first and is a little time consuming, it is a good time to have friends or family involved in stuffing and rolling the vine leaves as it's really fun and a grounding way to connect with loved ones.*

For the beans:
2 cups (400g/14oz) dried cannellini
  or haricot (navy) beans, soaked
  overnight in twice their volume of
  cold water, drained and rinsed
1 small onion, peeled
2 dried bay leaves
3 fresh sage leaves
1 tsp sea salt

For the meat:
2 tbsp olive oil
500g (1lb 2oz) veal shin, cut into chunks,
  or lamb chops
1 onion, peeled
2–3 cups hot chicken stock

For the leaves:
450g (1lb) fresh, young, tender vine
  (grape) leaves or brine-preserved
  leaves

For the filling:
500g (1lb 2oz) minced (ground) lamb
  or beef
2/3 cup medium-grain rice, soaked in
  hot water for 10 minutes, rinsed and
  drained
1/2 cup finely chopped flat-leaf parsley
  (use leaves and tender stems)
1/2 cup finely chopped fresh dill
2 tbsp olive oil
1/2 cup canned chopped tomatoes
1 tsp tomato paste
1 tsp sea salt
1/2 tsp finely ground white pepper

Cook the beans: Put the beans in a large pan with enough cold water to cover by 2.5cm (1in). Add the onion and bay and sage leaves. Bring to a boil. Cover, reduce the heat and simmer for 1½ hours or until they are tender but not mushy. The cooking time depends on the quality and age of the beans. Check frequently as they cook, adding more hot water as necessary. Add the salt in the last 10 minutes of cooking. When the beans are tender drain in a colander and discard the onion and herbs.

Cook the meat: Heat the oil in a large, deep, heavy-based pan over a medium-high heat. Add the veal or lamb and cook until lightly browned. Add the onion and pour enough hot stock to cover. Bring to a boil. Cover, reduce the heat and simmer for 50 minutes or until the meat is very tender. Add hot water as necessary. Reserve the cooking liquid and keep at a simmer.

Prepare the leaves: Blanch the vine leaves in boiling water for 3 minutes, in batches, then refresh in cold water and drain. Drape the vine leaves over the edge of a colander to drain thoroughly.

Make the filling: Combine all the ingredients in a large bowl.

Stuff the leaves: Lay a few vine leaves at a time on a work surface, vein side up, with the stem towards you. Place a tablespoon of the filling in the centre of each leaf near the stem end. Fold both sides inward over the filling and roll up snugly into a cigar shape. Repeat with the remaining leaves until all the filling is used.

To cook: Add half the cooked beans to the pan with the meat. Arrange the stuffed leaves side-by-side, seam side down, over the beans, packing them tightly in concentric circles. Place the sliced tomatoes over the stuffed vine leaves. Scatter over the remaining beans. Weigh the stuffed vine leaves down with an inverted heatproof plate large enough to fit the pan to keep the *yaprakes* from unravelling during cooking. Combine the hot reserved cooking liquid from the meat, lemon juice, oil, hot water and salt and pepper in a jug and pour down the inside of the pan, just enough to cover the *yaprakes*. Bring to a boil. Cover, reduce the heat and simmer for about 45 minutes or until the filling has cooked. Shake the pan from time to time so that the cooking liquid circulates. Add hot water as necessary. Add the cornflour mixture to the sauce and cook for a further 5 minutes, swirling the liquid around for the sauce to seep through evenly. Test one stuffed leaf to ensure the leaves have softened and the filling is cooked. Taste for salt and lemon juice.

For cooking:
2 ripe tomatoes, thickly sliced
3 tbsp fresh lemon juice
3 tbsp olive oil
1 cup hot water
sea salt and finely ground white pepper
1 tsp cornflour (cornstarch) dissolved in
   2 tbsp cold water

For serving:
2 tbsp extra-virgin olive oil
2 lemons, cut into wedges

To serve: Remove the plate and carefully transfer the contents into a deep serving bowl. Drizzle with olive oil and serve hot with a tomato rice pilaf (p172) and lemon wedges.

 TWISTS ON TRADITION:
- *You can substitute 3 × 400g (14oz) cans cannellini beans, rinsed and drained, for the dried beans.*
- *3–4 whole garlic cloves can be slipped in between the stuffed leaves before cooking.*

In Ladino slang, vegetables often denoted characteristics of a person:

piminton (bell pepper) – quick temper, cheekiness or liveliness;

kalavasa (pumpkin) – absent-minded;

kavesa di apio (a head of celery) – forgetful, vague;

okra used in this phrase, *si tupo en negra bamia,* was used to describe someone who finds

themselves stuck in a problematic situation

buen pipino – what a cucumber – what a problem!

Mediterranean vegetables stuffed with meat and rice

verduras reynados

Mediterranean vegetables, such as aubergines, tomatoes, courgettes and bell peppers, are hollowed out and stuffed with a fragrant rice and meat filling and then simmered on a bed of vegetables. Also known as Tomat a la Turka *by the Sephardim from Rhodes, it is one of the dishes traditionally prepared for Rosh Hashanah, the Jewish New Year. This colourful entrée looks spectacular as part of a buffet and, like other stuffed vegetables, is best prepared a day ahead for the flavours to deepen. I like to cook and serve in the same oven-to-table casserole, which besides making cleaning up easier gives a casual feel to the meal.*

For the vegetables:
4 plump baby aubergines (eggplants) – about 7.5cm (3in) long and 5cm (2in) wide
6 small, ripe red tomatoes
4 firm, thick courgettes (zucchini), about 7.5cm (3in) long
4 small yellow or orange bell peppers
sea salt
1 tsp fresh lemon juice
olive oil (enough for shallow-frying)

For the filling:
450g (1lb) minced (ground) beef
2 garlic cloves, finely grated
½ cup medium-grain rice, soaked in hot water for 10 minutes, rinsed and drained
1 cup canned chopped tomatoes
1 cup roughly chopped flat-leaf parsley (use leaves and tender stems)
¼ cup pine nuts, toasted (p287)
¼ tsp ground cumin
2 tbsp olive oil
1 tsp sea salt
½ tsp finely ground white pepper

For the vegetable base:
¼ cup olive oil
1 large onion, roughly chopped
1 large potato, peeled and diced
reserved pulp of aubergines, tomatoes and courgettes, roughly chopped
1 cup canned chopped tomatoes
1 tbsp tomato paste
½ tsp sugar
1 cup hot chicken stock
sea salt and finely ground white pepper

Prepare the aubergines: Cut the stems off the aubergines and remove the caps. Using a very sharp knife, peel 1cm (½in) strips at intervals along the length of the aubergines, leaving them striped. Push a corer into the cut end of the aubergine, going as deep as possible, and rotate it to scoop out the pulp, leaving a 6mm (¼in) shell. Be careful not to pierce the skin. Reserve the scooped out pulp for the vegetable base. Soak the aubergine shells in water with 1 tsp salt and 1 tbsp lemon juice for 30 minutes, then drain. Heat enough oil for shallow-frying in a frying pan over a medium-high heat. Cook the aubergine shells in the sizzling oil until lightly browned. Drain on paper towels.

Prepare the tomatoes: Slice off around the stem end of the tomatoes, reserving for the lids. Keep the lids matched to the appropriate tomato. Hollow out the tomatoes using a spoon and carefully scoop as much pulp and seeds from each tomato as you can without piercing the skin. Lightly sprinkle a little salt in the tomato shells and turn them over to drain for 10 minutes. Deseed and chop the tomato pulp and reserve for the base.

Prepare the courgettes: Blanch in boiling water for 5 minutes, refresh in cold water and drain. When cool, slice off the stem end. With a long, narrow vegetable corer*, push the corer into the courgette at the cut end and hollow out, scooping out the pulp and leaving a thin even shell. Be careful not to pierce the shell. Reserve the pulp for the base. Put a pinch of salt in each cored courgette and let them drain in a colander until needed.

Prepare the bell peppers: Slice off 1.25cm (½in) from the stem end, keeping the stem intact and reserving for the lids. Keep the lids matched to the appropriate pepper. Scoop out the hard ribs and seeds.

Make the filling: Combine all the ingredients in a large bowl.

Make the vegetable base: Heat the oil over a medium-high heat in a large, shallow, heavy-based, oven-to-table casserole with a lid. Add the onion, potato, reserved aubergine and courgette pulp and cook for 10 minutes, stirring occasionally, until softened. Add the reserved tomato pulp, canned tomatoes, tomato paste, sugar and hot stock. Season with salt and pepper. Bring to a boil. Cover, reduce the heat and simmer for 30 minutes or until the vegetables are tender.

Stuff the vegetable shells: Fill the prepared vegetables with the filling to three-quarters full, as the rice mixture swells during cooking. (Use a coffee spoon for filling the courgettes.) Place the reserved matched lids over the tomatoes and peppers.

- *Corer: For best results use a vegetable reamer or a long, thin* ma'anara *corer (found at Middle Eastern stores) for scooping the pulp from the courgettes.*

To cook: Pack the stuffed vegetables upright, close together, in a single layer over the vegetable base. Arrange the tomatoes on the outer edge of the casserole as they cook the quickest. Add enough hot water to reach about 2.5cm (1in) below the top of the vegetables. Bring to a boil. Cover, reduce the heat and simmer for 45 minutes or until the filled vegetables are cooked. Shake the pan from time to time to prevent the vegetables from catching. Add hot water as necessary.

To serve: Preheat the oven to 190°C (375°F). Place the rack in the top third of the oven. Put the uncovered casserole in the oven for the tops of the vegetables to brown lightly. Usually 15 minutes is enough, but keep watching. Serve hot in the casserole with a vermicelli rice pilaf (p177) and a green spring salad (p48).

Dinguno save lo ki ay en la oya mas ke la kutchara ke la maneya

(Lit: No one knows what is in the pot other than the spoon that stirs it)

Never judge a person until you've walked a mile in their shoes

tomatoes and onions stuffed with meat
tomat i sevoya reynavas

This is one of my favourites of the stuffed vegetable dishes. Preparation is a little more labour intensive than other stuffed vegetables as the stuffed onions and tomatoes are lightly coated in egg and flour and briefly sautéed. However, this step adds another layer of flavour and texture which I find simply delicious. People often rediscover onions through this dish – not realizing just how sweet and delicate this vegetable can be.

10 small oval-shaped onions
10 small, ripe red tomatoes

For the filling:
500g (1lb 2oz) minced (ground) beef
¾ cup finely chopped flat-leaf parsley
   (use leaves and tender stems)
½ cup finely chopped spring onions
   (scallions)
1 large ripe tomato, halved, seeded and
   coarsely grated (about 2 tbsp)
4 slices white bread, crusts removed,
   dampened in ½ cup water, squeezed and
   torn into small pieces
1 egg, lightly beaten
1 tsp sea salt
½ tsp finely ground white pepper

For the vegetable base:
3 tbsp olive oil
1 large onion, roughly chopped, plus
   reserved chopped onion
4 spring onions, roughly chopped
2 tender celery stalks with leaves, chopped
2 large potatoes, peeled and diced
½ cup canned chopped tomatoes, plus
   reserved tomato pulp
½ cup hot water
½ tsp sugar
sea salt and finely ground white pepper

For shallow-frying:
vegetable or grape-seed oil

For coating:
prepare ½ cup plain (all-purpose) flour in a
   shallow bowl and 2 eggs, lightly beaten,
   in another

For cooking:
2 cups hot chicken stock

You will need:
a shallow casserole, about 33cm (13in)
   in diameter, with a lid

Prepare the onions: Discard the outer skin and halve the onions lengthways. Retain the outer two layers as cases for stuffing. Reserve the remainder of the onions and chop for the base.

Prepare the tomatoes: Cut the tomatoes vertically in half through the core. Hollow out the tomatoes using a spoon and carefully scoop as much pulp and seeds from each tomato as you can, without piercing the skin. Lightly sprinkle a little salt in the tomato shells and turn them over to drain for 10 minutes. Deseed and chop the tomato pulp and reserve for the vegetable base.

Make the filling: Combine all the ingredients in a large bowl.

Make the vegetable base: Heat the oil in an ovenproof casserole over a medium-high heat. Add all the chopped vegetables and cook for 4 minutes, stirring occasionally. Stir in the canned tomatoes and reserved tomato pulp, hot water, sugar, and season with salt and pepper. Bring to a boil. Cover, reduce the heat and simmer for 20 minutes or until the vegetables are tender. Add hot water as necessary.

Stuff the onions and tomatoes: Fill the cavities with the meat mixture and flatten to the level of the brim of the vegetable shells. Heat 1.25cm (½in) oil in a large frying pan over a medium-high heat. In batches, lightly coat the filled side only with the flour then dip the floured side of the stuffed vegetable into the egg. Fry the filled side and the base of the onions until golden brown. Fry the tomatoes on the filled-side only. Drain the fried vegetables on paper towels.

To cook: On the prepared vegetable base, arrange the stuffed onions in the centre of the pan and the stuffed tomatoes on the perimeter, meat side up. Pour in enough hot stock to come midway up the stuffed vegetables. Bring to a boil. Cover, reduce the heat and simmer for 45 minutes or until the vegetables and meat are cooked through. Shake the pan from time to time to prevent the vegetables from catching. Add hot water as necessary.

To serve: Preheat the oven to 200°C (400°F). Place the rack in the top third of the oven. Put the uncovered casserole in the oven for the tops of the vegetables to brown lightly. Usually 15 minutes is enough but keep watching. Serve hot in the casserole with a Spanish fried rice pilaf (p169).

vine leaves stuffed with rice and fresh herbs
yalandji de oja de parra kon arroz

Most Sephardic meze and festive tables will include a platter of plump, glistening vine leaves stuffed with rice, fresh aromatic herbs, spring onions and pine nuts. They are also known as yalandji falso, *meaning 'false' or 'lying' in Judeo-Spanish, as they contain no meat. Served chilled or at room temperature, they are ideal as an appetizer at a summer lunch accompanied with yoghurt garlic dip (p47).* Yalandjis *keep well, covered, for a few days in the fridge.*

450g (1lb) fresh, young, tender vine (grape) leaves or brine-preserved leaves

For the filling:
3 tbsp olive oil
½ cup pine nuts
1 large onion, coarsely grated
1 cup finely chopped spring onions (scallions)
1½ cups medium-grain rice, soaked in hot water for 10 minutes, rinsed and drained
1 cup canned chopped tomatoes
1 tbsp tomato paste
½ tsp sugar
1 cup hot vegetable stock
1 tsp sea salt
½ tsp finely ground white pepper
½ cup finely chopped fresh dill
½ cup finely chopped flat-leaf parsley (use leaves and tender stems)
⅓ cup finely chopped fresh mint

For cooking:
1 large potato, peeled and thickly sliced
2 medium ripe tomatoes, thickly sliced
3 garlic cloves
½ cup fresh lemon juice
⅓ cup olive oil
2 cups hot chicken or vegetable stock
½ tsp sea salt
½ tsp sugar

Prepare the leaves: Blanch the vine leaves in boiling water for 3 minutes, in batches, then refresh in cold water and drain. Drape the leaves over the edge of a colander to drain thoroughly.

Make the filling: Heat the oil in a large, shallow, heavy-based pan (that has a lid) over a medium-low heat. Add the pine nuts and fry for 2 minutes until just golden. Drain on paper towels. Turn the heat to medium-high, add the onion and spring onions and cook for 10 minutes, stirring occasionally, until softened. Add the rice, stirring well for 2 minutes. Stir in the tomatoes, tomato paste, sugar, hot stock, salt and pepper. Bring to a boil. Cover, reduce the heat and simmer for 15 minutes until the rice is partially cooked (*al dente*, to the bite) and most of the liquid has been absorbed. (The rice will finish cooking later.) Remove from the heat. Toss in the dill, parsley, mint and pine nuts and combine.

Stuff the leaves: Lay a few vine leaves at a time on a work surface, vein side up, with the stem towards you. Cut off the stems. Place a tablespoon of the filling in the centre of each leaf near the stem end. Fold both sides inward over the filling and roll up snugly into a cigar shape. Repeat with the remaining leaves until all the filling is used.

To cook: Line the bottom of a large, heavy-based pan with the sliced potato and tomatoes. Arrange the stuffed leaves, side-by-side, seam side down, over the vegetable base, packing them tightly in concentric circles. Slip the cloves of garlic in between the parcels. Combine the lemon juice, olive oil, hot stock, salt and sugar in a jug and pour over the vine leaves. Weigh the stuffed vine leaves down with an inverted heatproof plate large enough to fit the pan to keep the *yalandjis* from unravelling during cooking. Bring to a boil. Cover, reduce the heat and simmer for about 30 minutes, until most of the liquid has been absorbed and the rice is tender but not mushy. Remove from the heat. Place paper towels between the lid and the pan to absorb the steam for about 20 minutes.

To serve: Turn the *yalandjis* out onto a serving platter. Discard the potato and tomatoes. Serve chilled or at room temperature.

 TWIST ON TRADITION:
♦ *Swiss chard leaves make a tasty and light substitute for vine leaves. Cut away the stalks and ribs and cut the leaves into 17 × 9cm (6½ × 3½in) pieces. Blanch a few at a time in boiling water for 5 seconds and refresh in a bowl of cold water for 1 minute. Drain. Fill and cook as above.*

Meat & Poultry

chargrilled minced lamb kebabs with fresh tomato sauce
kyeftes asados kon salsa di tomat

Succulent chargrilled kebabs, made from minced lamb, are superb mixed together with parsley and spices. The sausage-shaped kebabs are moulded on flat-blade skewers and served over chunks of warmed pita bread with an aromatic fresh tomato sauce and toasted pine nuts. Alternatively, shape into patties and grill in a very hot, lightly oiled griddle pan and serve with buns and a dollop of creamy garlic and potato dip (p46).

500g (1lb 2oz) well-marbled lamb, from the shoulder, minced (ground) twice
2 tbsp lamb fat
1 medium onion, coarsely grated
½ tsp baharat spice mix (p287) or ground cumin
½ cup finely chopped flat-leaf parsley (use leaves and tender stems)
1 tsp sea salt
¼ tsp freshly ground black pepper

For basting:
1 tbsp extra-virgin olive oil

For serving:
fresh tomato sauce (see below)
1 tbsp extra-virgin olive oil
4 pita breads, cut into bite-sized chunks
2 tbsp pine nuts, toasted (p287)

You will need:
6 long, flat-blade steel skewers (see p291)

MAKE the tomato sauce (see below).

PUT the minced lamb and fat in a food processor and pulse briefly. Add the onion, oil, baharat or cumin, parsley, salt and pepper. Knead together thoroughly. Refrigerate for 1 hour for the flavours to develop.

PREHEAT a barbecue or ridged cast-iron griddle until very hot.

Shape the kebabs: With dampened hands, shape the meat mixture into 12–14 oval portions and gently mould 2–3 ovals compactly around each skewer with the palm of your hand. Place the kebabs on a lightly oiled tray.

PREHEAT the oven to 180°C (350°F). Drizzle olive oil over the pita chunks and seal tightly in foil.

To cook the kebabs: Brush the meat with oil and grill for 8–10 minutes, turning once, until char-marked and cooked through. As the kebabs are cooked, wrap in foil to keep hot while you are cooking the rest of the kebabs.

WHILE grilling the kebabs, warm the foil-wrapped pita in the preheated oven.

To serve: Scatter the pita chunks on a warmed platter and spoon some of the tomato sauce over the pita. Carefully slide the kebabs off the skewers and arrange on top. Sprinkle with toasted pine nuts. Serve immediately along with the remaining tomato sauce.

fresh tomato sauce
salsa di tomat fresko

450g (1lb) ripe tomatoes
2 tbsp olive oil
1 medium onion, finely chopped
½ tsp Turkish red pepper flakes
1 tsp sugar
1 tbsp fresh thyme leaves, stripped from the stem
sea salt
1 tsp red wine vinegar

HALVE the tomatoes crossways and squeeze out the seeds. Grate the tomato halves by rubbing the cut side against a coarse grater down to the skin. Discard the skin. Heat the oil in a medium-sized pan. Add the onion and cook, stirring frequently, for 5 minutes, until softened. Add the tomatoes, red pepper flakes, sugar and thyme and bring to a boil. Add the salt and vinegar, reduce the heat and simmer, uncovered, for 20 minutes, until the sauce has thickened.

El escarso bive prove para morir riko

(Lit: The miser lives poorly to die rich)

lamb kebabs
şiş kebab de kordero asado

Juicy cubes of marinated lamb are threaded onto metal skewers and interspersed with wedges of red onions and squares of tomatoes. The tantalising aroma of kebabs being grilled over a charcoal brazier evokes in me the magic of street food in Turkey. The succulent kebabs are wonderful sprinkled with an onion, parsley and sumac relish and wrapped in warm pita bread. These are simply superb for a casual lunch accompanied with a refreshing cabbage salad (p42).

For the marinade:
1 medium onion
¾ tsp Turkish baharat spice mix (p287)
1 tsp paprika
½ tsp Turkish red pepper flakes
1 tsp sea salt
¼ tsp freshly ground black pepper
1 tbsp fresh thyme leaves
2 tbsp olive oil
¼ cup red wine vinegar

1kg (2¼lb) boned lamb shoulder, cut into
  2.5cm (1in) cubes
2 small red onions
2 ripe tomatoes

For basting:
1 tbsp olive oil

For serving:
10 pita breads
extra-virgin olive oil
onion, parsley and sumac relish (see below)
2–3 lemons, cut into wedges

You will need:
10 flat-bladed steel skewers

Make the marinade: Grate the onion coarsely into a strainer (sieve) set over a small bowl and let stand for 10 minutes. Press down with the back of a spoon to squeeze out the juice. Discard the onion. Combine the onion juice and remaining marinade ingredients in a large bowl.

ADD the cubed lamb to the marinade, turning the pieces over so they are well coated. Cover and refrigerate for 2–3 hours.

CUT the onions into wedges and the tomatoes into 2.5cm (1in) squares.

REMOVE the lamb from the fridge and let the meat come to room temperature before grilling. Drain the marinade and thread 6–8 cubes of lamb onto each skewer, alternating with the pieces of onion and tomato, packing the meat and vegetables close together.

PREHEAT a barbecue or ridged cast-iron griddle pan until very hot.

BRUSH the kebabs with oil and cook for 4–5 minutes, turning frequently, until the lamb is nicely charred on the outside and still a little pink inside.

To serve: Slide the meat onto the pita breads. Sprinkle with onion-sumac relish and a squeeze of lemon juice. Roll the bread tightly around the kebabs or simply serve on a bed of vermicelli rice pilaf (p177).

 STELLA'S HINTS:
- *For tastier kebabs, string one or two pieces of lamb fat between the meat chunks or leave a little fat on the lamb cubes as this keeps the meat moist and succulent and drips off during cooking.*
- *You can substitute beef fillet for the lamb.*

onion, parsley and sumac relish
prichil, sevoya kon sumac

2 medium red onions, peeled
1 tsp sea salt
2 tsp ground sumac (p58)
2 tsp Turkish red pepper flakes
1 cup roughly chopped flat-leaf parsley
  (use leaves and tender stems)

CUT the onions in half lengthways, and finely slice each into half-moon slices. Place the slices in a small bowl and rub the salt into them with your fingers to extract some of the juice, until they soften. Rinse the onion slices and squeeze between your palms to remove excess water. Mix the sumac, red pepper flakes and parsley with the onions, tossing well together.

meatballs poached in a fresh tomato sauce
albondigas di karne kon tomat

Meatballs, fragrant with fresh herbs, are poached in a fresh tomato sauce. This dish, albondigas *as it is known in Ladino, is derived from the Moorish Spanish* al bundo, *meaning round. These tasty meatballs are wonderful for casual family gatherings served with a Spanish fried rice pilaf (p169) and a green (p48) or cabbage salad (p42).*

For the meatballs:
1 small onion
1 egg, lightly beaten
3 slices white bread, crusts removed, dampened in ½ cup water, squeezed and torn into small pieces
500g (1lb 2oz) lean minced (ground) beef or veal
1 ripe plum tomato, halved and coarsely grated (about 1 tbsp)
½ cup finely chopped flat-leaf parsley (use leaves and tender stems)
¼ cup finely chopped fresh dill
1 tbsp olive oil
sea salt and finely ground white pepper

For the tomato sauce:
2 cups peeled, seeded and chopped ripe tomatoes or canned chopped tomatoes
2 tender celery stalks with leaves, cut into chunks, or 4 fresh sage leaves
2 tbsp olive oil
1 tsp sugar
sea salt and finely ground white pepper

For dredging:
½ cup plain (all-purpose) flour spread on a shallow plate

For serving:
1 tbsp fresh lemon juice
1 tbsp each of finely chopped flat-leaf parsley (use leaves and tender stems) and fresh dill

Prepare the meatballs: Grate the onion finely into a strainer (sieve) set over a small bowl. Sprinkle with salt and leave to stand for 10 minutes. Press down with the back of a spoon to squeeze out the juice. Discard the onion. Combine the onion juice with the remaining meatball ingredients in a large bowl. Knead well. Cover with plastic wrap and refrigerate for about 15 minutes.

Make the tomato sauce: In a large, shallow, heavy-based pan bring all the tomato sauce ingredients to a boil over a medium-high heat. Reduce the heat to medium and cook for 5 minutes.

SHAPE the meatballs with dampened hands into about 30 small meatballs. Dredge the meatballs in the flour, to coat lightly, patting off the excess.

DROP the meatballs gently into the pan with the tomato sauce. When all the meatballs have been added, pour in a little simmering water so that the sauce comes about halfway up the meatballs. Cover and continue to cook at a very low simmer for 20 minutes, until the meatballs are tender and the sauce has thickened. Shake the pan from time to time to ensure the sauce evenly coats the meatballs and prevents them from sticking to the pan. Add a little more hot water if necessary.

To serve: Drizzle in the lemon juice and scatter with the fresh herbs.

 STELLA'S HINTS:
- *I like to use the brand Wonder bread in the U.S.*
- *Use a 4½cm (1¾in) ice-cream scoop to form evenly sized meatballs.*

 TWIST ON TRADITION:
- *Add 1 tsp ground cumin to the meatball mixture and a pinch Turkish red pepper flakes to the tomato sauce to add another layer of flavour.*

El mojado no se espanta de a luvya

(Lit: The one that is wet is not afraid of the rain)

meatballs Rhodes Island style
keftes de karne

Tasty, moist meatballs, lightly coated in flour and egg and then sautéed, are delicious for everyday fare, a buffet spread or part of a meze. Keftes (patty-shaped meatballs) were always a favourite with my children, who insisted they should be served with French fries and ketchup! The addition of tomatoes to the mixture is typical of the cuisine of the Dodecanese Islands and likely an influence of the Italians during their occupation of Rhodes between 1911 and 1947.

3 slices white bread, crusts removed, dampened in ½ cup water, squeezed and torn into small pieces
500g (1lb 2oz) lean minced (ground) beef
1 large ripe tomato, halved, seeded and coarsely grated (about 2 tbsp)
1 spring onion (scallion), finely chopped
1 tbsp finely chopped onion
½ cup roughly chopped flat-leaf parsley (use leaves and tender stems)
1 tsp dried Greek oregano, crumbled
1 tbsp olive oil
2 eggs, lightly beaten
sea salt and freshly ground black pepper

For shallow-frying:
vegetable or grape-seed oil

For dredging:
1 cup plain (all-purpose) flour spread on a shallow plate
2 eggs, lightly beaten in a shallow soup plate

COMBINE the bread, minced meat, tomato, spring onion, onion, parsley, oregano, oil and eggs in a large bowl. Season generously with salt and pepper. Knead the mixture thoroughly. Shape the meatballs with dampened hands into about 18 meatballs. Place them on a tray lined with plastic wrap and refrigerate for 20 minutes.

HEAT 3.5cm (1½in) of oil in a heavy-based frying pan over a medium-high heat. Dredge 4–5 meatballs with flour and flatten slightly, then dip into the beaten egg. Gently drop them in the oil and cook in small batches. Turn over once or twice until crisp and golden brown. Remove with a slotted spoon and drain each batch in an ovenproof dish lined with paper towels. Keep in a warm oven until all the meatballs have been cooked.

SERVE with a warm fresh tomato sauce (p148), a green spring salad (p48) and a chickpea rice pilaf (p169) or in warm hamburger rolls, with sliced tomato and onion for the children!

 STELLA'S HINTS:
- *I like to use the brand Wonder bread in the U.S.*
- *For Passover, substitute ¼ cup of matza meal for the bread and coat the meatballs with matza flour.*
- *To freeze: Pack the cooked meatballs into a plastic container with a tight-fitting lid. Allow to defrost to room temperature before reheating.*
- *To reheat: Place the meatballs in an ovenproof dish covered with foil in a preheated 180 °C (350 °F) oven, until warmed through.*
- *Use a 6cm (2¼in) ice-cream scoop to form evenly sized meatballs.*

 TWIST ON TRADITION:
- *Meatballs simmered in tomato sauce (Keftes kon kaldo di tomat): Leftover fried meatballs can be simmered in a tomato sauce for a hot entrée served with rice.*

For the tomato sauce:
1 tbsp olive oil
2 tbsp tomato paste
1 tender celery stalk with leaves, cut into chunks
1 tbsp fresh lemon juice
1 cup boiling water
sea salt and freshly ground black pepper
½ tsp sugar
1 tsp sweet paprika (optional)

COMBINE all the tomato sauce ingredients in a shallow, heavy-based pan with a lid. Simmer, partially covered, for 10 minutes and then add the cooked meatballs. Scoop some of the sauce over the meatballs and continue to simmer for another 10 minutes. Gently shake and tilt the pan from time to time to ensure the tomato sauce evenly coats the meatballs and prevents them sticking to the pan.

slow-cooked lamb with potatoes
kuzi de pesah

An easy one-pan lamb and potato dish which is perfect as a family meal on a chilly night. The lamb is gently simmered on the stovetop then briefly browned in the oven. Traditionally this flavoursome dish is served for the Passover dinner, paired with a green spring salad (p48) or braised green beans (p76).

1.5kg (3¼lb) shoulder of lamb, cut
    through the bone into even chunks*
5 tbsp olive oil
2 onions, roughly chopped
2 fresh bay leaves
2 small sprigs fresh rosemary
sea salt and freshly ground black pepper
3–4 cups hot chicken stock
1kg (2¼lb) waxy potatoes, peeled and
    quartered lengthways
3 tbsp roughly chopped flat-leaf parsley
    (use leaves and tender stems)

You will need:
an enamelled, cast-iron, shallow oven-to-
    table casserole

TRIM excess fat from the lamb.

HEAT 4 tbsp olive oil in the casserole over a medium-high heat. Add the lamb and cook in batches on all sides until lightly browned. Remove the lamb with tongs and keep in a heatproof dish.

ADD the onions to the casserole and cook for 5 minutes, stirring frequently, until softened. Return the browned meat to the pan. Add the bay leaves, rosemary sprigs and season with salt and pepper. Pour in enough hot stock to just cover the lamb. Bring to a boil. Cover, reduce the heat and simmer for 3–4 hours or until the meat is tender, adding more hot stock as necessary. Skim the fat off the cooking juices in the pan.

MEANWHILE boil the potatoes until just tender and drain.

SCATTER the potatoes over the lamb and sprinkle with half the parsley. Drizzle remaining olive oil over the potatoes and season with salt and pepper.

PREHEAT the oven to grill/broil 15 minutes before serving. Place under the grill for 15 minutes or until the potatoes are golden brown. Serve at once with the remaining parsley sprinkled on top.

 STELLA'S HINTS:
- **Ask your butcher to cut the shoulder into roughly 5–6cm (2–2½in) chunks.*
- *Lamb chops can be used instead of shoulder, which will save cooking time.*

En boka serada no entra moshka

(Lit: In a closed mouth a fly cannot enter)

Silence is golden

chicken kebabs
kebab de gayina asada

Cubes of chicken, made tender and flavourful in a lemon-garlic marinade and then grilled on skewers, makes a perfect addition to your barbecue repertoire. Serve the kebabs on a bed of chickpea rice pilaf (p169) or wrapped in pita bread with a tangy garlic and potato dip (p46).

900g (2lb) boneless, skinned, free-range
    chicken breasts, cut into 2.5cm (1in)
    cubes
2 small red onions
2 ripe tomatoes
2 yellow bell peppers

For the marinade:
3 tbsp olive oil
2 garlic cloves, finely grated
2 tbsp fresh lemon juice
1 tsp paprika
½ tsp sea salt
¼ tsp freshly ground black pepper

For basting:
1 tbsp olive oil
sea salt

You will need:
8 stainless steel skewers about 30cm
    (12in) long or sticks of fresh rosemary,
    lower leaves removed and the point
    sharpened with a knife

COMBINE all the marinade ingredients in a large bowl. Add the cubed chicken, turning the pieces over so they are well coated. Cover and refrigerate for 2 hours.

CUT the onions into wedges and the tomatoes and yellow peppers into 2.5cm (1in) squares.

REMOVE the chicken from the fridge and let it come to room temperature. Drain the marinade and thread the chicken cubes onto skewers or rosemary sticks, alternating with the vegetables. Be careful not to cram them too tightly to ensure that they cook evenly.

PREHEAT a barbecue or ridged cast-iron griddle pan until very hot.

BRUSH the kebabs with oil and season lightly with salt. Cook the kebabs for 6 minutes, turning frequently until the chicken is nicely charred on the outside and cooked through but still moist. Serve immediately.

 STELLA'S HINT:

♦ *To serve chicken kebab with pita: Split each pita bread in half, opening at the seam. Lay half a pita on a plate, rough side up and spread with garlic and potato dip. Push the chicken off the skewers on top of the garlic dip. Scatter with pickles or Turkish diced salad (p32) and roll the bread tightly around the filling. Cover the bottom half of each wrap with paper napkins.*

 TWIST ON TRADITION:

♦ *For an easy, spicy Moorish marinade add 1 tbsp harissa paste (see below) to 3 tbsp olive oil and 1 tsp sea salt.*

hot chilli paste
harissa

I find this hot chilli paste to be a useful and versatile condiment, especially for those who like a fiery kick to their food. It is good to have on stand-by as it keeps well in the fridge for up to a month. You may want to wear rubber gloves when preparing the chillies. If you have already experienced the store-bought harissa, try this homemade version – I find the colour and texture is superior and you can vary the heat so it's just right for your palate.

500g (1lb 2oz) fresh hot red chillies
2 tbsp coriander seeds
1 tbsp cumin seeds
1 tsp caraway seeds
3 garlic cloves, crushed
¼ cup extra-virgin olive oil, plus extra
    to pour over the top
¾ tsp salt

RINSE the chillies in running water. Break off the tops and slit lengthways. Scrape out the seeds and membranes.

TOAST the coriander, cumin and caraway seeds in a frying pan, stirring frequently over a medium heat, until the aroma of the spices starts to rise.

PUT the chillies, spices, garlic, olive oil and salt in a blender or processor fitted with a metal blade. Process until a smooth thick paste is formed. Spoon the harissa into a sterilised glass jar, smooth the top and cover with a thin layer of olive oil. Seal and refrigerate.

saffron-glazed baby chickens stuffed with couscous and almonds

gayina kon asafran, couscous i almendras

Imagine a celebratory dish of crisp saffron-glazed baby chickens, stuffed with couscous and almonds, stacked around a mound of fried potatoes or plain couscous in the centre. This makes a magnificent dinner party dish.

6 × 400g (14oz) free-range baby chickens
  (*petit poussins*), rinsed and patted dry
sea salt and freshly ground black pepper
3 tbsp olive oil
2 large onions, finely sliced
1 tsp ground cinnamon
1 tsp *ras-el-hanout* (optional)
2 tbsp vegetable oil
½ tsp saffron threads
1 cup hot chicken stock
1–2 tbsp runny honey
1 tbsp icing (confectioner's) sugar
½ cup golden raisins, soaked in 1 cup
  hot water with ½ tsp ground
  cinnamon for 10 minutes

For the stuffing:
½ cup couscous
1 cup hot chicken stock
a pinch saffron threads
2 tbsp vegetable oil
½ cup golden raisins, soaked in 1 cup hot
  water for 10 minutes and drained
1 tsp ground cinnamon
1 tbsp icing (confectioner's) sugar
1 tbsp runny honey
1 cup whole blanched almonds, toasted
  and roughly chopped in a food
  processor
sea salt and finely ground white pepper

You will need:
a shallow braising pan with a lid that will
  fit the birds snugly, breast-side up

Prepare the stuffing: Place the couscous in a bowl and pour in the hot chicken stock and a pinch of saffron threads. Lightly work with your hands to break up any lumps. Add the oil to the grains and fluff up lightly with a fork. Cover tightly with plastic wrap and set aside for about 10 minutes or until the liquid has been absorbed. Add the raisins, cinnamon, icing sugar, honey and half the chopped almonds to the couscous. Season with salt and pepper to taste and mix gently with a fork. Set aside.

SEASON the baby chickens inside and outside with salt and pepper. Spoon the couscous stuffing into the chicken cavity until approximately three-quarters full. Secure the skin with a toothpick.

HEAT 1 tbsp olive oil in the braising pan over a medium-high heat and cook the onions with the cinnamon and *ras-el-hanout* (if using) until softened.

BLEND the vegetable oil with the saffron and rub over the chickens. Place them breast-side up in the braising pan over the onions. Pour in the hot chicken stock and bring to a boil. Cover, reduce the heat and simmer for 30 minutes, basting the chickens with the pan juices from time to time. Turn the chickens often and add hot water as necessary. Cook until tender and the juices run clear when the thighs are pierced with a skewer.

TRANSFER the baby chickens to a large plate. Bring the pan juices to a rapid boil, reducing the cooking liquid to 1 cup. Add the honey, icing sugar and the raisins with the soaking liquid to the sauce. Stir to blend well and taste. Adjust seasoning for salt and pepper and sweetness.

HEAT the remaining 2 tbsp of olive oil in a large frying pan, over a medium-high heat and transfer the chickens to the frying pan. Carefully fry them, turning until they are glossy and golden brown.

To serve: Heap plain couscous or fried potatoes in the centre of a large, warmed platter. Stack the baby chickens around the couscous or potatoes. Spoon the saffron sauce over the chickens and scatter with the remaining chopped almonds. Serve immediately.

Pensando al envierno no se goza el enverano

(Lit: Thinking of the winter one does not enjoy the summer)

Enjoy the present

spicy piri-piri baby chicken

Growing up in landlocked Rhodesia (in what is now Zimbabwe), our family spent many holidays in Beira, a seaside resort on the Mozambique coast off the Indian Ocean. Our frequent trips were prompted by my father's need to secure timber from the many sawmills in the country for his furniture factory. We relished the Portuguese flavours in Mozambique and became addicted to their fiery blend of African bird's eye chilli, garlic and lemon basted piri-piri chicken. As children we opted for the mild version, served with a heaping of potato chips (French fries) and a Turkish diced salad (p32).

4 × 450g (1lb) free-range baby chickens
(*petit poussins*), rinsed and patted dry

For the marinade:
½ cup fresh lemon juice
4 garlic cloves, finely grated
2 heaped tsp sweet paprika
1 tsp dried oregano
2 tsp sea salt

For basting:
6 dried bird's eye chillies or 4 fresh
chillies, seeded and finely chopped
3 garlic cloves, roughly chopped
¼ cup olive oil
1 tsp sea salt
2 bay leaves, preferably fresh
2 tbsp whisky (optional)

 TWIST ON TRADITION:
◆ *Za'atar chicken: Alternatively you can use a za'atar marinade: 2 tbsp za'atar spice blend; a pinch ground cinnamon; ¼ cup fresh lemon juice; 4 garlic cloves, grated; 3 tbsp olive oil. Marinate with half of this mixture and use the remaining marinade for basting when browning the cooked chickens. Za'atar is a spice blend consisting of thyme, ground sumac and roasted sesame seeds and is available from Middle Eastern speciality stores.*

Butterfly the chickens: To remove the backbone, position the chicken on a chopping board, breast-side down, so the drumsticks are facing towards you. With kitchen shears, snip closely along the backbone and remove. Turn the chicken breast-side up and press down firmly on the breastbone to flatten the chicken. Make a few slashes where the flesh is thickest to ensure that it cooks evenly all the way through. Trim off excess fat and repeat with remaining chickens.

Make the marinade: Mix all the ingredients together.

POUR the marinade in a shallow bowl large enough to fit the chickens. Rub the marinade over the chickens, turning them over so that they are well coated. Cover and marinate in the fridge for at least 2 hours or preferably overnight.

Make the basting: With a mortar and pestle crush the chillies and garlic to a paste. Stir in the oil, salt, torn bay leaves and whisky (if using). Taste and adjust the seasoning. Add more chilli according to your taste. Set aside.

REMOVE the chickens from the fridge 30 minutes before cooking to return to room temperature.

PREHEAT the oven to 200°C (400°F). Foil-line a roasting pan large enough to hold the chickens in a single layer.

TRANSFER the chickens, skin-side up, to the prepared tray. Sprinkle with salt, cover with foil and roast for 45 minutes until cooked through and the juices run clear when the thigh is pierced with a sharp knife.

REMOVE the foil, lift the chickens out and discard the marinade. Return the chickens to the pan and brush with half the basting sauce. Place the chickens under a hot grill for 4–5 minutes on each side and continue basting with the remaining sauce until golden brown and crisp. Allow to rest for 5 minutes to reabsorb the juices. Serve with a tomato rice pilaf (p172) or fried potato chips.

 STELLA'S HINT:
◆ *Baby chickens, also known as spatchcocks, are available from butchers.*

Berekyet versin

(Lit: Giving thanks after a meal for abundance)

Rice Pilafs & Noodles

Sephardic Rice Pilaf

Rice, the preferred grain of the Sephardim, was introduced to Spain in the 8th century by the Moors and has remained a constant in Sephardic cuisine ever since. Rice traditionally symbolises fertility, purity, prosperity and abundance.

The basic rice pilaf is made by soaking the uncooked grains and then briefly sautéing them in oil. A measured amount of hot stock is added and the rice is then covered and simmered undisturbed. This method of cooking the white rice pilaf is the basis for making the fresh tomato and saffron pilafs, as well as the more elaborate and sumptuous pilafs that are cooked with chickpeas, aubergines and toasted nuts.

If cooked correctly, each grain of rice should be tender to the bite and plump and separate easily from one another. Overall the rice pilaf should be fluffy. At all costs avoid rice that my mother derisively refers to as *lapa* – soggy rice.

- I use basmati rice, preferably Indian or Pakistani, with its long grain for the best results (not the pre-steamed processed variety). It has a good texture and absorbs the flavours of the other ingredients with which it is cooked.
- One cup of long-grain basmati rice absorbs about 2 cups boiling water and will yield 3 cups cooked rice. I find cooking 2 cups rice sufficient to feed 4–6 people as an accompaniment to a main course.
- Experiment with a brand of long-grain basmati rice to assess the precise quantity of liquid required as the absorption by the grains differs with each variety.
- First, soak the rice in a generous amount of boiling water for 10 minutes. Then drain and rinse under cold running water in a fine-mesh sieve until the water runs clear, removing as much of the starchy water as possible. Drain again.
- I recommend the use of a deep, heavy-based, straight-sided pan to ensure even distribution of heat. A tight-fitting lid is essential. The capacity of the pan should be at least six times the volume of the uncooked rice as the rice expands to about three times its original volume.
- For rice pilafs and noodles you can use one half of a chicken or vegetable stock cube for 2 cups water or 1 tsp of concentrated chicken or vegetable stock paste.
- Be sure to stir only once when adding the stock and salt. Thereafter resist the temptation to stir as it is important that you allow the rice to steam undisturbed. Stretch a clean folded tea towel over the top of the pan and press the lid tightly on top, securing it in place. This will absorb excess moisture.
- To store cooked rice: When the rice is at room temperature, place in an airtight container and refrigerate for up to 2 days.
- To reheat cooked rice: Sprinkle about 1 tbsp hot water over the rice and place on a low heat. Cook until piping hot, killing any bacteria.

In our home, a rice or vermicelli pilaf is served once or twice a day accompanying the main dish. The techniques for making a perfect pilaf are soon mastered, resulting in perfectly balanced and satisfying flavourful meals. I encourage you to make these rice pilafs as part of your everyday home cooking.

Esta arroz alvanta muncha agua

(Lit: This rice will absorb a lot of water)

This will take a lot of sorting out

wedding pilaf
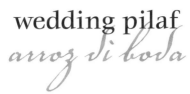
arroz di boda

Wedding rice pilaf, crowned with a crunchy topping of mixed nuts, is an elegant way of presenting the classic white rice pilaf for a festive table. This rice pilaf is a boon for easy entertaining as you simply pack the base of an oiled ring-shaped mould with the toasted nuts before pressing the cooked white rice on top. This can be prepared in advance and heated through just before serving.

¾ cup mixed nuts of your choice, such as blanched almonds, blanched pistachios and pine nuts
1–2 tbsp sunflower or olive oil

MAKE the basic white rice pilaf (p168).

FRY the nuts, except pistachios, in a small frying pan, with a little vegetable oil, over a medium heat, shaking the pan until they colour. Remove with a slotted spoon and drain on paper towels.

SPREAD the toasted nuts and pistachios evenly over the bottom of an oiled ring mould just large enough to hold all the rice. Pack the cooked rice into the mould, pressing down firmly over the nuts. Cover the mould with foil.

To serve: Preheat the oven to 150°C (300°F) 30 minutes before serving in the dish. Place the mould into a baking dish and pour 2.5cm (1in) of hot water into the dish. Place in the preheated oven for about 20 minutes or until heated through. Discard the foil.

SET a large, warmed serving platter over the open end of the mould. Carefully invert, turning the rice out onto the platter, and serve.

Ken se aharva kon sus manos ke no yore

(Lit: Someone who strikes himself with his hands let him not cry)

Someone who finds himself in trouble through his own fault must not complain

basic white rice pilaf
arroz blanko

This simple everyday pilaf, which the Spanyolim affectionately refer to in Ladino as arroz a la muestra *(rice our way), complements grills, roasts, stews and stuffed vegetable dishes. This is the basic version for most variations of rice pilafs made by the Sephardim from Rhodes, Salonica, Greece and Turkey. I particularly like to pair* arroz blanko *with the more elaborate and colourful dishes to create balance and contrast.*

2 cups water

3 tbsp sunflower or olive oil

1 generous cup long-grain basmati rice, soaked in boiling water for 10 minutes, rinsed and drained

½ chicken or vegetable stock cube

1 tsp salt

BRING the water to a boil. Reduce the heat and keep at a simmer.

HEAT the oil in a deep, heavy-based pan over a medium-high heat. Add the rice and cook, stirring constantly for 1 minute, until the grains are well coated and become opaque.

POUR the simmering water into a heatproof measuring jug, crumble in the stock cube and stir in the salt.

CAREFULLY pour the hot stock into the pan with the sizzling fried rice, as it will splatter. Stir once. Bring to a boil. Cover with a tight-fitting lid, reduce the heat to medium and simmer undisturbed for about 12 minutes or until the rice has absorbed all the liquid and little holes appear on the surface. Do not stir. The grains should be just tender to the bite. Turn off the heat. Stretch a clean folded tea towel over the top of the pan and press the lid tightly on top, securing it in place. Leave the pilaf to stand on the warm stovetop for 10 minutes. The rice grains should be plump, tender and separate from one another.

To serve: Fluff up the rice with a fork and tip into a deep serving dish.

 TWIST ON TRADITION:

- *Rice pilaf with fresh herbs is often served at New Year, auguring a good year. Add 1 cup finely chopped mixed fresh herbs (including flat-leaf parsley, coriander (cilantro), dill and chives) or a few finely sliced spring onions (scallions) to the rice while cooking, when the water is totally absorbed. To serve: Fluff up the rice with a fork, mixing in the steamed herbs, and tip into a deep serving dish.*

saffron rice pilaf
arroz kon zafran (arroz di shabbat)

Medieval Moors in Spain introduced saffron to their cooking, which tinted their food with a golden yellow colour, signifying joy. Fragrant saffron rice pilaf still appears at our celebratory tables at the New Year and the Sabbath and at other joyful festivities.

¾ tsp saffron threads, crushed

2 tbsp hot water

CRUMBLE the saffron threads with your fingertips and soak in the hot water. Let it steep for a few minutes for the colour and fragrance to be extracted.

MAKE a basic white rice pilaf (p168). When adding the simmering stock and salt, also add the saffron and water mixture.

chickpea rice pilaf
arroz kon garavansos

Rice laden with golden nutritious chickpeas makes a wholesome pilaf. I like to serve this glorious dish alongside stews and grilled food or as part of a buffet.

2 cups water

3 tbsp sunflower or olive oil

1 large onion, finely chopped

1 cup canned chickpeas, drained and rinsed

1 generous cup long-grain basmati rice, soaked in boiling water for 10 minutes, rinsed and drained

½ chicken or vegetable stock cube

1 tsp salt

TWIST ON TRADITION:

♦ *For an aromatic flavour, add ¼ tsp ground allspice and ½ tsp ground cinnamon together with the chickpeas.*

BRING the water to a boil. Reduce the heat and keep at a simmer.

HEAT the oil in a deep, heavy-based pan over a medium-high heat. Add the onion to the pan and cook for 5 minutes, stirring frequently, until softened. Add the chickpeas and rice, stirring constantly for 1 minute, until the rice grains are well coated and become opaque.

POUR the simmering water into a heatproof measuring jug, crumble in the stock cube and stir in the salt.

CAREFULLY pour the hot stock into the pan with the sizzling fried rice, as it will splatter. Stir once. Bring to a boil. Cover with a tight-fitting lid, reduce the heat to medium and simmer undisturbed for about 12 minutes or until the rice has absorbed all the liquid and little holes appear on the surface. Do not stir. The grains should be just tender to the bite. Turn off the heat. Stretch a clean folded tea towel over the top of the pan and press the lid tightly on top, securing it in place. Leave the pilaf to stand on the warm stovetop for 10 minutes. The rice grains should be plump, tender and separate from one another.

To serve: Fluff up the rice and chickpeas with a fork and tip into a deep serving dish.

Spanish fried rice pilaf
arroz frito

Arroz frito is like a rice mosaic with fried golden brown grains speckled amongst the white rice. The golden grains can be added while cooking to soften, or at the end to add extra crunch – highly sought after in my home.

2 cups water

3 tbsp sunflower or olive oil

1 generous cup long-grain basmati rice, soaked in boiling water for 10 minutes, rinsed and drained

½ chicken or vegetable stock cube

1 tsp salt

STELLA'S HINT:

♦ **For a crunchier texture, toss the reserved fried golden rice into the cooked white rice and serve.*

BRING the water to a boil. Reduce the heat and keep at a simmer.

HEAT the oil in a deep, heavy-based pan over a medium-high heat. Add 3 tbsp rice and cook until golden brown for 1–2 minutes. Remove with a slotted spoon and set aside*. Add the remaining rice and cook for 1 minute, stirring constantly, until the grains are well coated and become opaque. Add the reserved fried golden rice.

POUR the simmering water into a heatproof measuring jug, crumble in the stock cube and stir in the salt.

CAREFULLY pour the hot stock into the pan with the sizzling fried rice, as it will splatter. Stir once. Bring to a boil. Cover with a tight-fitting lid, reduce the heat to medium and simmer undisturbed for about 12 minutes or until the rice has absorbed all the liquid and little holes appear on the surface. Do not stir. The grains should be just tender to the bite. Turn off the heat. Stretch a clean folded tea towel over the top of the pan and press the lid tightly on top, securing it in place. Leave the pilaf to stand on the warm stovetop for 10 minutes. The rice grains should be plump, tender and separate from one another.

To serve: Fluff up the rice with a fork and tip into a deep serving dish.

aubergine pilaf with pine nuts

arroz pilaf kon berendjena i pinyones

Turkish-inspired aubergine pilaf is redolent with warming spices, toasted pine nuts and succulent morsels of cooked aubergine. Try this aromatic pilaf as it is a sumptuous accompaniment to roasts and grilled food and makes a tasty change from the basic white rice pilaf.

2 plump aubergines (eggplants), about 450g (1lb)
1 tbsp kosher or coarse salt
1 tsp fresh lemon juice

For the rice:
1¾ cups water
3 tbsp extra-virgin olive oil
1 large onion, finely chopped
2 garlic cloves, grated
1 tsp sugar
½ tsp ground cumin
½ tsp ground coriander
1 cinnamon stick
1 cup long-grain basmati rice, soaked in boiling water for 10 minutes, rinsed and drained
1 tsp tomato paste
1 cup peeled, seeded and chopped ripe tomatoes or canned chopped tomatoes
½ tsp paprika
½ chicken or vegetable stock cube
1 tsp sea salt

For shallow-frying:
vegetable or grape-seed oil

For serving:
2 tbsp finely chopped fresh dill
½ cup pine nuts, lightly toasted (p287)

Prepare the aubergines: Cut the stems off the aubergines. Using a very sharp knife, peel 1.25cm (½in) strips at intervals along the length of the aubergines, leaving it striped with some peel. Cut each aubergine into slices about 1.25cm (½in) thick. In a large bowl, dissolve 1 tbsp coarse salt into 2.4lt (5pt) water and add 1 tsp lemon juice. Immerse the aubergine slices and place a weighted plate on top to keep them submerged. Soak for 45 minutes. Rinse under cold running water and drain. Pat dry with paper towels.

Cook the aubergines: Heat enough oil for shallow-frying in a large frying pan over a medium-high heat. Cook the aubergine slices in the sizzling oil, in batches, for 3–5 minutes per side, until fork tender and lightly golden on all sides. Replenish the oil as necessary and adjust the temperature of the oil if it becomes too hot. Lift the aubergines out with a slotted spoon and drain on a plate lined with paper towels. Press lightly with paper towels to soak up excess oil.

Make the rice: Bring the water to a boil. Reduce the heat and keep at a simmer. Heat the oil in a deep, heavy-based pan over a medium-high heat. Add the onion to the pan and cook for 5 minutes, stirring frequently, until softened. Add the garlic and stir in the sugar, cumin, coriander and cinnamon stick. Add the rice, stirring constantly for 1 minute, until the grains are well coated and become opaque. Stir in the tomato paste, tomatoes and paprika.

POUR the simmering water into a heatproof measuring jug, crumble in the stock cube and stir in the salt.

POUR in the hot stock and stir once. Bring to a boil. Cover with a tight-fitting lid, reduce the heat to medium and simmer undisturbed for about 12 minutes or until the rice has absorbed all the liquid and little holes appear on the surface. The grains should be just tender to the bite. Turn off the heat. Stretch a clean folded tea towel over the top of the pan and press the lid tightly on top, securing it in place. Leave the pilaf to stand on the warm stovetop for 10 minutes. The rice grains should be plump, tender and separate from one another. Discard the cinnamon stick. Toss in the aubergines, dill and pine nuts. Fluff up with a fork and tip into a deep serving dish.

 STELLA'S HINT:

♦ *To reheat, place covered in a 180°C (350°F) preheated oven for 15 minutes or until heated through.*

Nasido de syete mezes

(Lit: Premature born at 7 months)

Person always in a hurry wanting immediate results

tomato rice pilaf

arroz kon kaldo de tomat

Known as 'pink rice' in our home, the love for this dish has been instilled in my grandkids who always ask for it shortly after I arrive for one of my visits. For the Sephardim in Turkey this pilaf made with ripe fresh tomatoes is known as arrosito a la Judia *(rice the Jewish way).*

1½ cups water

3 tbsp sunflower or olive oil

1 cup peeled, seeded and puréed ripe
   tomatoes

½ tsp sugar

1 cup long-grain basmati rice, soaked in
   boiling water for 10 minutes, rinsed
   and drained

½ chicken or vegetable stock cube

1 tsp salt

BRING the water to a boil. Reduce the heat and keep at a simmer.

HEAT the oil in a deep, heavy-based pan over a medium-high heat. Add the tomatoes and sugar carefully as it will splatter. Reduce the heat to medium and cook uncovered, stirring occasionally, until the tomatoes thicken slightly – about 5 minutes.

ADD the rice, coating it in the tomato sauce, stirring gently for a further 1 minute.

POUR the simmering water into a heatproof measuring jug, crumble in the stock cube and stir in the salt.

POUR the hot stock into the rice mixture and stir once. Bring to a boil. Cover with a tight-fitting lid, reduce the heat to medium and simmer undisturbed for about 12 minutes or until the rice has absorbed all the liquid and little holes appear on the surface. The grains should be just tender to the bite. Turn off the heat. Stretch a clean folded tea towel over the top of the pan and press the lid tightly on top, securing it in place. Leave the pilaf to stand on the warm stovetop for 10 minutes. The rice grains should be plump, tender and separate from one another.

To serve: Fluff up the rice with a fork and tip into a deep serving dish.

 STELLA'S HINT:

♦ *2 tbsp tomato paste may be used instead of the puréed tomatoes.*

TWIST ON TRADITION:

♦ *Fry 1 small onion, finely chopped, in the oil until softened. Then add the tomatoes and sugar and continue cooking as above.*

Este es nacido de Viernes

(Lit: He is born on Friday)

He is an intelligent, talented person (The popular belief that being born on a Friday one is mysteriously gifted with extraordinary intelligence and attributes)

toasted noodles in a tomato sauce
fidéyos tostados

The Sephardim have a distinctive way of cooking angel hair noodles. The noodles are toasted and then simmered with just enough tomatoes and chicken stock to cook them. The browning stage imparts a nutty, toasted flavour. This noodle dish, also called fidellos *in Ladino, was brought to Spain in the 13th century by the Arabs. It makes a tasty and unusual accompaniment to any non tomato-based dish, instead of rice pilaf. My mother makes this dish with coiled ribbon-like egg pasta –* tagliatelli *or the diminutive* stellini *(little stars) – a delicious alternative that my grandchildren love. If using vermicelli, the strands should be broken into thirds or halved.*

250g (9oz) vermicelli, coiled angel hair
   noodles or other thin pasta
3 tbsp sunflower oil
1 cup canned chopped tomatoes, puréed
1 tbsp tomato paste
1 tsp salt
2 cups chicken or vegetable stock

PREHEAT the oven to 180°C (350°F).

Toast the noodles: Spread the coiled noodles on a baking tray. Place in the oven to toast for about 15 minutes or until a light golden colour, stirring or shaking the tray so that the noodles colour evenly. Watch carefully as the noodles tend to brown quickly. Then toss the coloured noodles into a bowl to cool.

HEAT the oil in a large, heavy-based pan over a medium-high heat. Stir in the tomatoes, tomato paste and salt. Reduce the heat and simmer for about 5 minutes or until the tomatoes thicken, stirring occasionally.

POUR the hot stock carefully into the tomato sauce and stir once. Bring to a boil. Add the noodles, reduce the heat to a simmer and cook for about 15 minutes, partially covered, until the liquid has been absorbed and the noodles are tender. Stir occasionally, lifting the noodles with a fork to prevent them sticking together and to break up the coils. A little boiling water may be added to the noodles if they seem too dry. However, if the noodles seem too moist, leave the lid off to dry out a little.

REMOVE from the heat and tip the noodles into a deep serving dish.

 STELLA'S HINTS:

◆ *Alternatively: To brown the noodles you can fry them. Heat 2 tbsp of sunflower oil in a deep, wide frying pan over a medium-high heat. Add the noodles in batches and cook until lightly golden, stirring constantly, so that the colour shades evenly. Remove the noodles using a slotted spoon and drain on paper towels.*
◆ *To reheat, place on the stovetop over a gentle heat with the lid on, carefully lifting the noodles from time to time with a fork.*

Mujer kon meoyo, mazal i repozo

(Lit: A woman with brains, good luck and rest)

To be assured of a good life, choose a wise woman

vermicelli rice pilaf

arroz kon fideyos

Vermicelli rice pilaf makes for an unusual and tasty accompaniment to grilled meats, stuffed vegetable dishes and stews. This rice pilaf includes pieces of vermicelli tossed in hot oil until it begins to colour, which gives a nutty flavour to the dish.

2 cups water

3 tbsp sunflower or olive oil

½ cup vermicelli noodles, broken into
  2.5cm (1in) lengths

1½ cups long-grain basmati rice, soaked
  in boiling water for 10 minutes,
  rinsed and drained

½ chicken or vegetable stock cube

1 tsp sea salt

BRING the water to a boil. Reduce the heat and keep at a simmer.

HEAT the oil in a deep, heavy-based pan over a medium-high heat, add the vermicelli and cook, stirring constantly, until it turns light golden in colour. Watch carefully as it browns rapidly. Add the rice and cook, stirring constantly for 1 minute, until the grains are well coated and become opaque.

POUR the simmering water into a heatproof measuring jug, crumble in the stock cube and stir in the salt.

CAREFULLY pour the hot stock into the pan with the sizzling fried rice, as it will splatter. Stir once. Bring to a boil. Cover with a tight-fitting lid, reduce the heat to medium and simmer undisturbed for about 12 minutes or until the rice has absorbed all the liquid and little holes appear on the surface. Do not stir. The grains should be just tender to the bite. Turn off the heat. Stretch a clean folded tea towel over the top of the pan and press the lid tightly on top, securing it in place. Leave the pilaf to stand on the warm stovetop for 10 minutes. The rice grains should be plump, tender and separate from one another.

To serve: Fluff up the rice with a fork and tip into a deep serving dish.

 STELLA'S HINT:

♦ *You can toast the vermicelli on a baking tray in a preheated 180°C (350°F) oven. Be sure to stir often so that the pasta colours evenly.*

Arvole sin solombra

(Lit: A tree without shade)

An expression said of one who is selfish and does not give to others

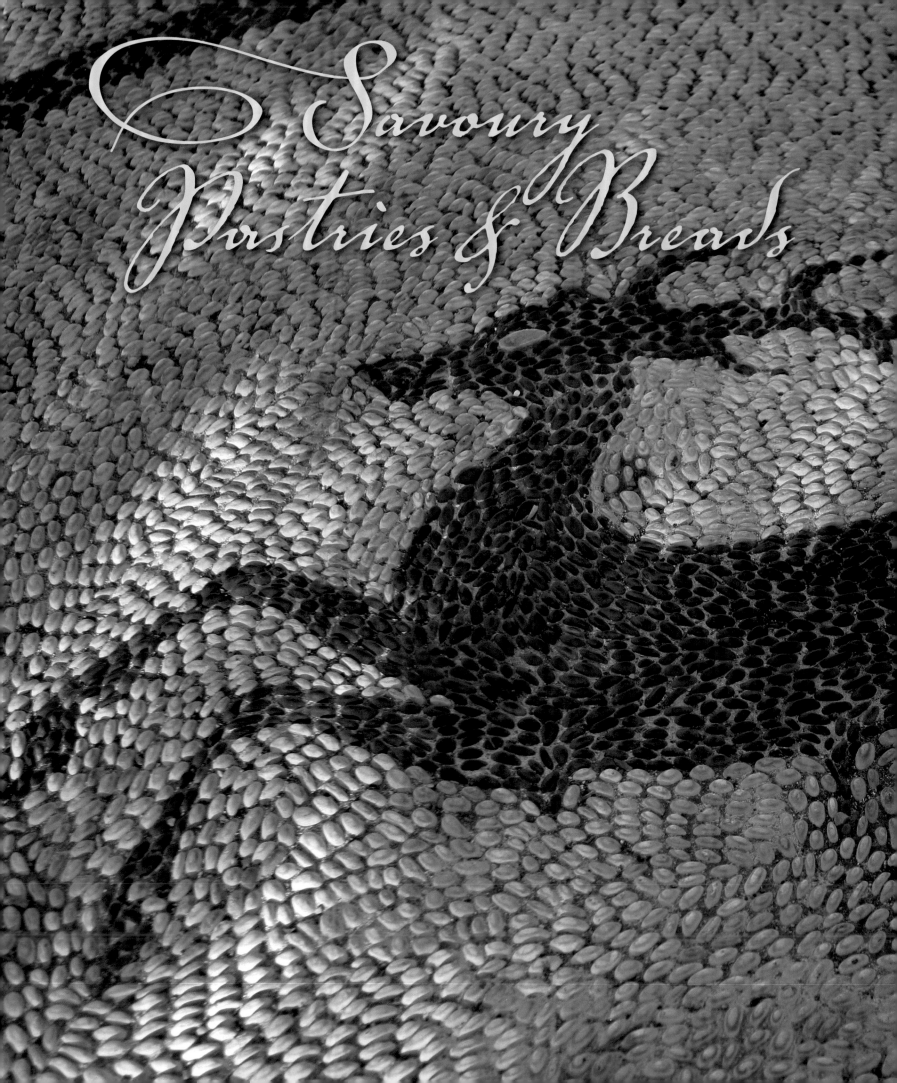

Savoury
Pastries & Breads

cheese and potato tartlets
gizadas de patata i kezo

*These dainty, cupcake-like tartlets (*gizadas* – derived from the Spanish* quesadilla *for cheese turnovers) are a speciality of the Greek Islands. Made with a pleated, star-shaped pastry, encasing a luscious potato and cheese filling, handcrafted* gizadas *make elegant savoury nibbles for a party or gathering.*

For the filling:
½ cup grated or crumbled ricotta
½ cup grated kefalotiri or Parmesan
    cheese
3–4 eggs, lightly beaten
3 large potatoes (about 500g/1lb 2oz),
    boiled, skinned and mashed
salt and finely ground white pepper

For the pastry:
3 cups plain (all-purpose) flour, sifted
½ tsp baking powder
½ tsp salt
¼ cup olive oil
¼ cup vegetable oil, plus extra for
    brushing
¾ cup iced water

For the egg wash:
1 egg yolk mixed with 1 tbsp milk

For the topping:
2 tbsp finely grated kefalotiri or
    Parmesan cheese

Prepare the filling: Combine the cheeses and the eggs in a large bowl. Then add the potato and season with salt and pepper. Mix well.

Prepare the pastry: Put the flour, baking powder and salt in a large bowl and make a well in the centre. Add the oils and water and incorporate gradually until the dough begins to hold together and makes a smooth elastic dough. If the pastry is too soft to retain its shape, add a little more flour.

Make the tartlets: Divide the dough into four portions. Take one portion and roll the pastry very thinly. If you have a pasta machine you can put the dough through it. Keep the remaining portions covered with plastic wrap until required. Cut circles out of the rolled pastry using a 7cm (2¾in) biscuit cutter. Place a teaspoon of filling in the centre of each circle, leaving a 1.25cm (½in) margin. Carefully work around the edges of the pastry circles using your thumb and forefinger to pinch upright pleats around the filling, leaving the cheese filling exposed. The closer and tighter the pleats are pinched together the better the filling will be held. Repeat this process with the remaining pastry.

PREHEAT the oven to 190°C (375°F). Lightly brush two large baking trays with oil.

ARRANGE the filled shells on the baking trays. Brush the tops with the egg wash and sprinkle with grated cheese. Bake for about 30 minutes or until the pastry is crisp and lightly golden. Transfer to wire racks. Serve hot or at room temperature.

 STELLA'S HINT:
♦ *To freeze baked tartlets: Place the tartlets between layers of baking paper in an airtight container and freeze for up to 1 month. To serve, defrost in the container for 1–2 hours. Preheat the oven to 180°C (350°F) and reheat the tartlets on a baking tray for 10 minutes.*

cheese scones
boyikos de kezo (boyikos de rayo)

These easy-to-make cheese scones are good for newcomers to baking and are also really fun for kids to make (and eat). The name boyikos de rayo, *derived from* rayo *in Ladino (grater), refers to the decorative imprint that was traditionally made on the scone with a grater. These savoury bites are customarily served after the Fast of Tisha b'Av and for the festival Shavuot. They are best eaten warm with cheese and olives for a weekend brunch or a teatime treat.*

1½ cups cake flour
1 tbsp baking powder
a large pinch salt
¾ cup crumbled feta cheese
¾ cup coarsely grated kefalotiri or
    Parmesan cheese
½ cup full-fat milk or cream
1 egg, lightly beaten
⅓ cup vegetable oil

For the egg wash:
2 egg yolks, lightly beaten, mixed with
    1 tbsp milk

For the topping:
3 tbsp finely grated kefalotiri or
    Parmesan cheese

PREHEAT the oven to 200 °C (400 °F). Line two large baking trays with baking paper.

IN a large bowl, sift together the flour, baking powder and salt and stir in the cheeses. Make a well in the centre of the dry ingredients and pour in the milk or cream, egg and oil. Mix the ingredients together with a spatula until well combined.

TURN onto a lightly floured surface and knead briefly. Do not overwork the dough. Roll into about 30 walnut-size balls with your hands and flatten slightly.

ARRANGE the scones on the baking trays 2.5cm (1in) apart. Brush the tops with the egg wash and sprinkle with grated cheese. Bake for 20 minutes or until lightly golden. Transfer to wire racks. Serve warm.

 STELLA'S HINTS:

- *In Turkey ½ tsp cayenne pepper or ¼ tsp red pepper flakes are added to the dough to give the scones a spicy bite.*
- ***To freeze baked scones:*** *Open-freeze on a plastic wrap-lined tray. Store in an airtight container and freeze for up to 1 month. To serve, defrost in the container for 1–2 hours. Preheat the oven to 180 °C (350 °F) and reheat the scones on a baking tray for 10 minutes.*

Dame godrura te dare ermozura

(Lit: Show me a plump woman, I will show you beauty)

festive bread

roska

Roska *is a sweet festive bread; some variations are eaten simply day-to-day for breakfast or coffee, while more elaborate types are made for Jewish holidays and milestone events.*

With origins in the Greek egg and sugar bread called tsoureki, *this bread is typified by a slightly sweet flavour and long-stranded texture when broken apart.* Roska *is topped with sesame seeds, and traditionally whole blanched almonds are added for celebrations.*

As in many religions and traditions, particularly in the east Mediterranean, bread plays an important and symbolic role in the Jewish tradition. For the blessing at the Friday night Sabbath meal, or the next day for brunch after the morning service, roska *braided as the traditional Sabbath bread,* challah, *is served.* Roska *is shaped into ring-shaped loaves representing eternity and auguring abundance for Rosh Hashanah, and for the meal to break the Fast where it is dipped into olive oil.*

A version of this ancient bread, called roska reynado, *is prepared for a bride's shower, which typically takes place on the Friday prior to the wedding. For this celebration an opulent stuffing of homemade marzipan (p232) or the* travado *filling (p214) is rolled into the dough, which is then shaped into a ring or spiral.*

For casual fare, the roska *is shaped into small coffee rolls,* roskitas *or* panizikos. *The baked* roskitas *are delicious warmed through and served for breakfast or teas accompanied with olives, sliced ripe tomatoes and cubes of feta cheese. My family loves to eat them piping hot and fresh from the oven with a fruit preserve.*

For the starter:
4 tsp active dried yeast (rapid-rise)
1½ cups warm water (about 55 °C/130 °F)
1 tbsp caster (superfine) sugar

For the dough:
5 large eggs, at room temperature
1½ cups caster sugar
¾ cup vegetable oil, plus extra for
    coating the bowl and brushing
1 tsp orange blossom water
2 cups warm water
11–12 cups unbleached plain (all-purpose)
    flour, sifted with 1 tsp salt, plus extra
    flour for kneading

For the egg wash:
2 egg yolks mixed with 1 tsp milk

For the topping:
½ cup sesame seeds placed in a flat dish
¼ cup whole blanched almonds
    (optional)

Prepare the starter: Dissolve the yeast and sugar in the warm water in a small bowl. Stir, cover with plastic wrap and let stand for 5–10 minutes until frothy.

Prepare the dough: Using a heavy-duty electric mixer with a whisk attachment, beat the eggs with the sugar until pale and creamy. Slowly add the oil, the yeast starter, orange blossom water and 2 cups warm water and blend.

REMOVE the whisk attachment and fit the mixer with a dough hook. Turn the mixer on medium speed. Mix in 1½ cups of flour. Then gradually add flour, 1 cup at a time, and knead until the dough holds together and no longer sticks to the sides of the bowl. Place on a lightly floured surface and knead until smooth and elastic.

FIT the mixer with a mincing attachment. Break off a handful of dough at a time and dust with flour. Roll into logs and put each piece through the mincer set over a large lightly oiled bowl*. Cover with a loose piece of oiled plastic wrap and then with a tea towel. Let rise in a warm draught-free place for about 3 hours or until it doubles in bulk and is light and spongy. (The time depends on the temperature of the room.)

TRANSFER the dough onto a lightly floured work surface and punch down again. Knead briefly to get rid of any air pockets and divide into three portions.

LIGHTLY brush three foil-lined baking trays with oil and dust with flour.

 **STELLA'S HINTS:**

- *To make this quantity you will require a large, heavy-duty, free-standing mixer as a standard-size kitchen aid is too small. If you do not have one, beat the eggs with a hand-held electric beater and knead the dough by hand.*
- **The mincing process makes a lighter dough but can be omitted.*
- *For the first rise, the dough may also be placed in an oven that has been warmed to 150°C (300°F) and then turned off.*
- *I like to use Better for Bread flour when I am in the U.S.*
- *Roska and roskitas keep for 3 days in an airtight container. To serve, warm through.*
- **To freeze whole baked bread or rolls:** *Wrap a loaf or a small batch of rolls in heavy-duty foil and freeze for up to 1 month. Thaw at room temperature. Preheat the oven to 180°C (350°F) and reheat in the foil until warmed through.*

Shape the braided loaf:

- Divide one portion into three equal pieces and shape each piece into a ball.
- Roll each ball with your hands into a rope 56cm (22in) long that tapers slightly at each end.
- Working with three ropes at a time, fan out the strands evenly on a work surface, then pinch them firmly together at the top end.
- Braid by bringing the alternate outer ropes between the remaining two and repeat until the end of the ropes are reached.
- Finally, gently pinch the ends together to seal firmly.

REPEAT with remaining two portions of dough, making three loaves.

Alternatively: The three portions can be shaped into ring-shaped loaves or coiled into spirals.

Shape the rolls: Divide the dough into 40 × 100g (3½oz) portions. Shape them into equal balls or roll the dough into 20cm (8in) ropes and tie each rope into a loose knot.

BRUSH the tops of the bread or rolls with the egg wash, ensuring the tops and sides are well coated. Brush right into the crevices. Wet your fingers in water and then tap into the sesame seeds. Press lightly onto the tops of the bread or rolls to give a generous coating of seeds and decorate with a few blanched almonds (if using). Transfer the shaped loaves or rolls onto the baking trays and place the rolls 5cm (2in) apart. Loosely cover with a piece of oiled plastic wrap and let rise again in a warm draught-free place for 45 minutes or until doubled in bulk. Brush generously once more with egg wash to ensure a lacquer-like crust.

PREHEAT the oven to 180°C (350°F).

BAKE for 40 minutes for the bread and 20–25 minutes for the rolls or until the tops are golden brown and shiny and they sound hollow when tapped on the bottom. Transfer to a wire rack. Serve warm or at room temperature. Makes 3 loaves or 40 rolls.

Ke tengas una caza yena komo el huevo

(Lit: May your house be as full as an egg)

May your home be blessed with abundance

filo triangles with a meat filling
hojaldres de karne

These flaky gem-like pies make a stunning platter of crisp, golden, sesame-studded filo pastries enveloping a tasty meat filling. Vegetarian fillings of potato and cheese (p198) or pumpkin and cheese (p199) are delicious alternative fillers. In Turkey, these pastries are called filikas *or* hojaldries *(same as Ladino), from the Spanish* hoja *or leaf. I like to make a batch and freeze unbaked pastries, ready to pop in the oven for unexpected guests and my family's cravings. They are lovely served hot as a meze or at a brunch table.*

For the filling:
3 tbsp olive oil
500g (1lb 2oz) minced (ground) beef
salt and freshly ground black pepper
½ cup hot chicken stock
2 eggs, hard-boiled and coarsely grated
1 egg, beaten
3 tbsp finely chopped flat-leaf parsley
  (use leaves and tender stems)
500g (1lb 2oz) ready-made filo pastry
  sheets

For brushing:
½ cup vegetable oil

For the topping:
½ cup sesame seeds placed in a
  shallow dish

Prepare the filling: Heat the oil in a large, heavy-based pan over a medium-high heat. Add the meat and stir for 5 minutes, crushing the minced meat with a fork and stirring until it changes to a light brown colour. Season with salt and pepper. Add the chicken stock and bring to a boil. Reduce the heat and simmer, uncovered, until the liquid is reduced. Taste and adjust the seasoning. Transfer to a bowl and let cool. When cold, stir in the hard-boiled eggs, beaten egg and parsley.

Shape the triangles: Open a filo sheet on a flat work surface with the narrow end nearest you. Keep the remainder covered with a damp tea towel. Brush with oil and cut the filo with a sharp knife into rectangular sections 6–7cm (2½–2¾in) wide. Place a tablespoon of filling at the end of the filo strip about 2.5cm (1in) from the short edge. Now lift up the bottom corner and fold diagonally to make a triangle-shaped pastry. Continue to fold the triangle over itself until the whole strip is used. Make sure that any gaps are tucked closed so that the filling does not ooze out. Repeat with the remaining filo sheets and filling until all the meat mixture is used.

PREHEAT the oven to 180°C (350°F). Line two baking trays with baking paper and lightly brush with oil.

BRUSH the entire top of each triangle with oil and dip into the sesame seeds. Place on baking trays 1cm (½in) apart. Bake for 20 minutes or until crisp and golden. Serve immediately.

 STELLA'S HINTS:
- *For the vegetable fillings, top the filled pies with grated cheese.*
- ***To freeze unbaked pastries:*** *Open-freeze on plastic wrap-lined trays. Place the triangles between layers of baking paper in an airtight container and freeze for up to 1 month. Preheat the oven to 180°C (350°F). Place the frozen pastries on oiled baking trays and bake for 25 minutes or until crisp and golden.*

 TWIST ON TRADITION:
- *For a spicier version, omit the hard-boiled eggs and add ½ tsp ground allspice, 1 tsp ground cinnamon, ¼ tsp red pepper flakes and 2 tbsp lightly toasted pine nuts to the filling.*

Dar es honor, demandar es dolor

(Lit: To give is honourable, to beg is painful)

flaky filo-like savoury pastries
boyos de fila kon livadura

I think there is a subtle understanding among Sephardim that if you can make boyos *well, then you are de facto an accomplished cook. But I might be biased because I believe no one made* boyos *as well as my mother did. Her* boyos *were quite legendary among the Harare crowd.*

Boyos are the mainstay of the meze and buffet tables of Judeo-Spanish cuisine and are simply scrumptious with tea or coffee. Try not to be put off by the fact that this recipe uses yeast (my daughter was for years). In fact, in this particular recipe, you do not have to wait for the dough to rise – simply start making the pastries as soon as the dough has been made.

Prepare ahead the Swiss chard or potato
and cheese filling (p199, 198)

For the starter:
¼ tsp active dried yeast (rapid-rise)
1 cup warm water (about 55°C/130°F)
1 tsp sugar

For the dough:
3¼ cups plain (all-purpose) flour,
or as needed
a pinch salt
2 tsp unsalted butter
½ cup warm water

For brushing:
mix ½ cup melted butter with ½ cup
vegetable oil in a small bowl

For sprinkling:
mix ½ cup flour with 1 tbsp grated
kefalotiri or Parmesan cheese

For the topping:
½ cup grated kefalotiri or Parmesan
cheese

You will need:
1 rectangular dish, 30 × 24cm
(12 × 9½in) with enough vegetable
oil to cover 20 balls of dough

Prepare the starter: Dissolve the yeast in the warm water with the sugar. Stir, cover with plastic wrap and let stand for 5–10 minutes, until frothy.

Prepare the dough: Put 2½ cups flour with the salt in a large bowl. Work the butter into the flour with your fingertips. Make a well in the centre of the flour and add the starter. Add the warm water and mix well until a sticky dough mass begins to form. Transfer the dough onto a lightly floured surface. Knead the dough for about 10 minutes until smooth and elastic, adding a little flour if still sticky.

DIVIDE the dough into 20 golf ball-sized pieces. Roll each piece into smooth balls between your palms and immerse in the prepared dish of oil. Turn balls over once to coat well and let sit in the oil.

TAKE one ball at a time, starting with the ones first placed in the oil, and press between your palms to flatten. Place on a work surface and, with the fingertips of both hands, press the dough outwards as much as possible. Then, working around the flattened dough, gently lift and stretch the edges outwards with your fingertips until paper thin and about 30cm (12in) in diameter. Brush lightly with the melted butter and oil mixture and cut off any thick edges with a sharp knife and discard. Sprinkle with a little of the prepared flour and cheese mixture.

Shape and fill the dough: Fold a third of one side over to the centre of the stretched dough. Fold the remaining third to overlap, making three layers into a narrow rectangle. With the narrow side facing you, place a generously heaped tablespoon of your chosen filling on the narrow edge of the rectangle and fold the dough parcel into triangles.

PREHEAT the oven to 190°C (375°F). Line two large baking trays with baking paper.

TRANSFER the filled pastries onto the baking trays, leaving a little space between them. Brush the tops lightly with the remaining melted butter and oil mixture and sprinkle with grated cheese. Bake for 30–40 minutes, until golden brown and crisp. Place on a wire rack. Serve immediately or at room temperature, traditionally with hard-boiled eggs and olives. Makes 20.

 STELLA'S HINTS:
- *When stretching the dough, do not worry if it tears or holes open – they will not be noticed once the pastry is folded.*
- *To reheat baked pastries: Preheat the oven to 180°C (350°F), then switch off the oven. Place the pastries in the oven for about 15 minutes.*
- *To freeze the baked pastries: Place the pastries between layers of baking paper and freeze in an airtight container for up to 1 month. To reheat, place the frozen pastries in a 180°C (350°F) preheated oven for about 20 minutes.*

meat and rice-filled pies
pastelikos de karne

The pièce de resistance *of Sephardic pies are the small meat and rice-filled pies shaped like little pots with straight sides and decoratively crimped lids to seal in the filling. You can also substitute with an aubergine, onion and tomato filling (p198) which, besides being vegetarian, is so tasty. Although it takes patience and practice to shape the pies, the technique is soon mastered. Enlist the help of a family member or friend for a faster assembly line. For best results I like to make two batches of dough for this amount of filling. I prepare the second batch of dough once the first batch of meat and rice pies have been filled and shaped as the dough tends to dry out fairly quickly.*

For the meat filling (konducho):
¼ cup olive oil
1 cup finely chopped onion
500g (1lb 2oz) minced (ground) beef
1 tsp salt
a pinch finely ground white pepper
2½ cups hot chicken stock
1 cup canned chopped tomatoes, puréed
¾ cup basmati rice, soaked for 5 minutes
    in boiling water, rinsed and drained
¾ cup finely chopped flat-leaf parsley
    (use leaves and tender stems)

For the dough:
1 cup vegetable oil
2 cups hot water
1 tsp salt
4½ cups cake flour

For the topping:
½ cup sesame seeds

For brushing:
½ cup vegetable oil

Prepare the meat filling: Heat the oil in a large, heavy-based pan over a medium-high heat. Add the onion and cook for 3 minutes, stirring frequently, until softened. Add the meat and stir for 5 minutes, crushing the meat with a fork and stirring until it changes to a light brown colour. Season with salt and pepper. Add ½ cup of the hot stock and the tomatoes. Bring to a boil. Reduce the heat and simmer, uncovered, until the liquid is reduced. Taste and adjust the seasoning.

MAKE a well in the centre of the meat, add the rice and the remaining 2 cups hot stock. Return to a high heat and bring to a boil. Cover, reduce the heat to medium-low and simmer for 15–20 minutes until the liquid is absorbed and the rice is soft. Remove from the heat and let cool. Stir in the parsley and mix well. Transfer to a bowl and cover with plastic wrap until required. This amount of filling will require two batches of dough.

Prepare the dough: Combine the oil, water and salt in a medium-sized pan and bring to a boil. Remove the pan from the heat and place on a dampened tea towel on a work surface. Add the flour, 1 cup at a time, into the pan and stir vigorously with a wooden spoon until well blended. Do not overwork the dough. Transfer the dough onto a work surface.

Shape and fill the pies: While the dough is still hot, take two-thirds and shape into 3cm (1¼in) walnut-sized balls, for the pots. Shape the remainder of the dough into 1.75cm (¾in) smaller balls for the lids. Cover the dough that is not being worked with a tea towel so it does not dry out. Hollow the larger balls with your thumbs and fingers and shape into little pots with straight-sides 3.5cm (1½in) deep and 3.5cm (1½in) wide, making the walls as thin as possible, about 3mm (¼in). Fill the pots to the top with a heaped teaspoon of filling.

To cover the filled pots: Take one of the smaller balls, lightly dip into the sesame seeds and then flatten between both palms. Fit the lid over the filled pot. Pinch the edges of the dough together all around to seal the pies. Using a small sharp knife, at a 45° angle, serrate the top circumference of the closed pie edges into a crisscross fringe. Finally lift up the sides of the finished pastry to a uniform height and then rotate the pie between the palms of your hands (like a potter's wheel).

STELLA'S HINTS:

- *The filling can be prepared ahead and refrigerated. Bring back to room temperature before using.*
- *To freeze unbaked pastelikos: Open-freeze on a plastic wrap-lined tray. Store in a single layer in an airtight container and freeze for up to 1 month. To serve, preheat the oven to 200°C (400°F) and generously brush the tops of the frozen pastries with oil. Bake the pies on oiled baking trays for 40–45 minutes or until crisp and golden brown.*

AT this point prepare the second batch of dough to complete using the entire filling.

PREHEAT the oven to 200°C (400°F). Generously brush two baking trays with oil.

BRUSH the tops of the pies with oil. Place on the baking trays and bake for 30–40 minutes or until they are crisp and a deep golden colour. Transfer to a wire rack. Serve at once or at room temperature with warm hard-boiled eggs (p113).

 TWISTS ON TRADITION:

- *To crimp aubergine, tomato and onion filling, firmly pinch the dough around the edges into a thin flat hem. Then, using your thumb and index finger, twist, giving the border a quarter turn inwards and creating diagonal pleats resembling a twisted cord, sealing the pie.*
- *For a quick and easy version to assemble: Shape the dough into walnut-sized balls and roll into about 8cm (3¼in) discs. Spoon a heaped teaspoon of your chosen filling into an oval and place into the middle of each disc. Fold up the sides of the pastry, bringing them together to make a raised pastry, pinching with your fingertips along the length of the crest to seal the pastry completely. Brush with oil and dab the sides with sesame seeds. Bake as above.*

pumpkin and cheese coiled pastries
boyos de kalavasa — rodanchos

Pumpkin coiled boyos *are a sweeter variant of the filo-like flaky pastries made with a yeast dough. They are shaped into a long roll and twisted into a coil or 'rose', symbolic of the Island of the Roses (the name the Italians gave to the beautiful island of Rhodes). These mouthwatering pastries, fragrant with the warming spices of cinnamon and cloves, are traditionally made for the Jewish New Year dinner and the Festival of Sukkot. These can be served as a starter on their own or with your favourite sundowner.*

Prepare ahead the pumpkin and cheese
    filling (p199)

For the starter:
¼ tsp active dried yeast (rapid-rise)
1 tsp sugar
1 cup warm water (about 55°C/130°F)

For the dough:
3¼ cups plain (all-purpose) flour,
    or as needed
a pinch salt
2 tsp unsalted butter
½ cup warm water

For brushing:
mix ½ cup melted butter with ½ cup
    vegetable oil in a small bowl

For sprinkling:
mix ½ cup flour with 1 tbsp grated
    kefalotiri or Parmesan cheese

For the topping:
½ cup grated kefalotiri or Parmesan
    cheese

You will need:
1 rectangular dish, 30 × 24cm
    (12 × 9½in), with enough vegetable
    oil to cover 20 balls of dough

Prepare the starter: Dissolve the yeast and sugar in the warm water in a small bowl. Stir, cover with plastic wrap and let stand for 5–10 minutes, until frothy.

Prepare the dough: Put 2½ cups flour with the salt in a large bowl. Work the butter into the flour with your fingertips. Make a well in the centre of the flour and add the starter. Add the warm water and mix well until a sticky dough mass begins to form. Transfer the dough onto a lightly floured surface. Knead the dough for about 10 minutes until smooth and elastic, adding a little flour if still sticky.

DIVIDE the dough into 20 golf ball-sized pieces. Roll each piece into smooth balls between your palms and immerse in the prepared dish of oil. Turn balls over once to coat well and let sit in the oil.

TAKE one ball at a time, starting with the ones first placed in the oil and press between your palms to flatten. Place on a work surface and, with the fingertips of both hands, press the dough outwards as much as possible. Then, working around the flattened dough, gently lift and stretch the edges outwards with your fingertips until paper thin and about 30cm (12in) in diameter. Brush lightly with the melted butter and oil mixture and cut off any thick edges with a sharp knife and discard. Sprinkle with a little of the prepared flour and cheese mixture.

Shape and fill the dough: Spread about 3 tbsp of filling evenly along the long edge of the stretched dough and roll gently into one long cylinder about 3.5cm (1½in) in diameter. Then coil the roll into a spiral shape with the seam-side down. Repeat until all the pastry and filling are used up. Brush the tops lightly with the melted butter and oil mixture and sprinkle with cheese.

PREHEAT the oven to 190°C (375°F). Line two large baking trays with baking paper.

TRANSFER the filled pastries to the baking trays, leaving a little space between them. Bake for 30–40 minutes until golden brown and crisp. Transfer to a wire rack. Serve hot. Makes 20.

STELLA'S HINTS:

♦ *When stretching the dough, do not worry if it tears or holes open – they will not be noticed once the pastry is folded.*

♦ ***To reheat baked pastries:*** *Preheat the oven to 180°C (350°F), then switch off the oven. Place the pastries in the oven for about 15 minutes.*

♦ ***To freeze the baked pastries:*** *Place the pastries between layers of baking paper and freeze in an airtight container for up to 1 month. To reheat, place the frozen pastries in a 180°C (350°F) preheated oven for about 20 minutes.*

 TWISTS ON TRADITION:

♦ *For a sweet topping, brush with 1 beaten egg then sprinkle with cinnamon and icing (confectioner's) sugar*

♦ ***For a quicker and easier method:*** *You will need 500g (1lb 2oz) ready-made filo pastry sheets. Cut each filo sheet into rectangles measuring about 15 × 30cm (6 × 12in). Keep the filo sheets you are not working with covered with a damp cloth to prevent the pastry from drying out. Brush 1 filo rectangle with the melted butter and oil mixture and position with the length towards you. Spread a narrow line of about 3 tbsp of pumpkin filling along the longer edge of the filo. Fold the edge over to cover the filling and roll it away from you to form a cylinder. Then coil the roll into a spiral shape with the seam-side down. Repeat until all the filling and filo is used. Bake as above for about 25 minutes or until golden. Serve hot.*

Ken englute amargo no escupe dulse

(Lit: The one who swallows bitterness does not spit out sweetness)

No sweetness can come from an embittered person

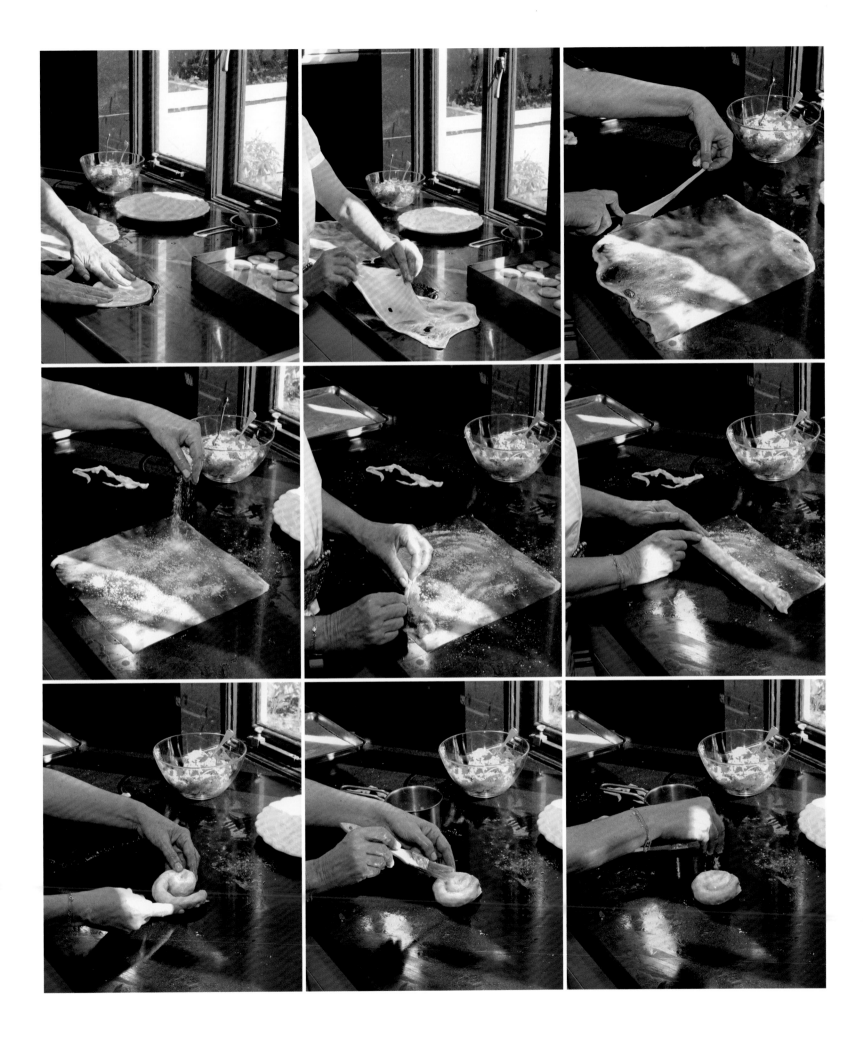

savoury pie fillings
gomo para desayuno

These are the vegetable pie fillings I loved most growing up. They are rich in flavour and exquisitely satisfying.

aubergine, onion and tomato filling
gomo de handrajo

3–4 medium aubergines (eggplants) –
    about 1kg (2¼lb)
1 tbsp kosher or coarse salt
1 tsp fresh lemon juice
¼ cup olive oil
1 cup finely chopped onion
2 cups canned chopped tomatoes, puréed
1 tsp sugar
salt and finely ground white pepper
¼ cup finely chopped flat-leaf parsley
    (use leaves and tender stems)

Prepare the aubergines: Peel, slice and finely dice the aubergines. In a large bowl, dissolve 1 tbsp coarse salt in 2.4lt (5pt) water and add 1 tsp lemon juice. Immerse the diced aubergines and place a weighted plate on top to keep them submerged. Soak for 45 minutes. Rinse under cold running water and drain. Pat dry with paper towels.

HEAT the oil in a large pan over a medium-high heat and cook the onion for 3 minutes, stirring frequently, until softened. Toss in diced aubergines and cook over a low heat for 15 minutes or until they are tender and cooked through. Stir frequently to prevent the aubergines from sticking to the pan. Stir in the tomatoes and sugar. Season with salt and pepper. Continue to cook over a low heat for 45 minutes, stirring from time to time, until all the liquid has been absorbed. Leave to cool.

ADD the chopped parsley. Taste and adjust the seasoning.

 STELLA'S HINTS:
- *I slice the peeled aubergine on a mandolin, 5mm (¼in) and then finely dice.*
- *This filling is best with the* boureka *dough (p200), brushed with egg wash and sprinkled with sesame seeds, or with the* pasteliko *dough (p191), brushed with oil and sprinkled with sesame seeds.*

potato and cheese filling
gomo de patata i keso

625g (1¼lb) (about 3 large) potatoes,
    unpeeled
1 heaped cup grated kefalotiri or
    Parmesan cheese
½ cup crumbled feta cheese
1 tbsp whole milk
1 tbsp unsalted butter, melted
3 eggs, lightly beaten
⅛ tsp baking powder (optional)
salt and finely ground white pepper

PUT the potatoes in a pan with enough cold salted water to just cover. Bring to a boil. Cover, reduce the heat and simmer for 30–40 minutes or until tender. Drain and, whilst still hot (using a fork to hold the potato steady and tongs to peel off the skin), peel and return to the pan for about a minute to dry off any excess moisture. Mash with a potato masher or, for smoother and fluffier results, put through a potato ricer.

IN a large bowl combine the cheeses, milk, butter and eggs. Then add the potato and baking powder (if using). Season with salt and pepper and mix well.

 STELLA'S HINTS:
- *If making ahead and refrigerating you may need to add a drop of milk before using as the filling tends to firm up.*
- *This filling is best with the* boureka *dough (p200), boyos dough (p188) or ready-made filo.*

 TWIST ON TRADITION:
- *My mother adds ¼ cup medium-grained rice for a textured, lighter filling. In a small pan bring 1 cup water and ½ tsp salt to the boil. Add the rice, reduce to medium heat and cook until soft. Drain off any excess water and stir gently into the potato and cheese mixture.*

pumpkin and cheese filling
gomo de kalavasa

1kg (2¼lb) pumpkin or butternut, peeled, seeded and cut into 5cm (2in) cubes
1 tsp caster (superfine) sugar
½ tsp salt
1 tsp ground cinnamon
a pinch ground cloves
1 cup grated kefalotiri or Parmesan cheese
½ cup crumbled feta cheese

For brushing:
1–2 tbsp olive oil

PREHEAT the oven to 190°C (375°F).

To roast the pumpkin: Line a baking tray with foil and brush with oil. Put the pumpkin on the tray. Toss to coat lightly in the oil and bake for about 1 hour or until soft.

Alternatively **to steam the pumpkin:** Pour water into a pan to a depth of about 2.5cm (1in). Place a steamer basket in the pan. The water should come just up to the bottom of the steamer. Cover and bring to a boil. Place the pumpkin in the basket. Cover the pan and let steam for 30–40 minutes or until tender. Place the hot pumpkin in a clean tea towel and squeeze out excess liquid.

PUT the cooked pumpkin in a bowl and mash. Add the sugar, salt, spices, cheeses and mix thoroughly.

 STELLA'S HINTS:
- *2 × 500g (1lb 2oz) cans pumpkin, drained and squeezed can be substituted for the fresh cooked pumpkin.*
- *This filling is best with the* boureka *dough (p200),* boyos *dough (p188) or ready-made filo.*

 TWIST ON TRADITION:
- *For the New Year I make a sweeter version by adding ½ cup caster (superfine) sugar and 1 cup finely chopped roasted walnuts.*

Swiss chard and cheese filling
gomo de pasi i keso

750g (1½lb) Swiss chard (silverbeet), stalks removed, washed, drained and finely shredded
1½ cups grated kefalotiri or Parmesan cheese
¾ cup crumbled feta cheese
3 tbsp dried breadcrumbs
salt and finely ground white pepper

DRY the shredded Swiss chard in a salad spinner and then spread out on paper towels to dry thoroughly. When completely dry, place on a tray and lightly mix in the cheeses and breadcrumbs. Season with salt and pepper. Turn the mixture over thoroughly with your hands as the cheese tends to sink to the bottom. Once the cheese has been added, use immediately to avoid the chard becoming soggy.

 STELLA'S HINTS:
- *I like to prepare the chard the night before to ensure that it is thoroughly dried.*
- *This filling is best with the* boureka *dough (p200) or* boyos *dough (p188).*

 TWIST ON TRADITION:
- *For a more fragrant filling, add 1¼ cups finely chopped flat-leaf parsley, ½ cup finely chopped fresh dill and 1 cup finely chopped spring onions (scallions), trimmed, white and light green parts.*

savoury turnovers with vegetable fillings
bourekas

Bourekas *are irresistible savoury turnovers made with a crisp, cheese pastry encasing a variety of delectable vegetable fillings. In the 15th century, the Jewish Iberian exiles blended their pie – the Spanish* empanada *– with the Turkish* borek *to create the popular and acclaimed* bourekas, *now found throughout the Middle East, Turkey and Israel.*

Bourekas (or as they are affectionately known, in the diminutive, as bourekitas) *feature as part of meze, brunch, teatime or at any festive table. Of all the savoury pie-making, these are the quickest and easiest to prepare.* Bourekas *are good to have stored in the freezer as they are easily warmed up. Do remember to prepare any of your chosen vegetable fillings ahead (p198–199). If needed, make two batches of dough to accommodate some of the fillings. Prepare the second batch of dough once the first batch of pies have been filled and shaped.*

For the dough (*masa fina*):
1 cup vegetable oil
1 cup iced water
½ tsp salt
1 cup finely grated kefalotiri or Parmesan
    cheese
3¾–4 cups plain (all-purpose) flour

For the egg wash:
2 egg yolks mixed with 2 tsp milk

For sprinkling:
½ cup grated kefalotiri or Parmesan
    cheese or sesame seeds

Prepare the dough: In a large bowl, combine the oil, water and salt and stir in the cheese. Gradually stir in 1 cup of flour at a time, enough to make a soft, slightly oily dough. Knead briefly with your hands to a smooth dough. Pinch off about 36 walnut-sized pieces and roll between your palms into smooth balls.

PREHEAT the oven to 180°C (350°F). Line two baking trays with baking paper.

Shape the *bourekas*: Traditionally the shape of *bourekas* differ depending on the vegetable filling. Collect any remaining scraps of dough and roll into additional balls. Repeat until both the dough and filling are all used up.

Potato and cheese-filled *bourekas*: Roll each ball of dough into about 8cm (3¼in) rounds using a small rolling pin. Take care not to roll the outer edges thinner than the centres. Place a heaped teaspoon of the filling in the centre of each round. Fold the round in half, forming a half-moon crescent. Firmly press the upper lid onto the lower rounded edges to seal the filling inside. Trim the edges with a 7cm (2¾in) pastry cutter.

Alternatively: Roll each ball into thin, long ovals. Place a heaped teaspoon of the filling at the lower edge and roll lightly into a sausage shape.

Pumpkin and cheese-filled *bourekas*: Roll each ball of dough into long, thin ovals. Place a heaped teaspoon of the filling at the lower edge and roll lightly into a sausage shape and finally curve slightly into a crescent.

Aubergine, onion and tomato or Swiss chard and cheese-filled *bourekas*: Roll each ball of dough into rectangles (10 × 8cm/4 × 3in). Place 1 heaped teaspoon of aubergine filling or 1 tablespoon of the Swiss chard filling in the centre of the rectangle. Lift and fold over half the long side towards the centre and then lift the other half over the filling, slightly overlapping and press to seal. On the short sides lift about 1cm (½in) and press down, securing the filling inside. Turn the pie over so that the sealed sides are underneath. Press all sides gently in to puff up and give it a raised parcel shape.

To bake: Transfer the pies onto the prepared baking trays, 1.25cm (½in) apart. Brush the tops and sides generously with the egg wash. Sprinkle the *bourekas* with grated cheese and, for the aubergine *bourekas*, with sesame seeds.

Bake for 25–30 minutes or until the pastry is golden and crisp. Transfer to wire racks. Serve warm.

 STELLA'S HINTS:

- *To freeze unbaked* bourekas: *Open-freeze on a plastic wrap-lined tray. Place the* bourekas *between layers of baking paper in an airtight container and freeze for up to 1 month. To serve, preheat the oven to 190°C (375°F) and brush the tops of the frozen* bourekas *with egg wash. Sprinkle with the appropriate topping. Bake on oiled baking trays for 30–35 minutes or until the pastry is golden and crisp.*
- *To freeze baked* bourekas: *Place the* bourekas *between layers of baking paper in an airtight container and freeze for up to 1 month. Preheat the oven to 190°C (375°F) and reheat the* bourekas *on a baking tray for 15 minutes.*
- *For a flakier pastry, my mother substitutes ¼ cup melted butter and ¾ cup vegetable oil in place of 1 cup vegetable oil and adds ½ tsp baking powder to the flour.*

Es komo trokar oro por lodo

(Lit: It's like swopping gold for dirt)

It's a really bad deal!

Swiss chard, fresh herb and cheese pie
kisirtma

This savoury pie is a favourite in my household. The pie has a rustic and crisp crust shaped in a half-moon, enclosing a flavour-packed filling of Swiss chard, spring onion, fresh herbs and cheese. I am sharing my mother's recipe here, which is inspired by her Turkish roots. I like to serve this fresh from the oven, cut into thick slices with a bread knife, either for meze or brunch. Kisirtma is also absolutely divine for a light summer vegetarian lunch with a Greek country salad (p48).

For the filling:

350g (12oz) Swiss chard (silverbeet), stalks removed, washed, drained and finely shredded

¾ cup grated kefalotiri or Parmesan cheese

½ cup crumbled feta cheese

¾ cup roughly chopped flat-leaf parsley (use leaves and tender stems)

½ cup roughly chopped fresh dill

¾ cup finely chopped spring onions (scallions), trimmed, white and light green parts

2 heaped tbsp dried breadcrumbs

salt and finely ground white pepper

For the starter:

1 tsp active dried yeast (rapid-rise)

½ cup warm water (about 55°C/130°F)

½ tsp sugar

½ cup plain (all-purpose) flour

For the dough:

3–3¼ cups plain flour, plus extra for dusting

1 tsp salt

1 tbsp unsalted butter, at room temperature

½ tbsp olive oil

½ tsp active dried yeast

1 cup warm water

For the topping:

1 tbsp vegetable oil

¼ cup grated kefalotiri or Parmesan cheese

 STELLA'S HINTS:

- *I use wooden toothpicks to keep the edges of the dough closed while baking. Remove after baking.*
- ***To freeze baked kisirtma:*** *Wrap in foil and then seal tightly with plastic wrap and freeze for up to 1 month. To reheat, defrost for about 2 hours. Remove the plastic wrap and place the foil-wrapped pie in a 180°C (350°F) preheated oven for about 15 minutes or until heated through.*

Prepare the chard: Dry the shredded Swiss chard in a salad spinner and spread out on paper towels to dry thoroughly. I like to do this step the night before so the chard dries thoroughly.

Prepare the starter: Dissolve the yeast in the warm water with the sugar in a small bowl. Stir in the flour. Cover with plastic wrap and let stand for 30 minutes until frothy.

Make the dough: Sift the flour into a large bowl and add the yeast starter, salt, butter and oil. Mix well with your fingertips. Add the yeast and the warm water a ¼ cup at a time and stir until the mixture comes together and forms a soft dough. Transfer the dough onto a lightly floured surface and knead vigorously for at least 10 minutes until the dough is smooth and elastic. Form the dough into a ball.

TURN the dough into a lightly oiled large bowl. Cover with a loose piece of oiled plastic wrap and then with a tea towel. Let rise in a warm draught-free spot for 1½–2 hours or until it doubles in bulk. The time depends on the temperature of the room.

Prepare the filling: Place the Swiss chard on a tray and mix in the cheeses, fresh herbs, spring onions and breadcrumbs. Season with salt and pepper. Turn the mixture over thoroughly with your fingers as the cheese tends to sink to the bottom. Use immediately to avoid the Swiss chard becoming soggy.

Shape and fill the pie: Place the dough onto a lightly floured work surface. Punch down and divide into two portions. While working with one portion, keep the remaining portion covered with a tea towel. With a lightly dusted rolling pin, roll the dough out into an oval shape about 5mm (¼in) thick. Spread half of the filling thickly and evenly on the front half of the dough, leaving a 2cm (¾in) edge. Lift and fold one half of the dough over the filling like a large turnover. Press the edges together with your fingertips. Pinch the edge of the dough between your thumb and finger, turning it 90° every centimetre (½in) to twist and plait. Repeat with the remaining dough and filling to make the second pie.

LINE two baking trays with baking paper and carefully transfer each pie onto the baking trays.

LIGHTLY brush the tops with the oil and sprinkle with the grated cheese. Loosely cover with a clean tea towel and let rise again in a warm draught-free place spot for 30 minutes or until doubled in bulk.

PREHEAT the oven to 180°C (350°F).

BAKE for 25–30 minutes or until the crust is crisp and the top is lightly golden. Slide onto a wire rack. Serve warm.

twice-baked bread rusks
biscotchadas

Twice-baked bread rusks are made from the festive bread (roska) dough and, like reshikas, are typically always available in Sephardic homes. Rusks are delicious for breakfast or at teatime served with kashkaval or feta cheese and plump marinated olives. I loved watching my parents' friends dunk these rusks into Turkish coffee just long enough that they wouldn't disintegrate and crumble! You have to work quickly in this recipe when shaping the twisted ropes of dough, so be prepared. Rusks keep for months but will probably be eaten within weeks!

Prepare the same dough as for festive
   bread on p182

For the egg wash:
2 egg yolks mixed with 1 tsp milk

For the topping:
½ cup sesame seeds

You will need:
2 rectangular, deep, straight-sided baking
   pans, about 35 × 28cm (13¾ 3 11in),
   lightly oiled

DIVIDE the dough into 60g (2oz) pieces and roll each piece into ropes 1cm (½in) thick.

TAKE two ropes and twist together. Arrange twisted ropes in lengths close together and lay them side-by-side in the pans with any excess dough hanging over the edge. Oil lightly between each row as you go. Continue until you have used all the dough. Cut away any overhanging rope so each row fits snugly in the inner edge of the pans. Cover with a clean tea towel and let rise in a warm, draught-free place for 1 hour or until doubled in bulk. As the dough rises the twisted ropes will come together.

BRUSH with egg wash and sprinkle with sesame seeds.

PREHEAT the oven to 180°C (350°F).

BAKE for 30 minutes or until the top is golden brown. Remove from the oven, leaving the oven on. Invert the baking pans onto a wire rack. When cool enough to handle, carefully separate each row of baked twists, either with two forks or with your fingers. With a sharp knife, cut into 7.5cm (3in) length rusks.

LAY the soft rusks flat on two baking trays and return one tray at a time to the oven for 5–8 minutes, until pale gold. Reduce the oven to 110°C (230°F). Pile all the rusks into one large, deep baking pan and return to the warm oven for about 1 hour, until completely dry and crisp. Turn off the oven, leaving the rusks in to crisp for another hour, taking care that they remain golden brown. Store the cooled rusks in an airtight container.

La buena mujer, yena la kaza

(Lit: The good woman, the house full)

A good woman's home is well stocked

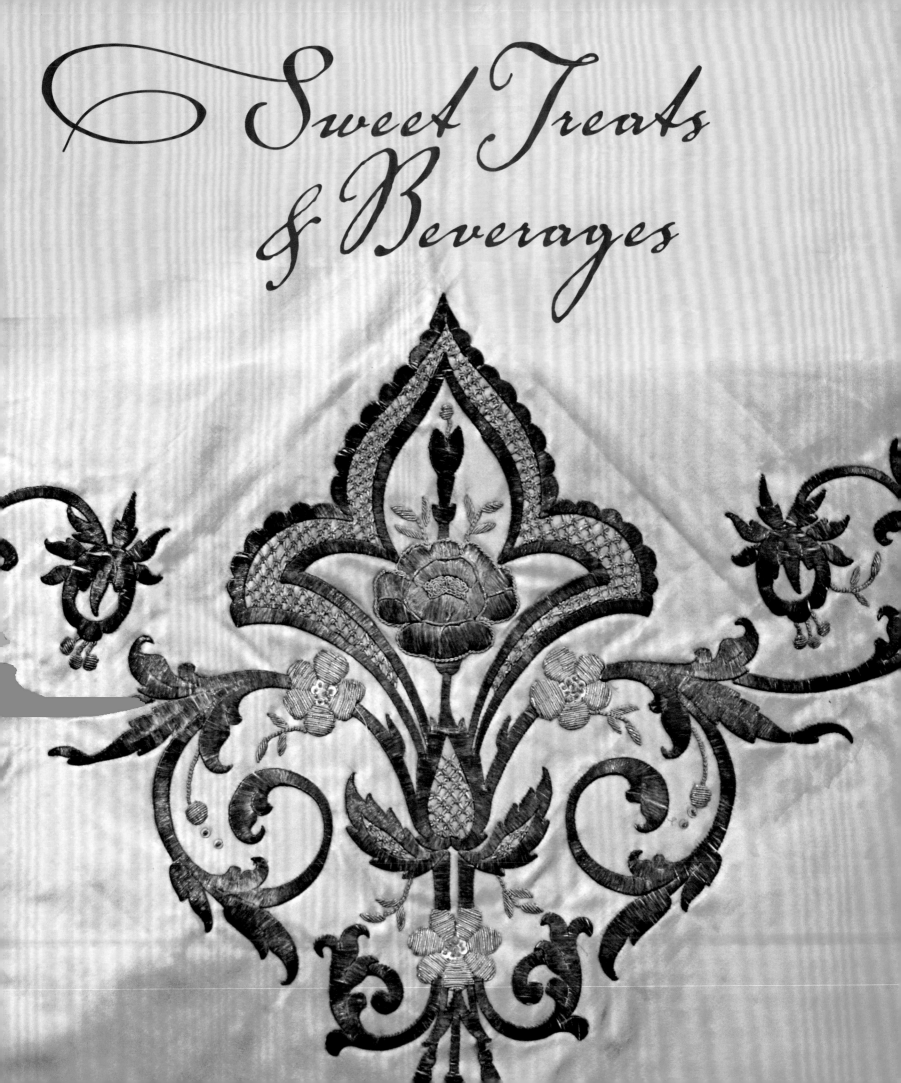

Sweet Treats
& Beverages

Sweet Treats

In Sephardic custom, homemade sugary treats are offered for everyday fare and at celebratory milestones, signifying sweetness and joy – *dulses d'alegria*. While most meals end with a platter of seasonal fruit to cleanse the palate, Sephardim are passionate about their sweets and relish them with strong Turkish coffee or a herbal tea.

There are a variety of sweet pastries and desserts, each with a unique origin and evolution. The love for almonds was inherited from our ancestors in Spain. Handcrafted marzipan, *masapan*, emblematic of Sephardic confectionery, traces its roots to sweet-making in the convents of medieval Spain. Marzipan appears in our dainty petit fours, which includes lemon fondant-filled marzipan, *pastel reale,* and macaroons baked in star-shaped pastry cases, *gizadas de masapan.* These magnificent marzipans are customarily offered on a large platter, interspersed with colourful sugar-crusted almonds, *bon bons*, at festivals and celebrations.

The iconic feather-light orange sponge cake, *pan d'Espanya*, originally made with Seville oranges, harks back to the Golden Age of Spain, as do doughnuts, *bimuelos*, soaked in a honey syrup.

The influence of the Ottoman Empire added more variety to the Sephardic desserts and sweets, notably almond frangipane-filled filo triangles, *filas d'almendra;* nut-filled *baklava* drenched in rosewater; deep-fried honey-coated pastry puffs, *piticas;* or almond and spice-filled crescents, *travados,* simmered in a honey syrup. Sephardim particularly love *shamali*, an almond semolina cake soaked in a citrus syrup. This all-in-one cake and dessert has versions that still appear in Greek and Turkish home cooking.

Biscuits are always a standby in our homes. These teatime delights range from sesame seed pretzel-shaped biscuits, *reshikas,* or the sugar and cinnamon coated *biskotchos,* to the Greek-inspired almond shortbread drenched in icing sugar, *kurabyes,* or the crumbly date and nut-filled bites, *menenas.*

The extraordinary choice of Mediterranean fruit has given rise to the art of making sweet fruit preserves or jam-like pastes – capturing the essence of each season in a jar. In Greek and Turkish Judeo-Spanish homes, ambrosial spoon sweets played an important role in their social life. Glistening fruit preserves were presented on a decorative silver platter, *tavla de dulsuras,* to welcome guests. The customary ritual was to sample a mouthful of the luscious spoon sweet or lemon fondant offered in crystal bowls with a little spoon from a silver spoon holder, *cuchariera,* accompanied with small glasses of chilled water to cleanse the palate.

The custom of offering a spoon sweet on a visit, *adulsar la vijita,* would invoke wishes and blessings appropriate to the occasion to the hostess by the guest. For example, if the occasion was an upcoming wedding a wish for the couple's happiness would be made, *Bueno ke pasen*, or generally, "May we only partake for festive and happy occasions", *Para fiestas i alegria siempre*.

More homely desserts, simple yet nourishing, can be whipped up at short notice, like the smooth ground rice or cornflour milk pudding topped with cinnamon. However, some of the pastries and confectionery may appear fiddly and intricate, but the visual guides and easy to follow steps simplify the process.

May the recipes you embark on, passed down from generations, bring you and your loved ones sweetness and joy.

Boka dulse avre puerta de fierro

(Lit: A kind word opens a gate of iron)

almond and sesame seed brittle
boulukunio

Toasted sesame seeds, honey and almonds make a deep-golden, chewy treat. Popular at any celebration, this ancient confection is traditionally offered over the Festivals of Purim and Hanukkah (Festival of Lights). These petite treats, not unlike the nut bars that are popular today, are utterly addictive.

5 cups hulled sesame seeds
1 tbsp plain (all-purpose) flour
170g (6oz) blanched split almonds,
    toasted

For the syrup:
1½ cups clear honey
1½ cups hot water
1½ cups sugar

SPRINKLE 1 cup of sesame seeds with a pinch of flour and toast lightly in a heavy-based frying pan over a medium heat for 4 minutes or until lightly golden. Shake the pan often and stir with a wooden spoon. Transfer to a bowl. Repeat this process, 1 cup at a time, with the remaining four cups of sesame seeds.

HEAT the honey, water and sugar in a large, heavy-based pan over a medium heat. Bring to a boil, stirring until it thickens and reaches the soft ball stage*. Remove the pan from the heat and pour the mixture into a very large, heatproof bowl.

ADD the almonds and 3 cups of sesame seeds and stir together vigorously with a wooden spoon. Spread the hot mixture onto an oiled worktop. Sprinkle in the remaining 2 cups of sesame seeds, working it a little at a time into the mixture. Dampen your hands with cold water and roll into four ropes about 2.5cm (1in) in diameter. Cut diagonally into 2.5cm (1in) sections using a sharp knife dipped into hot water. Allow to cool at room temperature until hardened.

 STELLA'S HINTS:
- **The soft ball stage is reached when a small drop of syrup forms into a little ball at the bottom of a cup of cold water. It will flatten and feel soft and pliable.*
- **To store:** *Place the brittle between layers of baking paper and store in an airtight container for up to 1 month.*

Amigos i hermanos seremos, las bolsas no tokaremos

(Lit: Let's be friends and brothers, let's not touch our purses)

Between family and friends avoid money matters to maintain good relationships

almond brittle candy

crocan

This delectable nutty candy can be served with coffee or tea or you can crush the brittle into smaller pieces and use it as a topping on ice cream or rice pudding.

3 cups sugar
500g (1lb 2oz) blanched split almonds, toasted

You will need:
an oiled baking tray, marble slab or worktop
2 unwaxed lemons, washed and dried with a cloth

Make the caramel: Heat the sugar in a large, heavy-based pan over a medium-high heat. As soon as the sugar begins to melt around the sides of the pan, begin stirring with a metal spoon. When most of the sugar has turned to a liquid syrup with a few small lumps floating in it, reduce the heat to low. Continue cooking, crushing the solid lumps with the spoon until the sugar is completely dissolved and turns a pale caramel.

PUT the almonds into the caramel straight away, stirring vigorously over the heat until the nuts are well coated in the caramel. If the caramel continues to darken, remove from the heat and immediately dip the base of the pan into a bowl of cold water to slow the cooking process and maintain the caramel colour.

CAREFULLY pour the hot mixture onto the oiled worktop. Hold a whole lemon in each hand and press into the mixture. Spread evenly to form a thin brittle. Finally dampen your hands with cold water and smooth and flatten the surface.

USING a sharp knife, cut the brittle into diamond shapes while it is still warm. It is important to work quickly and not allow the brittle to harden or snap into uneven chunks. Leave to cool at room temperature until hardened.

 STELLA'S HINT:
- *To store: Place the brittle between layers of baking paper and store in an airtight container for up to 1 month.*

 TWIST ON TRADITION:
- *Place pieces of brittle in the bowl of a food processor and process in short bursts until crushed. Sprinkle this crushed praline over rice pudding or ice cream spiked with a shot of freshly brewed espresso coffee.*

Si era riko, otra gayo me kantava

(Lit: If I were rich, another rooster would be crowing for me)

If I were wealthy, this would have been another story

almond frangipane-filled filo triangles
filas d'almendra (sansaticos)

These elegant, mouthwatering, triangle-shaped filo pastries are filled with ground almond paste scented with orange blossom water and dusted with icing sugar. In the Rhodesli community these prized pastries are served especially at the ritual Bridal Bath, Banyo de Novia. Quick and easy to prepare, the frangipane-filled pastries make a marvellous dessert. Paired with vanilla ice cream and mixed berries, they are bound to impress your guests.

250g/9oz (about 8 sheets) ready-made filo pastry, at room temperature

For the filling:
175g (6oz) blanched almonds, finely ground
2 tbsp caster (superfine) sugar
2 tbsp heavy cream
½ cup melted unsalted butter
1 tsp almond extract
pinch mastic ground with 1 tsp sugar (optional)
2 tbsp orange blossom water

For brushing:
½ cup melted butter or light vegetable oil

For dusting:
1 cup icing (confectioner's) sugar

PREHEAT the oven to 180°C (350°F). Line two baking trays with baking paper and lightly brush with some of the melted butter or oil.

Prepare the filling: Combine the filling ingredients in a bowl.

Shape the triangles: Open a filo sheet on a flat work surface with the narrow end nearest you. Keep the remainder covered with a damp tea towel. Brush with oil and cut the filo with a sharp knife into rectangular sections 6cm (2½in) wide. Place 1 heaped teaspoon of the filling at the short end of the filo strip, 2.5cm (1in) from the edge. Now lift up the bottom corner and fold diagonally to make a triangle-shaped pastry. Continue to fold the triangle over itself until the whole strip is used. Repeat with the remaining filo sheets and filling.

TRANSFER the pastries, seam-side down, onto the prepared baking trays, spaced 1cm (½in) apart. Bake for 20 minutes or until crisp and golden. Transfer to a wire rack. While the pastry is still warm, sprinkle with sifted icing sugar and serve.

 STELLA'S HINTS:
- *To freeze unbaked pastries: Open-freeze on a baking tray lined with plastic wrap. Store between layers of baking paper in an airtight container and freeze for up to 1 month. To serve, defrost and bake as directed.*
- *To store baked pastries: Place the triangles between layers of baking paper and store in an airtight container for up to a week. Allow to thaw and serve at room temperature.*

 TWIST ON TRADITION:
- *The baked pastries can be coated in a warm honey syrup (p214) and sprinkled with 2 tbsp blanched, peeled and finely ground unsalted pistachios or toasted sesame seeds.*

Esta haziendo un borako en la agua

(Lit: He is trying to make a hole in the water)

He is getting nowhere

almond-filled, honey-drenched crescents

travados

Travados are crescent-shaped almond and spice-filled biscuits, soaked in a hot honey syrup and sprinkled with toasted sesame seeds. The honey-drenched travados *keep well in an airtight container for a week and are delicious with coffee or tea or as that sweet something after a meal. These irresistible nutty indulgences are particularly popular at all celebrations, especially at the religious festivals of Purim and the New Year and at the meal to break the Fast of Yom Kippur.*

For the filling:
250g (9oz) unblanched almonds, lightly toasted
1 tbsp fresh orange juice or water
½ cup clear honey
1½ tbsp brandy, preferably Greek Metaxa
1 tsp ground cinnamon
½ tsp ground cloves
1 heaped tbsp sesame seeds, lightly toasted

For the dough:
1 cup vegetable oil
½ cup caster (superfine) sugar
¾ cup water
3¼ cups cake flour, plus extra for dusting
1 level tsp baking powder

For the syrup:
½ cup sugar
1 cup clear honey
½ cup water
a 2.5cm (1in) strip orange zest
1 tsp fresh lemon juice
1 tbsp orange blossom water

For the topping:
½ cup toasted sesame seeds or finely ground unblanched almonds

Prepare the filling: Pulse the almonds in a food processor until they are coarsely ground. In a bowl combine the rest of the filling ingredients, add the almonds and mix to a paste that is quite soft to the touch.

Prepare the dough: Combine the oil, sugar and water in a bowl. Add the flour and baking powder a little at a time. Mix, without kneading, to form a soft, pliable dough. If it seems too oily add a little more flour. Do not overwork the dough. Let it rest for 5 minutes at room temperature.

PREHEAT the oven to 180°C (350°F). Line two baking trays with baking paper.

Make the biscuits: Pinch off 40 walnut-sized pieces of dough and roll into smooth balls. Flatten each ball between your palms to make discs about 3mm (⅛in) thick. Place each disc on a lightly floured work surface and create a ridged pattern by gently pressing the tines of a fork on one side of the pastry. Turn the discs over and place 1 heaped teaspoon of the prepared paste in the centre. Fold over and press the edges with your fingers to seal, and curve the pastries slightly into half-moon crescent shapes. Repeat the rolling, filling and shaping of the pastry until all the filling has been used. Place the biscuits on the prepared baking trays and bake for 30 minutes or until lightly golden. Cool on wire racks.

Make the syrup: Combine the sugar, honey, water and orange zest strip in a small pan and bring to a boil, stirring constantly. Reduce the heat and simmer, uncovered, without stirring, for 5 minutes. Add the lemon juice and orange blossom water and simmer until the syrup has thickened slightly and the short-thread stage is reached*. Discard the strip of orange zest.

TURN the heat down to the lowest setting. Gently drop a few biscuits at a time into the hot syrup and use a spoon to submerge them for 2 minutes to absorb the syrup. Scoop them out with a slotted spoon and place the syrup-drenched *travados* in a large, deep heatproof dish, in a single layer. Ladle the remaining syrup over the biscuits and sprinkle with sesame seeds or coat with finely ground unblanched almonds. Makes about 40.

 STELLA'S HINTS:
- *To freeze baked* travados*: Place the* travados *between layers of baking paper in an airtight container and freeze for up to 2 months. To serve, defrost and crisp in a 180°C (350°F) preheated oven for 5 minutes. Then proceed with the honey syrup.*
- **Short-thread stage: At this stage, the hot syrup is thick and sticky. You test it by placing a small amount onto a teaspoon. Dip wetted thumb and index finger in the syrup and pull them apart a couple of times to see if threads of about 1.5cm (½in) in length form.*

TWIST ON TRADITION:
- *You may prefer less sweet, drier* travados*. If so, simply serve the baked biscuits sprinkled with icing (confectioner's) sugar.*

almond semolina cake
soaked in a honey-citrus syrup
shamali (tishpishti)

This luscious, syrup-soaked cake is a delight served for afternoon tea or coffee. The ground mastic adds a pine-scented depth to this moist cake. Shamali also makes a spectacular finale to a meal, accompanied with whipped cream and fresh berries that help balance the intense sweetness of this cake. This prepare-ahead dessert tastes even better the day after it has been made, when the syrup has been fully absorbed. Shamali is served on the Festival of Shavuot, and for the New Year is customarily made with blanched almonds, which give the cake a lighter colour. This is symbolic of the wish for the year to be 'sweet, bright and light', 'dulse i aclarada!'

For the syrup:

1 cup caster (superfine) sugar

1 cup clear honey

1¼ cups water

1 small cinnamon stick

1 tbsp fresh lemon juice

a 2.5cm (1in) strip of lemon zest

For the cake:

4 eggs, separated

¾ cup caster sugar

½ cup vegetable oil, plus extra for
  brushing

¾ cup plain (all-purpose) flour

½ cup fine semolina

2 heaped tsp baking powder

170g (6oz) unblanched almonds, finely
  ground

1 piece of mastic, ground with 1 tsp sugar

½ tsp ground cinnamon

For the topping:

30 whole blanched almonds, toasted

You will need:

a rectangular or oval 30 × 22cm
  (12 × 9in) ovenproof dish that is
  at least 6.5cm (2½in) deep

Prepare the syrup: Combine the sugar, honey and water in a small, heavy-based pan. Bring to a boil, stirring constantly, until the sugar has dissolved. Add the cinnamon stick, lemon juice and zest. Boil for 5 minutes without stirring. Let cool and discard the cinnamon stick and lemon zest.

PREHEAT the oven to 180°C (350°F). Lightly oil the dish and dust with 1 tbsp flour. Place in the fridge.

Make the cake: In the bowl of an electric mixer beat together the egg yolks and sugar on high speed, until pale and thick. Beat in the oil.

IN a medium-sized bowl combine the flour, semolina, baking powder, almonds, mastic and cinnamon.

WHISK the egg whites in a clean bowl until soft peaks form. In two batches, gently fold into the egg and sugar mixture. Then fold in the dry ingredients, scraping down the sides of the bowl, until well incorporated.

POUR the batter into the prepared dish, smoothing it out evenly. Bake in the centre of the oven for 35 minutes or until golden brown and a skewer inserted in the cake comes out clean. Remove the cake from the oven*.

REDUCE the oven temperature to 150°C (300°F). While the cake is still in the dish, cut deeply into approximately 4cm (1½in) diamond shapes with a sharp knife. Gently spoon the cooled syrup evenly over the entire hot cake. Press a halved toasted almond onto the centre of each diamond shape. Return to the oven for 5 minutes for the syrup to be absorbed. Let stand at room temperature for at least 2 hours for the syrup to soak in. Serve at room temperature either from the dish or arrange the cut pieces on a cake platter.

 STELLA'S HINTS:

♦ **To freeze the cooled baked cake: Seal the cake in the dish in plastic wrap and freeze for up 1 month. To serve, defrost, then make the hot syrup. Cut the cake deeply into diamond-shapes and spoon over the hot syrup. Top with almonds.*

♦ *The finished* shamali *keeps for a week covered with plastic wrap in the fridge.*

 TWIST ON TRADITION:

♦ *For a festive flavour, add 2 tbsp of the Greek brandy Metaxa to the syrup instead of the lemon juice and zest.*

almond shortbread
kurabyes

Rich, shortbread-like kurabyes *are delicious little biscuits that crumble and melt in your mouth (my grand-children love them for this reason). They look impressive heaped on a plate, drenched in icing sugar, as an after-dinner petit four or for afternoon tea.*

1 cup unsalted butter, at room
    temperature
¾ cup icing (confectioner's) sugar, plus
    extra for dusting
1 tsp vanilla extract
½ cup sunflower oil
1 tbsp brandy or ouzo (raki)
170g (6oz) blanched almonds, lightly
    toasted and finely ground
3 cups plain (all-purpose) flour
¼ cup cornflour (cornstarch)
1 tbsp sesame seeds, toasted (optional)

For shaping:
1 tsp rose water diluted in 1 cup water

For topping:
24 blanched almonds or pistachios

For serving:
icing (confectioner's) sugar

BEAT the butter on medium speed in the bowl of an electric mixer for about 8 minutes, until pale and creamy. Gradually add the icing sugar and vanilla extract and beat for 2 minutes. Beat in the oil and mix in the brandy or ouzo.

STIR in the almonds and the sifted combined flours, gradually working in lightly with your hands until a very soft dough forms. Be careful not to overwork it*. The sesame seeds (if using) can be added at this point. Cover in plastic wrap and refrigerate for 30 minutes.

PREHEAT the oven to 160°C (325°F). Line two baking trays with baking paper.

PINCH off about 24 pieces of dough. Moisten your hands with diluted rose water and shape into balls. Press gently to flatten slightly. Squeezing with both forefingers and thumbs, shape into triangles about 3.5cm (1½in) wide and 1.25cm (½in) in height. Arrange on the prepared baking trays, leaving some space between them as they spread while baking. Press an almond or pistachio in the centre of each biscuit.

BAKE for about 20 minutes or until they are just beginning to colour. They should be pale, slightly cracked on the top and barely golden around the edges. Do not overcook. Let cool on the baking trays for 5 minutes before removing with a metal spatula and setting on wire racks. To serve, dust generously with icing sugar and stack on a platter.

 STELLA'S HINTS:
- *Grind the toasted almonds finely but not to a powder – they should be like sand with coarser bits giving the biscuit more crunch.*
- **Handle the dough lightly and work as quickly as possible.*
- *The biscuits will keep for up to 2 weeks in an airtight container in a cool dry place.*
- ***To freeze the baked biscuits:** Place the biscuits between layers of baking paper in an airtight container and freeze for up to 1 month. Allow to thaw and dust with icing sugar.*

Kada flor tiene su guesmo
(Lit: Every flower has its own fragrance)

Everyone has their own special qualities

baklava

These pastries are, of course, very well known in the east Mediterranean. Apart from the classic baklava, *the Sephardim in Rhodes made a triangular version with walnuts called* trigonas. *I like to make individual flower-shaped* baklava *with lavish pistachio and almond filling, often seen in Lebanon and other countries in the Middle East. These petal-shaped treats make a spectacular dessert or an indulgent snack with a cup of strong Turkish coffee.*

¾ cup unsalted melted butter mixed with
    ¾ cup vegetable oil
500g (1lb 2oz) ready-made filo pastry
    (about 16 sheets), at room temperature

For the filling:
3 egg whites
½ cup caster (superfine) sugar
250g (9oz) blanched almonds, coarsely
    ground
250g (9oz) unblanched pistachios,
    coarsely ground
1 tsp orange blossom water

For the syrup:
1 cup caster sugar
1 cup clear honey
1½ cups water
1 tsp fresh lemon juice
1 cinnamon stick
1 tsp orange blossom water

For the topping:
½ cup coarsely ground blanched
    pistachios

Prepare the filling: Beat the egg whites in the clean bowl of a free-standing electric mixer, with the whisk attachment, until foamy. Then beat in the sugar. With a spatula, gently fold in the ground almonds and pistachios and the orange blossom water.

Prepare the syrup: Dissolve the sugar, honey and water in a small, heavy-based pan over a low heat, stirring constantly, for about 2 minutes. Stop stirring and bring to a boil. Add the lemon juice and cinnamon stick. Reduce the heat and simmer, uncovered, for about 15 minutes or until the syrup is thick enough to coat the back of a spoon. Stir in the orange blossom water. Discard the cinnamon stick. Remove from the heat and set aside to cool.

PREHEAT the oven to 180°C (350°F). Lightly brush a 39.5 × 27cm (16 × 10in) ovenproof baking dish with straight sides with some of the butter and oil mixture.

Assemble the baklava: Lay a sheet of filo on a work surface and cover the rest with a slightly damp tea towel. Brush lightly with the melted butter and oil mixture ensuring it is evenly coated. Cover with another sheet of filo and brush with the melted butter and oil. Repeat until you have a stack of seven sheets.

CUT the buttered stack into 7cm (2¾in) squares with kitchen scissors or a sharp knife. Place 1 tbsp of the filling in the centre of each square. Gently squeeze the pastry around the filling, two-thirds of the way up so that the points of the filo open out like the petals of a flower*. Continue with the remaining pastry squares and filling. Arrange the pastries close together in rows in the baking dish so that the petals do not open.

To bake: Place the dish on the middle rack of the oven and bake for 30 minutes or until the pastries are crisp and lightly golden.

LADLE half the cooled syrup evenly over the hot baklava. Sprinkle the ground pistachios over the centre of the pastries. Drizzle over the remaining syrup. Makes 40.

 STELLA'S HINTS:
- **Be sure not to squeeze the corners of the filo too hard as the layering is important so as not to lose the effect of the multi-layered petals.*
- *Store at room temperature, covered with a cake net.*
- *To freeze the unbaked pastries: Store in a single layer in airtight containers and freeze for up to 1 month. To serve, make the syrup and bake the frozen pastries. Ladle the syrup and sprinkle the pistachios as directed above.*

clementine and almond cake
pan de mandarina i almendra

Puréed, boiled clementines lend themselves to an indescribably moist, citrus-flavoured, flourless almond cake. This cake has proven very popular with family and friends as a dessert or for tea with lightly whipped cream. In Zimbabwe clementines are known as naartjies, *which is an Afrikaans word from neighbouring South Africa. It is a fruit that is grown in profusion in the Mazowe citrus estates close to Harare. It is ideal as a flourless cake for Passover with baking powder omitted*. For a festive touch I scatter glistening slices of candied clementine on the top or simply dust with icing sugar.*

4–5 whole clementines
250g (9oz) caster (superfine) sugar
6 eggs, separated
250g (9oz) blanched almonds, finely
    ground
1 heaped tsp baking powder
a large pinch saffron threads

For the syrup:
1 cup reserved clementine juice
2 tbsp caster sugar

For greasing:
1 tbsp soft unsalted butter

For dusting:
icing (confectioner's) sugar

For candied clementines:
4 clementines
140g (5oz) caster sugar
140ml (¼pt) water

 STELLA'S HINTS:
* *You can substitute clementines with tangerines or mandarins.*
* *To get the lining for the base of the cake pan just right, lay the cake pan on a sheet of baking paper and trace an outline. Cut it to fit snugly in the base of the tin.*
* **For the Passover add 1 extra beaten egg white and omit the baking powder.*

Prepare the clementines: Put the unpeeled clementines in a pan and cover with cold water. Bring to a boil. Cover, reduce the heat and simmer for about 2 hours or until tender. Remove the clementines from the pan and discard the liquid. When the clementines have cooled, cut them open and discard the pips. Place in a clean tea towel and squeeze to remove all excess liquid, reserving 1 cup for the syrup. Whizz the cooked clementines in a food processor until smooth.

Prepare the syrup: Heat the clementine juice with the caster sugar in a small pan over a medium-high heat. Stir occasionally until the syrup thickens. Pour into a serving jug.

PREHEAT the oven to 180°C (350°F). Lightly grease the base and sides of a 23cm (9in) spring-form cake pan. Cut out a circle of baking paper and line the base.

Make the cake: In the bowl of a free-standing electric mixer, beat the sugar and egg yolks at high speed until pale and creamy. In a separate bowl combine the ground almonds, baking powder and saffron threads and fold gently into the egg and sugar mixture.

BEAT the egg whites in a clean bowl with the whisk attachment, until stiff peaks form. Then, in two batches, gently fold the egg whites into the mixture using a large metal spoon, until incorporated. Pour the mixture into the prepared pan.

BAKE for 45–60 minutes or until the top is golden brown and a skewer inserted in the centre comes out clean. Let the cake cool in the pan on a wire rack for 10 minutes. Then invert onto the wire rack to cool completely. When cold, transfer to a serving plate. At this point make the candied clementine slices or dust with sifted icing sugar.

SERVE a slice of the cake, spooning over a little of the syrup together with lightly whipped cream or Greek yoghurt.

Make the candied clementine slices: Slice the clementines to a 5mm (¼in) thickness. Place the sugar and water into a small pan over a medium heat and simmer, stirring constantly, to dissolve the sugar. Immerse the clementine slices and bring the syrup to a boil. Cut a circle of baking paper to fit in the pan to keep the fruit submerged for 30 minutes until the slices are glossy and translucent. Remove with a slotted spoon and cool on top of baking paper. Arrange the clementine slices, slightly overlapping, on the outer edge of the cake.

dates filled with almond paste
and wrapped in filo

fila di datli kon almendra

These elegant, quick and easy sweet finger foods make a spectacular impact on a dessert tray. They are bound to make a lasting impression especially when served with vanilla ice cream.

250g (9oz) plump fresh dates (medjool)

12 sheets ready-made filo pastry, at room temperature

For the almond paste:

75g (2½oz) unsalted butter, softened

50g (1½oz) unblanched almonds, finely ground

50g (1½oz) sugar

1 egg

For brushing:

½ cup melted unsalted butter

For sprinkling:

¼ cup icing (confectioner's) sugar mixed with 1 tsp ground cinnamon

PREHEAT the oven to 210°C (410°F). Lightly butter two baking trays.

MIX all the ingredients for the almond paste together well in a bowl.

CUT a slit 2.5cm (1in) long and 1.25cm (½in) deep in the side of each date using a small sharp knife and remove the pip. Stuff the dates with 1 tsp of almond paste.

OPEN a filo sheet on a flat work surface. Keep the remainder covered with a damp tea towel. Brush with melted butter and cut the filo with a sharp knife into 10cm (4in) squares. Place each filled date in the centre, towards the edge of the filo. Wrap and twist both ends like a wrapper for a sweet. Arrange on the prepared baking trays and bake for 5–6 minutes.

REMOVE from the oven and arrange on a platter. Lightly dust the hot pastries with icing sugar and cinnamon. Serve at once or at room temperature.

 STELLA'S HINT:

♦ *To freeze baked pastries: Place the filas between layers of baking paper in an airtight container and freeze for up to 1 month. Allow to thaw and dust with icing sugar.*

doughnut puffs
bimuelos (beignets)

Doughnuts, or deep-fried fritters, are the symbolic food amongst Judeo-Spanish communities on Hanukkah, when the Festival of Lights, the miracle of the burning oil lamp in the ancient temple in 166 BCE, is celebrated. Bimuelos is derived from the Spanish word bunuelo, *which was a popular yeast dough fritter in medieval Spain.*

I am offering my mother's recipe that she recalls from her adolescence growing up in the Belgian Congo, called beignets. *This delicious alternative is lighter and quicker to make using baking powder instead of yeast. Drizzle warm honey syrup over these golden doughnut puffs and then sprinkle with cinnamon and/or finely chopped pistachios. Bimuelos are customarily served with a delicious homemade raisin syrup (see below).*

1 egg
1 cup whole milk
2 tsp vanilla extract
1 heaped cup plain (all-purpose) flour
1 heaped tsp baking powder
½ tsp salt

For the syrup:
½ cup sugar
½ cup water
3 tbsp clear honey

For deep-frying:
canola, grape-seed or other neutral oil

For the topping:
ground cinnamon
finely chopped pistachios (optional)

BEAT the egg, milk and vanilla together in a bowl with a balloon whisk. Sift in the flour, baking powder and salt. Fold the mixture together until the batter is well combined.

PREHEAT the oven to 180°C (350°F).

Prepare the syrup: Dissolve the sugar in the water in a small pan over a medium heat. Add the honey and bring to a boil. Reduce the heat and simmer uncovered, without stirring, until thick enough to coat the back of a spoon. Keep warm over a very low heat while you fry the doughnut puffs.

HEAT 7.5cm (3in) oil in a deep, medium-sized, heavy-based pan and place over a medium heat until a drop of batter sizzles in it.

Very gently ladle about 2 tablespoons of the batter into the sizzling oil. Fry for 2 minutes. Then, using a slotted spoon, turn over and fry for a further 1–2 minutes until a deep golden brown. Transfer to an ovenproof dish and keep warm in the oven. Repeat with the remaining batter. Fry in batches, of no more than 3 at a time. Adjust the oil temperature as necessary.

DRIZZLE the warmed honey syrup over the puffs, dust with cinnamon and nuts (if using) and serve immediately. Makes 25.

 STELLA'S HINT:
♦ *Ideally these should be fried as near to serving time as possible.*

 TWIST ON TRADITION:
♦ *Icing (confectioner's) sugar and cinnamon can be sprinkled on the doughnut puffs instead of the warm honey syrup.*

Raisin syrup (arrope):
3 cups (450g/1lb) dark raisins
5 cups water
1 tbsp fresh lemon juice
½ cup sugar

IN a large, heavy-based pan, soak the raisins in the water for 15 minutes to plump up. Bring to a boil over a medium-high heat. Cover, reduce the heat and simmer, stirring occasionally, for 2 hours until soft. Place the raisins and cooking liquid in a processor and pulse to a purée. Strain through a fine mesh sieve, pushing through the pulp. Return to the pan, add the lemon juice and sugar and simmer for about 30 minutes, uncovered, over medium heat, stirring occasionally until syrupy.

POUR into a glass preserving jar and store in the fridge. This syrup can also be served with fried matza fritters (p110) over Passover.

fragrant rice flour and milk pudding

sutlach

Called sutlach *by the Sephardic communities of Turkey and Greece, this is a light but nourishing rice pudding. Traditionally it is served on Friday night, after Saturday Sabbath morning services, as part of the meal breaking the fast on Yom Kippur, or for the Jewish festival of Shavuot. My mother would make individual bowls of* sutlach *and sprinkle my sister's and my initials on the top using ground cinnamon, a practice my children and grandchildren also love.*

In this recipe from Rhodes, ground rice flour is used, which gives the dessert a gloriously creamy texture. It is infused with rose water and sprinkled with ground cinnamon. Though easy to make, this pudding requires a little patience as it takes about 15 minutes of constant stirring over very low heat to thicken. There is a quicker alternative using cornflour, which I describe below. I prefer sutlach *chilled alongside fresh berries.*

4 heaped tbsp ground rice flour
½ cup water
4 cups (850ml/1½pt) whole milk
3 tbsp caster (superfine) sugar, or to taste
1 tbsp rose water or vanilla extract

For the topping:
ground cinnamon

You will need:
4 small, shallow heatproof bowls or
    6 ramekins

BLEND the rice flour and water in a small bowl and stir until smooth.

COMBINE the milk and sugar in a large, deep, heavy-based pan and set over a medium-high heat. Bring to a boil, stirring frequently using a balloon whisk. When the milk comes to a boil, remove from the heat. Stir the rice flour mixture into the milk. Return the pan to the heat, stirring continuously for 2 minutes, and then reduce to a medium heat. Continue stirring in the same direction for about 15 minutes or until the pudding thickens and coats the back of a spoon. Be sure to stir constantly and scrape the bottom and sides of the pan as this prevents the pudding from forming lumps and catching to the bottom of the pan. Remove from the heat and stir in the rose water or vanilla extract.

STRAIN the pudding into a jug and pour immediately into individual serving bowls or ramekins. Seal each bowl with plastic wrap to prevent a skin forming.

SERVE at room temperature or chilled, sprinkled with ground cinnamon.

 TWISTS ON TRADITION:

♦ *You can use 3 tbsp cornflour (cornstarch) in place of the rice flour. This takes no more than about 5 minutes to cook.*

♦ *For a piney flavour, crush 1 mastic crystal to a powder with 1 tsp caster sugar and stir in very quickly when the heat is turned off.*

♦ ***Toppings:*** *You can substitute the cinnamon with toasted blanched almonds, coarsely chopped pistachios or desiccated coconut, and a little grenadine syrup poured on the top for a splash of deep pink colour. Rose petal preserve, found at Greek or Middle Eastern stores, is heavenly swirled into the pudding.*

La manseves es por penar, la vejes por descansar

(Lit: Youth is to struggle, the old age is time to take it easy)

Work while you are young so that you can rest when you are old

honeyed biscuit clusters

pinyonate

This confection consists of clusters of little biscuits covered in a caramel syrup and scattered with toasted almonds. It is quite unusual, particularly in presentation, as the pinyonate *is arranged on fresh lemon leaves, served on a large platter – really gorgeous on a table. It is also made at the celebratory tea for the Bridal Bath,* Banyo de Novia.

4 eggs
1 tbsp vegetable oil
2½–3 cups cake flour

For the syrup:
1 cup honey
1 cup sugar
3 cups water

For the topping:
½ cup blanched almonds, toasted

For serving:
fresh lemon leaves

BEAT the eggs and oil well in the bowl of an electric mixer. Gradually add the flour to make a soft, smooth dough.

DIVIDE the dough into six pieces. Roll each piece into a long rope about 1.25cm (½in) in diameter. Cut into 1.25cm (½in) pieces with a sharp knife and place on a clean tea towel sprinkled with a little flour, until all the pastry has been used.

Prepare the syrup: Put the honey, sugar and water in a large, heavy-based pan and bring to a rolling boil.

DROP the *pinyonate* into the syrup, a few at a time to prevent the temperature dropping. Cover, reduce the heat and simmer for 25 minutes, shaking the pan occasionally to prevent the *pinyonate* sticking to each other. Do not remove the lid during this stage. If the syrup boils over reduce the heat to the lowest setting.

REMOVE the lid and turn the biscuits gently with a wooden spoon to bring the *pinyonate* at the bottom of the pan up to the top. Replace the lid and continue to simmer for a further 30 minutes. Then remove from the heat, pour ½ cup of cold water into the syrup and toss in the toasted almonds.

WHEN the *pinyonate* cools, store in a wide-mouth glass container with an airtight lid. To serve, carefully break the sticky *pinyonate* into clusters and place on fresh lemon leaves. Arrange on a large platter and serve.

hot fresh apricots filled with almond paste

kayisi reynado kon masapan

I love to make this Turkish-inspired recipe with fresh, tart apricots filled with an almond paste. These are baked and served hot with lightly whipped cream or thick yoghurt and topped with pistachios. This quick and easy dessert makes a delicious finale to any meal.

For the paste:
200g (7oz) blanched almonds
100g (3½oz) caster (superfine) sugar
3 tbsp rose water
12 large fresh ripe apricots

For the topping:
¾ cup whole green blanched
    pistachios

For serving:
fresh heavy cream or thick Greek-
    style yoghurt

PREHEAT the oven to 180°C (350°F).

Make the paste: Blend the almonds, sugar and rose water to a soft paste in a food processor.

To assemble: Cut around one side of the apricots with a paring knife. With the tip of the knife gently dig the kernel (pit) out. Do not peel the apricots.

BREAK off pieces of almond paste the size of a hazelnut and roll into balls. Push them carefully into the slits in the apricots and press gently, encasing the filling.

ARRANGE the filled fruits in an ovenproof dish and bake in the oven for about 20 minutes or until the apricots have softened a little. Serve hot, sprinkled with the pistachios and accompanied with lightly whipped cream or thick yoghurt.

marzipan

marsapan

The recipe of this ancient confection, passed on from my ancestors from the island of Rhodes, has a less refined texture than the ready-made marzipan. Masapan, made with freshly ground blanched almonds and cooked with a sugar syrup, is handcrafted into orange blossom scented sweet treats. The Ladino expression, 'masapan blanko komo la inyeve', 'marzipan as white as snow', was a phrase expressing the superb expertise of the home cook. Masapan is offered at life-cycle celebrations (it was a big honour for young girls to hold the tray of marzipan at the synagogue entrance after a bar or bat mitzvah or wedding). Marzipan is served at all festivities and holidays or any time with Turkish coffee.

500g (1lb 2oz) blanched almonds
2¼ cups warm water
2¼ cups sugar
1 tsp fresh lemon juice

For shaping:
mix 1 cup water and 1 tsp orange blossom
    water in a small bowl

For decorating:
silver balls (*dragées*)

You will need:
fluted moulds about 4cm (1½in)
    in diameter

GRIND the almonds, a small batch at a time, in a food processor, until finely ground. Pulse, using the on-off action, to control that it does not grind to an oily paste. Put the warm water and sugar into a large, heavy-based, stainless-steel pan over a low heat. To avoid crystallisation, ensure that the sugar is completely dissolved before the syrup comes to a boil. Bring the syrup to a boil over a high heat, without stirring. As the sugar becomes more concentrated the syrup will feel tacky and a short thread, about 1.5cm (½in) in length, will form between your wetted finger and thumb when they are pulled apart. This takes 15–20 minutes.

REMOVE the pan from the heat, add the ground almonds and lemon juice, stirring vigorously with a wooden spoon. Return to a low heat and continue stirring constantly for about 12 minutes or until the paste comes away from the sides of the pan*. Be sure to stir continuously so that the mixture does not stick to the bottom of the pan or scorch. To test if the marzipan is ready, roll a small amount of the mixture, the size of a small marble, between your palms. If it stays in a ball and does not stick to your hands, remove from the heat. Beat the marzipan over a medium speed in the bowl of a free-standing mixer for 2 minutes.

Shape the marzipan: Dampen your hands in the scented water and roll the paste into ropes about 2.5cm (1in) thick. Cut into 3.5cm (1½in) diagonal sections and decorate with a silver ball in the centre. Alternatively roll into 2.5cm (1in) balls and press into the moulds. Tap it out of the mould and place on a tray and decorate with a silver ball. Makes 50.

STELLA'S HINTS:
- **I enlist the help of an extra pair of hands to alternate between holding the pan steady and energetically stirring the marzipan over the warm stove.*
- *If the marzipan seems dry when shaping, blend with up to ¼ cup of hot water, in small increments, in a food processor.*
- **To store:** *Place the* masapan *between sheets of baking paper and store in an airtight container in the fridge for up to 1 month.*
- **To freeze:** *Shape the* masapan *into ropes and seal in plastic wrap and freeze for up to 2 months. When required, let thaw and shape.*

Mira a la madre – toma la ija

(Lit: Look at the mother – take the daughter)

marzipan-filled pastries
gizadas de masapan

These baked pastries are the quintessential crown of Sephardic confectionery! Gizadas are star-shaped pastries that are filled with marzipan, similar to macaroons but just a little more refined. They make a gorgeous finale to a dinner party.

For the filling:
500g (1lb 2oz) blanched almonds
3 cups warm water
1¾ cups sugar
3 egg whites

For the pastry:
1½ cups sifted cake flour
2 egg yolks
1 whole egg
2 tsp vegetable oil
3 tbsp water

For decorating:
silver balls (*dragées*)

PREHEAT the oven to 180°C (350°F). Line two baking trays with baking paper.

Make the marzipan: Grind the almonds, a small batch at a time, in a food processor, until finely ground. Pulse, using the on-off action, to control that it does not grind to an oily paste. Put the warm water and sugar into a large, heavy-based, stainless-steel pan over a low heat. To avoid crystallisation, ensure that the sugar is completely dissolved before the syrup comes to a boil. Bring the syrup to a boil over a high heat, without stirring. As the sugar becomes more concentrated the syrup will feel tacky and a short thread, about 1.5cm (½in) in length, will form between your wetted finger and thumb when they are pulled apart. This takes 15–20 minutes.

Remove the pan from the heat and add the ground almonds, stirring vigorously with a wooden spoon. Return to a low heat and continue stirring constantly for about 12 minutes or until the paste comes away from the sides of the pan*. Be sure to stir continuously so that the mixture does not stick to the bottom of the pan or scorch. To test if the marzipan is ready, roll a small amount of the mixture, the size of a small marble, between your palms. If it stays in a ball and does not stick to your hands, remove from the heat. Allow to cool a little. Whisk the egg whites in a clean bowl until soft peaks form and then gradually fold into the almond mixture, a little at a time, with a metal spoon.

Make the pastry: Combine the pastry ingredients together in a large bowl to make a firm dough. Knead lightly. Working with small pieces of pastry at a time, roll the pastry very thinly on a lightly floured work surface. Keep the remaining dough covered with plastic wrap until required. Cut circles out of the rolled pastry using a 5cm (2in) biscuit cutter.

PLACE a teaspoonful of the filling in the centre of each circle. Carefully work around the edges of the pastry circle, using your thumb and forefinger of both hands. Pinch upright pleats to make a six-sided star around the almond filling. This takes some practice but you will soon become adept at pinching!

ARRANGE on prepared baking trays and place a silver ball in the centre of each filled pastry. Bake for 20–25 minutes until lightly golden. Leave to cool on wire racks.

 STELLA'S HINTS:
- **I enlist the help of an extra pair of hands to alternate between holding the pan steady and energetically stirring the marzipan over the warm stove.*
- *Instead of rolling the dough I use a pasta machine and feed it through until I achieve the desired thickness.*
- *For an easier method, press circles of pastry to fit tiny tartlet moulds. Fill the centre with the almond filling, pop a silver ball in the centre and bake as above.*
- ***To store the pastries:*** *Place the* gizadas *between layers of baking paper and store in an airtight container for up to 2 weeks.*

marzipan filled with lemon fondant
pastel reale – masapan kon sharope

This marzipan confection is usually made only for very special occasions. In this variation, marzipan is carefully handcrafted into dainty pie-like petit fours, filled with lemon fondant and crowned with a silver ball. Though time-consuming to make, they are impressive to serve displayed on a silver platter scattered with candy-coated almonds, bon bons.

½ quantity of marzipan recipe (p232)
¼ quantity of lemon fondant recipe
   (see below)

For shaping:
mix 1 cup water and 1 tsp orange
   blossom water in a small bowl

For decorating:
silver balls (*dragées*)

 STELLA'S HINT:
♦ *To store pastel reale: Place between layers of baking paper in an airtight container and store in the fridge for up to 2 weeks.*

MAKE the marzipan and the fondant ahead of time and keep refrigerated. If the marzipan has hardened, coarsely grate and then knead, adding a few drops of the water and orange blossom water mix to make it more malleable.

Shape and fill the marzipan: Dampen your hands in the scented water. Take two-thirds of the marzipan and shape into 3cm (1¼in) balls for the pots. Shape the remainder of the marzipan into smaller balls, about 1.75cm (¾in), for the lids. Cover the marzipan that is not being worked with a tea towel so it does not dry out. Hollow the larger balls with your thumbs and fingers and shape into little pots with straight sides 3.5cm (1½in) deep and 3.5cm (1½in) wide, making the walls about 3mm (⅛in) thin. Fill each pot with half a teaspoon of fondant.

To cover the filled pots: Take one of the smaller balls and flatten slightly between both palms. Fit and cover over the filled pot. Pinch the edges of the marzipan together all around to seal the pots. Using a small sharp knife, at a 45°angle, serrate the top circumference of the closed edges into a crisscross fringe called *varielle*. Finally, lift the sides of the finished sweet to a uniform height and then rotate between the palms of your hands (like a potter's wheel).

TOP each *pastel reale* with a silver ball.

lemon fondant
Dulse de sharope (Dulse blanco)

In Sephardic homes in Greece and Turkey this glossy white fondant is traditionally served as a symbol of purity at life-cycle events and on the New Year. One spoonful is all you really need to savour this very sweet treat. Chase it with a sip of chilled water and a cup of Turkish coffee.

4 cups warm water
3 cups caster (superfine) sugar
1 tbsp fresh lemon juice
a few drops orange blossom water

POUR the warm water into a heavy-based, stainless steel pan over a low heat. Add the sugar and stir gently with a metal spoon while the sugar is dissolving. Do not allow the water to boil before the sugar has dissolved. Boil the syrup on high heat and do not stir once the water starts to boil. As the sugar becomes more concentrated the syrup will feel tacky and a long thread, about 2cm (¾in) in length, will form between your wetted finger and thumb when they are pulled apart.

REMOVE from the heat and add the lemon juice. Place on a double-folded tea towel on a work surface to keep the pan steady, and stir briskly, using a circular motion in one direction only, for at least 20 minutes. This is important to give the correct texture and colour to the *sharope*. The fondant will thicken and whiten to a glossy paste during this process. As with the marzipan, I find it easier if someone helps me to hold the pan steady whilst I briskly stir the fondant.

KNEAD the fondant, a handful at a time, working quickly while still warm, adding a few drops of orange blossom water. Combine the handfuls together and place in an airtight glass container, in the fridge, where it will keep for months.

meringues with mastic

ashuplados kon almastica

These elegant, ivory-coloured meringues are crunchy to bite into yet soft and chewy inside because of their soft mastic- and vanilla-flavoured centres. They are utterly divine at afternoon tea, baked with your favourite topping. If making as a dessert, no topping is required before baking. My updated twist to transform this classic meringue into an exotic prepare-ahead dessert is to stack them on a platter and top with lightly whipped cream, freshly sliced mangoes and a drizzle of warm passion fruit (granadilla) syrup. Meringues are the ideal flourless sweet offerings for Passover.

6 egg whites

300g (10½oz) caster (superfine) sugar

2 crystals mastic, crushed with 1 tsp
    sugar

1 tsp vanilla extract

For the topping:

½ cup chopped pistachios

¾ cup flaked almonds or ½ cup cocoa
    powder

PREHEAT the oven to 120°C (250°F). Line two baking trays with baking paper.

PUT the egg whites in a clean bowl of a free-standing electric mixer fitted with a whisk attachment and beat until the whites double in volume and hold a slightly bent peak when you lift the whisk. Add half the sugar, a tablespoon at a time, incorporating each tablespoon completely before adding the next one. Tip in the remaining sugar and whisk until the whites are stiff and glossy. Fold in the ground mastic and vanilla extract with a metal spoon.

WITH two large metal spoons, take a big spoonful of the meringue mixture, the size of a small orange and scrape it off, placing it onto the baking tray. Repeat, spacing the meringues well apart. I like large individual spiky ones. Top with chopped pistachios, flaked almonds or sprinkle with cocoa powder when making for afternoon tea, or leave plain if using as a dessert.

BAKE for about 70 minutes or until they are crisp, depending on the size of the meringues. Check that the underside is firm to the touch and dry. Turn off the oven and allow the meringues to cool completely in the oven for 30 minutes, or overnight as I do.

 STELLA'S HINT:

◆ *The meringues can be stored in an airtight container for up to 2 weeks.*

 TWIST ON TRADITION:

◆ *Tropical meringue dessert: Whip 2 cups heavy cream with 1 tsp vanilla essence until thick but not stiff. Peel and slice 1 large ripe mango. Place 1 cup caster sugar, ½ cup water and 1 cup passion fruit pulp (about 12 scooped-out passion fruits) in a small pan over a medium-high heat and stir until the sugar has dissolved. Bring to a boil. Then reduce the heat and simmer for 8–10 minutes before serving so that the meringues remain crunchy. Have the cream, fruit and syrup ready. Stack the meringues high on a cake stand. Top with spoonfuls of whipped cream, scatter over mango slices and drizzle with the warm passion fruit syrup. Serve.*

milk pudding with fresh orange juice

sutlach kon portokal i agua di flor

This heavenly, delicate milk pudding is layered over a refreshing orange and cornflour base, sandwiched with a scattering of almonds or candied orange peel, and served chilled. I find it makes an elegant party dessert served in a deep glass dish.

For the milk pudding:
½ cup cornflour (cornstarch)
½ cup water
5 cups whole milk
1 cup sugar
2 tbsp orange blossom water

For the orange pudding:
¾ cup cornflour
½ cup water
3½ cups fresh orange juice
1½ cups sugar
¼ cup blanched flaked almonds
1 tbsp candied orange peel, chopped

Make the milk pudding: Blend the cornflour and water in a small bowl and stir to a smooth paste. Combine the milk and sugar in a deep, heavy-based pan and set it over a medium heat. Stir in the cornflour paste and bring gently to a boil, stirring constantly. Reduce the heat and continue stirring for a further 5 minutes. Stir in the orange blossom water and remove from the heat.

Make the orange pudding: Blend the cornflour and water in a small bowl and stir to a smooth paste. Pour the orange juice into a medium, heavy-based pan. Add the cornflour paste and sugar and stir constantly over a medium heat. Bring to a boil. Reduce the heat and continue stirring for a further 5 minutes.

POUR the warm orange pudding into a deep glass serving dish. Scatter with flaked almonds and candied orange peel. Gently ladle the milk pudding over the orange pudding.

SET aside until cool and then chill in the fridge for at least 1 hour before serving.

El mojado no se espanta de la luvyia

(Lit: The wet one is not afraid of the rain)

One who has passed through a difficult situation does not fear further challenges

orange Spanish sponge cake

pan d'Espanya (pan Esponjado)

This book would not be complete without featuring the quintessential orange sponge cake, which featured among the Jews of Medieval Spanish origin. Pan d'Espanya is traditionally served as part of the meal at the breaking of the Yom Kippur fast. This updated version is a feather-light orange chiffon cake, which can be turned into an irresistible finale served with strawberries soaked in rose water syrup (recipe below) and lightly whipped cream.

8 large eggs

1 cup caster (superfine) sugar

½ cup vegetable or sunflower oil

2 tsp finely grated orange zest

¾ cup fresh orange juice

1 tsp orange blossom water

2 cups sifted cake flour

2 heaped tsp baking powder

a pinch salt

¾ tsp cream of tartar

PREHEAT the oven to 180°C (350°F). You will need a 25cm (10in) ungreased chiffon cake pan (tube pan).

SEPARATE the eggs and place six egg yolks in a bowl. Put 8 egg whites in a large clean bowl and cover with plastic wrap, keeping at room temperature.

IN the bowl of a free-standing electric mixer, beat the sugar and egg yolks at high speed until pale and creamy. Stir in the oil, orange zest, orange juice and orange blossom water. In a separate bowl combine the flour, baking powder and salt. Reduce the speed to low and add the flour mixture to the sugar and egg mixture. Beat to combine, scraping down the sides of the bowl as needed.

BEAT the egg whites in a clean bowl with the whisk attachment, until foamy and shiny. Add the cream of tartar. Continue to beat until they hold stiff peaks.

IN two batches, gently fold the egg whites into the batter with a large silicone spatula or a metal spoon.

POUR the batter into the ungreased chiffon cake pan and smooth the surface with a spoon. Bake for 55–60 minutes or until the cake is firm to the touch and a skewer inserted in the centre comes out clean. Immediately invert the cake pan on a wire rack. Let the cake cool completely before removing from the pan (about 1½ hours). To remove the cake from the pan, loosen the outer edges of the cake with a long, thin knife around the inside of the pan and the centre core. Gently ease out onto a wire rack.

 STELLA'S HINT:

♦ *To freeze: Seal the cooled baked cake with plastic wrap and freeze for up to 1 month. To defrost, remove the wrapping and thaw for 3–4 hours at room temperature.*

 TWIST ON TRADITION:

♦ *For the rose water syrup: 2 cups water; 1 cup caster sugar; 2 tsp rose water; 1 tsp vanilla extract. In a small pan over a high heat, bring the ingredients to a boil. Reduce the heat to low and simmer for 3 minutes. Remove from the heat. Add a punnet of hulled and halved strawberries to the syrup and serve warm.*

Ojo ke vee, alma ke demanda

(Lit: The eyes see, the soul yearns)

oranges with dates and pine nuts
portokal kon datli i pinyones

This Moorish-inspired dessert is refreshing and colourful and very simple to make. Slices of fresh oranges or other citrus fruits are splashed with orange blossom-scented syrup and scattered with fleshy dates and pine nuts. Try adding limes, ruby grapefruit and tangerines for a splash of colour. I can assure you it will instantly become a hit with your guests.

6 large, juicy navel oranges or blood
    oranges

For the syrup:
2 tbsp clear honey
2 cups fresh orange juice
1 cinnamon stick
2 tsp finely grated orange zest
2 tsp orange blossom water

For the topping:
¾ cup fresh dates, pitted and cut
    lengthways into quarters
½ cup pine nuts, toasted (p287) or
    fresh pomegranate seeds

PEEL the oranges with a sharp knife, being careful to remove all the bitter white pith. Cut through the outer membrane, working over a colander placed in a bowl to catch any juice. Remove the seeds and place the segments into a shallow serving bowl. A bright contrasting colourful dish sets off the citrus magnificently. Squeeze the remains of the oranges over the bowl to extract all the juice.

Make the syrup: Put the honey, orange juice, cinnamon stick and zest in a small pan and simmer for 5 minutes. Add the orange blossom water and cool. Discard the cinnamon stick.

POUR the cooled syrup over the orange segments. Scatter with dates and toasted pine nuts or pomegranate seeds. Chill before serving.

No ay en el mundo amigo komo la madre

(Lit: There is no friend in the world like your mother)

Your mother is your best friend

sweet fruit and nut paste
harosi

Harosi is a delicious sweet paste made from dates, nuts, fresh apples, red wine and cider vinegar. This recipe was a favourite of the community of the island of Rhodes. The fruit and nut paste is served over Passover, symbolic of the mortar the Israelites used to build with when they were slaves in Egypt. The paste is one of the items on the Seder plate.

1½ cups walnuts
250g (9oz) blanched almonds
4 apples, peeled, cored and quartered
450g (1lb) dried pitted dates
½ cup cider vinegar, boiled and cooled
¼ tsp ground cinnamon
1 tsp sugar or honey, or to taste
½ cup sweet red Pesach wine

PULSE the walnuts and almonds in a food processor until finely chopped, but not ground, to give the paste more crunch.

PUT the apples and dates in a heavy-based pan with enough water to just cover. Bring to a boil. Reduce the heat and simmer for 15 minutes or until tender and the water has been absorbed. Strain the mixture into a bowl or blend it in a processor.

STIR in the nuts, cider vinegar, cinnamon and sugar or honey and enough wine to make a paste. Store in a glass, tight-lidded container in the fridge where it will keep well for a week.

SERVE with matza crackers at meals or as a snack.

 STELLA'S HINT:
- *Fresh dates are not suitable for this recipe.*

 TWIST ON TRADITION:
- *In Turkey, ½ cup of finely chopped dried figs, ¼ tsp ground cinnamon and ½ tsp ground cloves are added.*

Passover wine biscuits
masa de vino

Wine biscuits are a much-loved teatime nibble over Passover. These quick, simple, nutty biscuits are made with matza meal but are perfectly delicious throughout the year made with plain (all-purpose) flour.

1 cup vegetable oil
½ cup sweet red Pesach wine
½ cup caster (superfine) sugar
½ cup walnuts, finely chopped
3 cups matza cake meal (or 2½ cups matza cake meal and ½ cup potato starch)

For the topping:
25–30 walnut halves

PREHEAT the oven to 180°C (350°F). Line two baking trays with baking paper.

BEAT the oil, wine and sugar together with a whisk. Add the chopped walnuts and cake meal. If the mixture appears to be too soft, add a little more cake meal. On a board, lightly floured with matza cake meal, roll dough into small balls and flatten with the tines of a fork.

PLACE the biscuits on the prepared baking trays and press a walnut half onto the centre of each biscuit. Bake for 20 minutes or until golden and crisp. Remove from the oven and cool on wire racks. Makes 25–30.

STORE in an airtight container where they will keep well for a few weeks.

pastry puffs topped with honey, nuts and cinnamon
piticas

Piticas are crisp, thin, deep-fried pastries, drizzled with a floral honey just before serving and topped with nuts, toasted sesame seeds and dusted with ground cinnamon. They make a magnificent dessert stacked high on a large platter, and are delicious served on their own or with rice pudding or a scoop of your favourite ice cream and berries. For a speedier assembly line, my children would roll the dough thinly while I would fry them. As soon as the piticas *were made they would snatch a few and devour them, licking their sticky fingers.*

2 cups cake flour, as needed
¼ tsp bicarbonate of soda
½ cup vegetable oil
½ cup water

For deep-frying:
vegetable oil

For the topping:
1 cup Greek thyme or floral clear honey
½ cup unsalted pistachios or blanched
   and toasted almonds, finely chopped
½ cup toasted sesame seeds
ground cinnamon

SIFT the flour and bicarbonate of soda into a bowl and make a well in the centre. Pour in the oil and water and bring together with your hands, and then knead to make a smooth firm dough. Add more flour if necessary. Roll into walnut-sized balls, cover with plastic wrap and allow to rest for 1½ hours at room temperature.

ROLL out one ball at a time as thinly as possible on a work surface. Keep the remaining balls of dough covered with a tea towel.

HEAT enough oil for deep-frying in a large, heavy-based pan over a medium-high heat. When the oil is very hot, slowly lower one piece of dough into the oil and deep-fry. With a large spoon, continuously scoop hot oil over the pastry to make it puff up until it is crisp and pale golden (30–40 seconds). With a slotted spoon carefully transfer onto a tray lined with paper towels to drain. Repeat with another rolled piece of dough until all the dough is used. Reduce the heat if the oil becomes too hot.

GENTLY stack the fragile pastries on a large platter. Spoon the honey over the top, making sure each *pitica* is well covered. Sprinkle with chopped nuts, sesame seeds and ground cinnamon and serve.

 STELLA'S HINT:
♦ Piticas *can be made in advance and kept in an airtight container for up to 5 days without the honey and topping. When ready to serve, drizzle the honey and topping over the pastries.*

Si tu enemigo es una ormiga,
kontalo komo un gameyo

(Lit: If your enemy is an ant, treat it like you would a camel)

Do not underestimate your enemy

rice and rose water-scented milk pudding

arroz kon leche i agua di kondja al orno

Nourishing and creamy, with tender grains of rice, this rose water-scented pudding is served with the top lightly browned in the oven.

1 cup short-grain rice, rinsed and drained
5 cups whole milk
½ cup caster (superfine) sugar
¼ cup ground rice flour
¼ cup water
a pinch salt
1 mastic crystal, crushed with 1 tsp sugar
1–2 tbsp rose water

To sprinkle:
1–2 tbsp caster sugar

You will need:
8–9 ramekins, 7.5cm (3in) in diameter

PREHEAT the oven to 240°C (475°F).

PLACE the rice in a heavy-based pan and pour in enough water to just cover. Bring to a boil. Reduce the heat and simmer, uncovered, for about 12 minutes or until almost all the water has been absorbed and the rice is just tender.

POUR in the milk and bring to a boil. Lower the heat, stir in the sugar and simmer until the liquid starts to thicken. Raise the heat to medium-high and bring the mixture to a boil.

BLEND the rice flour and water in a small bowl and stir until smooth. Stir in some of the hot milk and slowly pour this into the simmering milk, stirring all the time with a balloon whisk.

GENTLY cook over a low heat for 20 minutes, stirring constantly to prevent lumps forming, until the mixture thickens to a pouring consistency. Add the salt, mastic and rose water.

LADLE the mixture into the ramekins and place in a roasting pan. Pour enough cold water into the pan to immerse the dishes up to two-thirds of their depth.

BAKE in the oven on the middle shelf for about 25 minutes.

WHEN the puddings have cooled to room temperature, sprinkle the tops lightly with caster sugar. Place under a hot grill or on the top shelf of the oven for 5 minutes until the tops are lightly browned.

SERVE at room temperature or chilled.

Mas vale un drama de mazal ke una oka de ducados

(Lit: A drop of luck is worth more than a barrel of coins)

sesame-studded biscuits
reshikas

In the old days, Reshikas *were a telltale sign you were in a Sephardic home. These simple, yet can't-get-enough-of-them sesame-studded, oil biscuits are baked twice; once to firm them up and a second time, at a low temperature to crisp them and give them a long shelf life.*

Like many good things, making these well doesn't come easy, as some skill and practice is required to form these twisted pretzel shapes consistently and at the same size. Being a good reshika *maker was like a badge of honour.*

Reshikas *are generally offered with feta cheese and olives or a fruit preserve with Turkish coffee or at any celebratory tea. My grandchildren order these biscuits from me way ahead of my trips to New York. In fact, they tend to prefer the bracelet-shaped, cinnamon sugared version,* biskotchos. *Each child has its own preference for eating the* biskotchos: *licking the cinnamon sugar first, nibbling it bit by bit, and even spooning up the crumbs of any broken ones in the biscuit tin.*

For the dough:
4 eggs
1 cup caster (superfine) sugar
1 cup vegetable or sunflower oil
1 cup freshly squeezed orange juice
7–8 cups cake flour, sifted
3 heaped tsp baking powder

For the topping:
1 cup sesame seeds or a mixture of
    2 tbsp caster (superfine) sugar and 2
    tsp ground cinnamon, placed in
    a shallow bowl

For the egg wash:
2–3 eggs, lightly beaten in a shallow bowl

PREHEAT the oven to 190 °C (375 °F). Line two baking trays with baking paper.

Make the dough: Beat the eggs and sugar in a free-standing electric mixer, fitted with a whisk attachment, until they are fluffy and pale. Over a low speed, beat in the oil and orange juice. Change to a beater attachment and add 3 cups of flour, a cup at a time, with the baking powder. Set the bowl aside, add the remaining 4–5 cups flour, kneading with your hands, to make a soft but not sticky dough*.

Shape the *reshikas*: Divide the dough into four portions. Cover three portions with a tea towel while you work with one portion. Break off into 20g (¾oz) pieces and evenly roll each piece into about 30cm (12in) pencil-shape lengths. Shape by looping the ends of the dough ropes over the middle to form the pretzel shape and press the ends lightly. Turn the top-side of the biscuit over into the sesame seeds, making sure that they are well coated.

ARRANGE the biscuits, with the topping side up, 2.5cm (1in) apart on the prepared baking trays. Brush the egg wash over the sesame seed-topped biscuits.

PLACE the tray in the centre of the oven and bake for 20 minutes or until the biscuits are firm and golden brown. While the first batch is baking, repeat with the remaining portions of dough.

TRANSFER the biscuits to a wire rack and allow to cool completely.

Crisp the *reshikas*: Pile them on a baking tray and return to the oven, turn off the heat and leave them in the oven to crisp for about 1 hour. Transfer again to a wire rack and allow to cool completely. Makes about 80.

 STELLA'S HINTS:

- **For a crisper biscuit put the dough through a mincer attachment of a free-standing mixer.*
- *Should the biscuits soften in damp weather, crisp in a preheated 150°C (300°F) oven for 10 minutes.*
- *To store reshikas: Store in an airtight container for up to 1 month.*

Biskotchos: Twisted ropes shaped into round bracelet-shapes are an alternative version of *reshikas*. To shape: Break off into 20g (¾oz) pieces and evenly roll each piece into very thin ropes, about 43cm (17in) in length. Fold each rope in half. Twist the ends in opposite directions, then press the ends gently together to close into a bracelet. Turn the top-side of the biscuit over into caster sugar and cinnamon mixture. The *biskotchos* can also simply be brushed with egg wash. Place on baking trays and bake as directed.

El Dio ke de vida par ver maraviyas

(Lit: May G-d grant you life to witness miracles)

shortbread filled with dates and walnuts

menenas

These biscuits are a little like shortbread but crumblier. They are made with semolina and flour and filled with a succulent spicy date and walnut paste. Traditionally the Rhodesli womenfolk moulded the menenas *into oval shapes and decorated the tops with a feathery design by pinching the dough with a pair of tweezers. An easier alternative is to use decorative wooden moulds with different ornate designs to shape the filled dough. These pale-coloured pastries, which are dusted in icing sugar, keep well for a month stored in an airtight container. They're lovely at teatime or as a festive treat.*

For the dough:
½ cup fine semolina
2¼ cups plain (all-purpose) flour
½ tsp baking powder
2 heaped tbsp icing (confectioner's) sugar
250g (9oz) unsalted butter, at room
    temperature
1 tbsp whole milk
1 tsp vanilla extract

For the filling:
170g (6oz) walnuts or unblanched almonds
200g (7oz) dried dates, pitted
¼ cup hot water
50g (2oz) unsalted butter
½ tsp ground cinnamon
¼ tsp ground cloves
1 tsp finely grated orange zest
1 tsp orange blossom water

For dusting:
icing sugar

 STELLA'S HINTS:

◆ *The hand-carved concave wooden moulds on thick handles, called* tabé, *can be purchased at Middle Eastern speciality stores or online – whatever the shape, the size of the mould is about 5cm (2in) in diameter and 1cm (½in) deep.*

◆ **To freeze baked** menenas: *Place the* menenas *between layers of baking paper in an airtight container and freeze for up to 1 month. When ready to use, let thaw and sprinkle liberally with icing sugar.*

◆ *The filling can be prepared ahead and kept overnight in the fridge.*

Prepare the dough: Combine the semolina, flour, baking powder and sugar in a large mixing bowl. Add the butter and, with fingertips, rub into the flour to a grainy texture. Add the milk and vanilla extract and combine until the dough begins to hold together. Using the palms of your hands, knead for 1 minute. Roll into a ball, wrap in plastic wrap and refrigerate for 15 minutes.

Prepare the filling: Pulse the walnuts or almonds in a processor until finely chopped, but not ground, to give the filling more crunch. Finely chop the dates with a sharp knife. Place the dates, hot water and butter in a heavy-based frying pan over a medium heat. Mash with a fork for 2 minutes until soft and paste-like. Stir in the ground cinnamon, cloves and orange zest. Remove from the heat, add the nuts and stir in the orange blossom water. Remove the paste from the pan and let cool on a plate. Take 1 heaped teaspoon of cooled date paste and roll into about 30 small balls. Set aside on a large plate.

PREHEAT the oven to 160°C (325°F). Line two baking trays with baking paper.

Fill the dough: Divide the dough into about 30 walnut-sized pieces and rolls with your hands into balls. The pastry balls should be twice the size of the date balls. Pierce a hollow into the centre of each pastry ball with your fingertip. With the index finger and thumb work around the inside and outside of the dough until you form a 5mm (¼in) thick shell. Push in one prepared date ball and mould the edges of the pastry together over the top. Gently pinch to enclose and seal in the filling, reshaping into a ball. The date filling should be enveloped in an even layer of dough. Repeat with the remaining dough and filling.

To shape the traditional way: Form the filled dough into oval shapes and arrange on a baking tray with smooth side on the top. To make a pattern on the surface of the shortbread, pinch a feathered design with tweezers or press with the tines of a fork.

To shape with a mould: Using a decorative wooden mould*, dust the mould lightly with flour and gently press the filled dough-ball into the mould, unpinched side down, with your palm. Flip the mould, then tap against a work surface and the *menena* will pop out. Place decorated side up, 1.25cm (½in) apart, on the prepared baking trays. Repeat with the rest of the filled pastry balls.

BAKE on the middle shelf for about 30 minutes until firm and pale in colour. Take care that the *menenas* do not over bake as they quickly become too hard and golden. Let stand on the baking trays for 1 minute, then carefully transfer to a wire rack. Sprinkle liberally with icing sugar while still warm.

Spoon Sweets

Spoon sweets and fruit preserves can keep for months if prepared and stored correctly. Here are a few helpful tips:

- Wash both jars and lids with hot soapy water and rinse. Put them in boiling water for 5 minutes. Remove and place upside down on a tray lined with paper towels to dry.
- Skim any foam off the surface of the preserves while they are simmering using a large metal spoon.
- There are two ways of checking to see if the syrup has set. Either the syrup will thickly coat the back of a spoon or alternatively dip a tablespoon into the hot syrup, remove and hold it vertically above the pan, allowing most of the syrup to drip back into the pan. Allow the final drops to drip over a small saucer and if they hold their shape the syrup is ready.
- Should the fruit turn too soft before the syrup is thick enough, you can remove the fruit and let the syrup cook longer.
- Pack the cooled fruit into the preserving jars, leaving a 1cm (½in) gap on the top and seal the lids.
- Once opened, store in the fridge.
- Add a little lemon juice if the syrup crystallises while stored.

apricot sweet paste

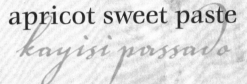

kayisi passado

This tart, amber-hued, apricot confection sets as a paste and is served in beautiful diamond-shaped wedges. I like to make it for the New Year and Passover as a sweet bite offered with herbal tisanes or strong Turkish coffee.

500g (1lb 2oz) dried apricots
2 tsp rose water
2¾ cups sugar

For the topping:
½ cup pine nuts or walnuts

You will need:
a 15.5 × 10.5cm (6 × 4in) heatproof dish,
   lightly oiled

PLACE the apricots in a bowl, cover with boiling water and leave to soak for 5 hours. Pour the apricots and the soaking liquid into a heavy-based, stainless steel pan and boil over a high heat until they are softened. Drain.

WHIZZ the apricots in a food processor in batches while still hot until a smooth purée forms.

TRANSFER the purée back into the pan and add the rose water and sugar. Stir vigorously with a wooden spoon over a medium heat, for 30–35 minutes, until the mixture thickens to a paste and leaves the sides of the pan.

SPREAD the paste into the prepared dish, smoothing the top with the back of a spoon and let set overnight to a firm paste that can be easily cut.

CUT into 3cm (1¼in) wide diamond shapes with a sharp knife. Serve either in the dish or remove each wedge and turn them over so the glossy side is up. Top with pine nuts or walnuts, pressed onto the centre of each wedge.

STELLA'S HINTS:
- *In the U.S. use Californian dried apricots as they give a lovely intense flavour.*
- *To store: Place the paste between layers of baking paper and store in an airtight container for up to a month in a cool dry place.*

La mujer i el vino kita a l'ombre del tino

(Lit: A woman and wine make a man lose his mind)

candied grapefruit peel

dulse de gajo

Strips of grapefruit peel are rolled tightly and coiled, then poached in a citrus syrup. Grapefruit makes an unusual glossy spoon sweet, wonderful served with thick Greek yoghurt or ice cream. After dinner, I like to offer the candied peel with Turkish coffee and glasses of chilled water.

4–5 large, thick-skinned pink grapefruit
    (about 2kg/4½lb), rinsed under hot
    water and dried

For the syrup:
9 cups caster (superfine) sugar
3 cups water
juice of 2 grapefruits and 2 oranges
1 cinnamon stick
2 tbsp orange blossom water

LIGHTLY grate the thin bitter zest of the grapefruit with a fine Microplane grater, without removing any of the white pith beneath. Discard the zest. With a sharp knife, score the grapefruit vertically into eight segments, avoiding cutting into the flesh. Carefully remove the peel from each segment, keeping the peel in one whole piece. Set aside the segments to be used as an alternative to oranges in the oranges with dates and pine nuts dessert (p244).

PLACE the peels in a large, heavy-based pan with cold water to cover and bring to a boil. Drain. Fill the pan with fresh water, return the peels to the pan, bring to a boil again for 10–15 minutes. Drain well. Roll each piece of peel into a tight coil. Push a wooden toothpick through the centres so they do not unravel.

Prepare the syrup: Rinse the pan and add the sugar and water. Dissolve the sugar in the water over a medium-heat for 5 minutes, stirring. Add the orange and grapefruit juices, cinnamon stick and peel. Boil for about 5 minutes without stirring, until it forms a thick syrup. Reduce the heat to medium-low and simmer, uncovered, for 45 minutes, stirring occasionally. Cook until the peel is soft and translucent and the syrup thickly coats the back of a spoon. Remove the pan from the heat, add the orange blossom water and let the preserve cool.

TRANSFER the peel into warm sterilised jars. Pour the syrup over the peel to cover. Seal the jars tightly and store in a cool dark place.

 TWIST ON TRADITION:
* *The same recipe can be used for 6 large, thick-skinned oranges. Simmer the orange peels for 35–40 minutes. Make the syrup with the juice of 2 lemons and 2 oranges.*

El ke oye a su mujer es bovo, el ke no la oye es loko

(Lit: The one who listens to his wife is stupid, the one who does not listen is crazy)

orange preserve
dulse de portokal

Whole oranges, preserved in syrup, are especially good spooned over creamy rice pudding or ice cream, or with coffee and festive bread rolls, roskitas (p182).

6 small oranges – about 1.5kg (3¼lb)
    whole weight
juice of 2 oranges
juice of 1 lemon
1kg (2¼lb) caster (superfine) sugar
½ cup blanched split almonds, toasted

STELLA'S HINT:
* *The same recipe can be used for tangerines and clementines (naartjies as they are known in South Africa). They will take about 15 minutes to become tender.*

PUT the whole oranges into a large pan and just cover with water. Cover with a lid and bring to a boil. Reduce the heat and simmer until tender but not soft, about 30 minutes.

DRAIN the oranges and reserve the liquid. When the oranges are cool to the touch cut the fruit into quarters, leaving the lower half uncut.

POUR the reserved cooled liquid into a large, heavy-based pan. Add the orange juice, lemon juice and sugar. Stir over a medium heat for about 5 minutes until the sugar dissolves. Gently drop the oranges into the pan and bring to a boil for 5 minutes without stirring for the syrup to thicken. Reduce the heat to medium-low and cook, uncovered, for about 1 hour, stirring occasionally, until the rind is translucent and the syrup thickens to coat the back of a spoon. Remove from the heat. Add the almonds and allow to cool.

TRANSFER the oranges into warm sterilised jars. Pour the syrup over the oranges to cover. Seal the jars tightly and store in a cool dark place.

candied quince paste
dulse de membrillo (bembriyo)

Serious Sephardic cooks waited for this treasured fruit to come into season to transform it into a luscious deep-coloured amber quince paste. This unique tasting candied quince is commonly offered on the festivals over the New Year and Passover. I like to serve this sweet after dinner with coffee. The recipe is relatively straightforward – the tricky part is all in arm strength. Help is a good idea on this one.

8 medium, hard and slightly unripe
    quinces (2kg/4½lb)
6 tbsp fresh lemon juice
3–4 cups sugar

You will need:
a 28 × 18cm (11 × 7in) heatproof dish,
    lightly oiled

STELLA'S HINT:
* *To store: Place the bembriyo between layers of baking paper and store in an airtight container at room temperature for up to 2 weeks.*

PEEL the quinces with a paring knife. Cut into 1.25cm (½in) slices and place into a stainless steel pan of cold water to which 3 tbsp lemon juice has been added, to prevent the quince from discolouring. Bring to a boil. Cover and cook over a medium-high heat for about 45 minutes, stirring often, until the quince is tender. Drain. Purée the quince in a food processor and then press through a strainer. Measure 1 cup of sugar for each cup of quince purée and return to the pan with the remaining 3 tbsp lemon juice. Stir over a low heat until the sugar has dissolved. Bring to a boil. Reduce the heat to medium-low and simmer, stirring frequently, for 30–35 minutes, until the mixture thickens and splutters and pulls away from the sides of the pan. Watch the pan carefully to ensure the paste does not stick or burn. When the quince pulls away from the sides of the pan remove from the heat.

SPREAD the paste into the prepared dish and smooth the top with the back of a spoon. Let cool to set and leave overnight to dry out a little. Do not refrigerate.

TURN out onto a work surface. Cut into 3cm (1¼in) wide diamond shapes with a sharp knife (dipping the knife into hot water to make sure you cut clean even shapes). Serve glossy side up.

candied pumpkin

Julse ke kalavasa

Deep orange coloured, luscious, candied pumpkin steeped in a ginger syrup with toasted almonds is a cherished childhood favourite of mine. Like all spoon sweets it keeps well and is wonderful to satisfy a sugary craving. You can use it on top of cakes instead of frosting or serve with Greek yoghurt for a quick dessert.

1kg (2¼lb) pumpkin, peeled
2 tbsp lime powder*

For the syrup:
1 cup honey
1½ cups sugar
1½ cups golden syrup
1 cup water
1 tsp ground ginger
1 cup whole blanched almonds, toasted

CUT the pumpkin into long thin strips 1 × 6cm (½ × 2in). Place in a dish with enough cold water to cover and add the lime powder. Allow to soak for 2 hours. This process firms up the pumpkin for preserving. Rinse thoroughly.

Prepare the syrup: In a large, heavy-based pan bring the honey, sugar, golden syrup and water to a boil. Add the pumpkin strips and allow to cook on medium heat for about 1 hour or until the syrup coats the back of a spoon. Remove from the heat and add the ginger and toasted almonds. Allow to cool.

TRANSFER the candied pumpkin and syrup into warm sterilised jars and store in a cool dark place.

 STELLA'S HINT:
* Lime powder is available from pharmacies.

whole pear and almond preserve

Julse de pera

Whole pears preserved and infused with fragrant cloves and toasted almonds are great with afternoon tea or coffee, or are sensational as a dessert served with your favourite ice cream. To enable you to indulge in this exquisite sweet, you will need to plan well ahead as this recipe takes three days to prepare.

24 small, firm unripe pears –
    about 2kg (4½lb)
6 cups cold water
¾ cup fresh lemon juice
6 cups sugar
12 whole cloves
1 cup whole blanched almonds, toasted

DAY 1: Peel the pears using a sharp knife or a potato peeler. Cut out the crown and core with an apple corer as far as possible without breaking the pear. Leave the stalk intact as they look attractive and it makes them easier to handle. Immediately submerge each peeled pear in a large bowl of fresh water, with a ¼ cup lemon juice, to prevent them from discolouring. Drain the peeled pears. Stand them in a large, deep-sided, heavy-based pan and cover with the sugar. Cover the pan with plastic wrap and leave overnight in the fridge. Spoon the syrup that forms over the pears from time to time to ensure they are well coated.

DAY 2: Place the pan over a medium-high heat and bring the pears in their syrup, which has formed overnight, to a boil. Reduce the heat and simmer for about 15 minutes or until the pears are tender. Remove the pan from the heat, allow the pears to cool and cover the pan with plastic wrap. Let the pears stand in the syrup overnight.

DAY 3: Carefully transfer the pears to a shallow dish. Add the cloves to the syrup, return the pan to the heat and simmer for about 40 minutes or until the syrup thickens to coat the back of a spoon. Add the toasted almonds and the remaining lemon juice and simmer for 2 minutes. Remove the pan from the heat and allow to cool.

TRANSFER the pears into warm sterilised jars. Pour the syrup with the almonds over the pears to cover. Seal tightly and store in a cool dark place.

fresh lemonade
limonada

We all know lemonade, but this one has an unusual twist that I feel makes it even more refreshing.

1 cup fresh lemon juice
½ cup caster (superfine) sugar, or to taste
4 cups chilled water
½ tsp orange blossom water

For the garnish:
a pinch chopped fresh spearmint leaves

PLACE the ingredients in a blender and whizz for a few seconds or simply mix in a pitcher and garnish with spearmint leaves.

 STELLA'S HINTS:

- *It is best to make this just before serving and pour into chilled glasses with ice cubes.*
- *Orangeade may be prepared the same way, substituting 1 cup fresh orange juice for the lemon juice – this is called* portokalada.

almond milk drink
almendrada

250g (9oz) blanched almonds, peeled
5 cups water
1 cup sugar
2 tsp orange blossom water

GRIND the almonds with 1 tsp water in a food processor, until it forms a pasty consistency. Pulse for 1 minute or until the paste holds together when squeezed with your hands.

PUT the almond paste in cheesecloth, bring the corners together and tie securely. Fill a bowl with the 5 cups of water and immerse the almond paste in the cheesecloth bag in the water. Leave in the fridge overnight. Squeeze and dip a few times until the water turns milky.

SQUEEZE the cloth tightly to extract as much flavour as possible. Discard the almond paste. Add sugar and orange blossom water to the milky liquid and refrigerate in a pitcher. Serve chilled.

Una puerta se sera, i sien se avren

(Lit: When one door closes, a hundred open)

melon-seed drink
pipitada

This delicious, refreshing melon-seed drink has a subtle almond taste, perfumed with orange blossom water. I simply adore this drink, as do most Sephardim I know. We'd usually just have pipitada to break the Yom Kippur fast as it helps rehydrate. This was customary in Sephardic communities from Rhodes and Salonica. Each year, I'd wonder why we didn't make it more often – maybe because it takes time to collect enough seeds for the recipe. My mother religiously collected seeds from cantaloupes or other melons when in season. For this recipe you need the seeds from 4–5 melons. Wash the seeds well in a colander to remove all the fleshy parts and lay out to dry on tea towels for a day or two in the sun, or if weather does not permit dry them in a 95 °C (200 °F) oven for 10 minutes. Dried seeds can be stored in an airtight glass jar for up to 1 year.

1 cup sweet melon seeds
3 cups water
2 tbsp caster (superfine) sugar
1 tbsp orange blossom water

GRIND the seeds to a fine powder in a food processor a day before you want to make the drink.

PUT the ground seeds in cheesecloth, bring the corners together and tie securely. Fill a bowl with about 3 cups of water and immerse the ground seeds in their cheesecloth bag in the water. Leave in the fridge overnight. Squeeze the cheesecloth from time to time to release the milky essence from the seeds into the water.

SQUEEZE the cloth tightly to extract as much moisture as possible out of the seeds. Discard the seeds. Add the sugar and orange blossom water to the milky liquid and refrigerate in a pitcher. Serve chilled.

 TWIST ON TRADITION:
◆ *For a creamier taste, my mother would add ½ cup finely ground blanched almonds to the powdered melon seeds when placing in the cheesecloth.*

Kon el tiempo, adulsa la uva

(Lit: Grapes ripen with time)

With time there is maturity

Turkish coffee

kave Turku

I recall returning home from school to the full-flavoured rich aroma of coffee beans being freshly roasted in my mother's oven. She would grind them in an old brass coffee mill that her family brought from Turkey when they emigrated to the Congo.

In our Sephardic community, as elsewhere in the east Mediterranean and Middle East, many hours are spent sipping small cups of strong, rich black coffee. A quintessential custom of our hospitality involves sweetening a guest's palate with a spoon sweet or even a sesame biscuit to dunk in the coffee. Upon drinking the coffee a common saying in Ladino is, Kaves d'alegria ke bevamos siempre, "May we always drink coffee on happy occasions."

A traditional pastime on completion of drinking the coffee would be fortune telling, meldar el findjan, *from the sediment of the emptied inverted cups on their saucers. As the grounds trickle down the sides of the cup they form images or symbols, which are interpreted by anyone who claims to be an expert coffee-cup reader.*

Making Turkish (or Greek) coffee is not as complicated as it's purported to be; I hope these instructions demystify this ritual. You will need a small long-handled, narrow-necked coffee pot, cezve, *usually made from tin-lined copper. The pot, which is wider at the bottom than the top, increases the creamy foam,* kaymak, *of the coffee that forms at the top as the coffee boils up. This is the hallmark of a well-made cup of coffee. The pots come in many sizes, from tiny for 1 cup to larger for 5 cups. The cups for Turkish coffee are espresso-cup size. I have given ingredients for one cup of coffee; simply increase all the ingredients by the number of cups you wish to make.*

Coffee is usually drunk sweetened according to personal taste. When ordering your coffee you will be asked how sweet – very sweet, medium, or unsweetened.

For a medium-sweet coffee:
1 Turkish coffee or espresso cup of
   cold water
1 heaped tsp of finely ground dark roasted
   plain Turkish (or Greek) coffee
1 tsp sugar, or to taste

MEASURE room temperature water into the coffee pot using a Turkish coffee or espresso-size cup. Put the coffee and sugar into the pot and stir well. Place over a high heat and bring to a boil, stirring from time to time. Watch the pot carefully until a froth forms on the surface and the coffee in the pot begins to rise. Immediately remove from the heat, not allowing it to boil. Spoon a small amount of the froth (not the liquid) that has collected at the top of the coffee into the cup.

RETURN the pot to the heat and boil briefly. Immediately pour the coffee into the cup, being careful not to disperse the foam, which will rise to the surface of the cup. Let the coffee rest for a minute for the grains to settle before serving. Do not stir. Only the clear liquid of the coffee is sipped, leaving the grounds that have settled at the bottom of the cup. Serve at once accompanied by a glass of cold water.

 STELLA'S HINT:
♦ *A cezve,* coffee pot, *can also be made in brass, enamel or stainless steel and can be found at Middle Eastern stores.*

Ken keri bivir sano kome poko I sena demprano

(Lit: Whoever wishes to live a healthy life should eat little and dine early)

Blessings, Home Remedies & Folk Beliefs

The women in the Judeo-Spanish communities in the Ottoman Empire practiced preventative and curative remedies and rituals that ensured the spiritual and physical well-being of their families. Some rituals, blessings and prayers were connected to Jewish traditions, while folk beliefs and superstitions had elements of the traditions of the Sephardic's Christian and Muslim neighbours. Many of these traditions were preserved by the older women in our community in Zimbabwe.

Blessings, *Bendisiones*: During my childhood numerous blessings and well-wishes were made throughout the day. Paramount were prayers and blessings for a healthy life – a common saying to this end was *Saludozos siempre*. Blessings of gratitude were also common and said at every meal or sacred occasion, for example the sayings praising G-d, *Alavado sea su nombre* or *Bendichio el Dio*.

Each time we entered or left home, we kissed the *mezuzah* affixed on our doorframe and said, *Kon il nombre del Dio*, "With G-d's presence." In times of adversity we would make the wish, *El Dio mos dara buelta i alegria*, "May G-d visit us and bring us happiness," or on going to school, *Los malachim ke te akompanyen*, asking the angels to be with us. As one was about to embark on a journey a wish was made by both the travellers and the ones being left behind, *Kon bueno ver las karas*, "May we only meet again in happy circumstances." When a new purchase was made the wish immediately expressed was *Kon salut ke lo gozes*, "May you enjoy it with good health."

When we would be sitting at a meal and a family member was absent, someone at the table would express the words, *De falta que no seyan*, "May our loved ones never be missing." At a festive table the host often made the wish *Pujados i non menguados*, "May our numbers always be increasing and not diminishing."

Home Remedies: My maternal grandmother, Vida, was our doctor of first call, and would prepare home remedies for various ailments that had been used on the island of Rhodes and Turkey. It turns out that a few of these remedies have some scientific basis for their curative properties, whilst others seem to belong more in the realm of superstition.

Some of the home remedies used to treat ailments included the following:

Stomach ache, *dolor di stomago*: Anise-scented ouzo, warmed with a little pepper and oil, was massaged onto the area of the stomach and then wrapped with an ouzo-doused cloth for a few hours.

Discomfort from teething, *dientando*: Ouzo or brandy was rubbed onto the gums to help numb the pain.

Panic attacks or fright, *espanto*: The sugar displayed symbolically on the New Year dinner table was saved for the coming year. To treat someone suffering from fear or stress, a sprinkling of this sugar was added to a cup of fresh marjoram tea, fragrant with orange blossom water, and slowly sipped.

Fever and headaches, *shakayika*: Slices of raw potato were tied to the forehead with a handkerchief to draw out the fever or pain.

Colds and flu, *abashada*: Hot tea, made with lemon, cinnamon and linden blossoms, *tilia*, was sipped and, of course, the Sephardic chicken and rice soup was a must.

Coughs, *tos*: My grandmother's cure of choice for those with chesty coughs was cupping therapy, *meter ventozas*. A few short small glasses were heated up by igniting pieces of cotton wool that were placed inside them. The hot glass was then placed mouth down onto the sick person's upper back. As it cooled, the air contracted creating a vacuum and suction effect on the surface of the skin. This increased the blood flow to the surface, drawing out the toxins.

Diarrhoea: Rice soup made with salt and a little lemon, or chicken and rice soup were the remedies offered to combat dehydration.

Urinary tract infection: Copious amounts of hot parsley tea were sipped throughout the day as a diuretic.

Folk Beliefs and Superstitions: The Sephardic belief in the evil eye, *ojo malo*, or *nazar* in Turkish, developed significantly during the years of the Ottoman Empire. Central to this belief is the idea that one can unintentionally or intentionally cause harm to a person simply through thinking or expressing praise. It was also believed that a negative power or harmful energy could be cast through envy, and that amulets afforded protection.

To counteract the evil eye, there was an array of protective talismans to choose from, often worn on a gold chain: blue beads, *nazarlik*, gold amulets, either with a *shaddai* – the three letters of the mystical name of G-d – or the *hamsa*, a symbol of a hand. Cloves of garlic, *klavos di ajo*, were positioned in a prominent place in the home, and later in cars and even in offices because of its alleged power to avert the evil eye.

To shield one vulnerable from envy, the protective custom on making a compliment regarding someone's success, family, new possession or home, was to preface a compliment with *Sin ojo!*, "Without evil eye!" or *Nazar no!* Thus Sephardim had a tendency to downplay success or

beautiful belongings to avoid triggering envy. Some people took this fear of the evil eye very seriously, as denoted in the expression *Mil mueren de ayinara i uno de su muerti*, "For every thousand that die from the evil eye, only one will die from natural causes."

Rue, *aruda*, is a verdant, strong smelling evergreen shrub bearing small yellow flowers. In Roman times rue was used as a protection from plagues and fleas. In Rhodes, it was believed to bring protection to one's home, warding off negative energy. It is also said to bring blessings and was placed on a bridal tray with marzipan, sprinkled with gold leaf, *alvarak*.

As in many cultures, if one felt depleted or out of sorts it was believed that salt should be used to clear one's energy or aura. In Rhodes a couple of handfuls of pure sea salt was dissolved in a large bowl of water. The patient was washed with the salty water while the healer made the incantation, *El Dio ke te guadre de todo modo de mal*, "May G-d protect you from all bad energy."

On hearing of the news of a tragedy, death or fatal illness, the immediate exclamation that it should not befall one's loved ones would often be one of these expressions, *Barminan!*, "G-d forbid!", *Leshos i apartados!*, "Far and apart!", or *Pishkado i limon!*, "Fish and lemon!"

The folk superstition woven with the lunar phases was prevalent with the Rhodeslis, as in other age-old cultures. The widespread lore was that new projects, including moving into a new home and weddings and celebrations, were encouraged to take place when the moon was waxing, *pujante*, and avoided when the moon was on the wane, *minguante*.

Faith Healing: Making a vow, *tomar neder*, was a practice which entailed a person making a vow to a person suffering from illness to do a good deed to restore their health, for

Detail from painting with protective talismans I created for my granddaughter Mia's nursery, 2011.

Sprig of fresh Rue.

Rabbi Chilebi Nissim Codron

Rabbi Yehuda Moshe Franco

Rabbi Yaacov Capouya

example, taking oil to light the candles in the synagogue, *encender el kal*, and handing out bread and money to the needy.

Another practice was name-changing for cases of severe illness. When a member of the family was critically ill, the person's name was changed at a prayer ritual in the synagogue in a desperate attempt to change their destiny by confusing the angel of death. If the patient recovered then the new name was kept thereafter. At the time my sister Vera's illness took a critical turn, her name was changed to Rifca at a prayer ceremony in a synagogue in Johannesburg. Sadly, in her case, the angel of death would not be confused.

Some community members in Rhodes were said to have the gift to heal through exorcisms and incantations, expelling malevolent spirits that allegedly caused illness. This practice was called *aprekantar*. They would chant *Ni venga, ni apareska*, warning the negative spirits not to dare appear and shooing them away with their hands saying, *Ajos i klavos a los de abasho*.

Lastly *enseredura*, retreat, was used for those suffering mental or emotional burnout. These people were isolated in a room when the moon was waning. During their retreat, which lasted three days, the patients were kept on a simple diet of yoghurt, rice pudding and sweet marjoram tea. At the end of the treatment the patients would be accompanied to the Turkish bath to wash off any traces of the 'condition' with a sulphur solution. After the ritual, the patients returned home 'healed'. The incantation, *Kitarte todo el mal, todo la estrechura, i echarlo a la profondina de la mar* would be said to remove emotional angst or depression and transfer it to the depths of the sea.

Some of these practices are faint memories now, but they do give us insight into our ancestors' daily lives during the Ottoman Empire. Personally, I believe giving blessings with loving intention is the best cure of all.

Celebrating Lifecycles

Both religious tradition and folk customs blend to mark lifecycle milestones with great celebration amongst the Sephardim. The emphasis of family and the deep sense of communal involvement is at the very heart of the rites and festivities. These ancient rituals date back centuries and vary where the exiled Jews from Spain made their adopted home in the Ottoman Empire. The customs presented here are those of my ancestors from the island of Rhodes.

Nacimiento (Paridura) – Birth

The birth of any child is greeted with great joy, not only by the family but the whole community. From the moment the expectant mother, *la parida*, announces the exciting news that she is pregnant she is deemed to have special status. Whoever she encounters wishes her a good and easy birth, *escapamiento bueno*. During the pregnancy appeasing any cravings she may have, *deseyos de la prenyada*, was a given. In fact, a taste, *gostar por guesmo*, of anything being prepared in the kitchen was and still is offered first to the expectant mother.

Kortar la fashadura – Preparing the layette

Five months into the pregnancy, it was customary for the women of the family and friends to attend a celebratory gathering to commence the preparation of making the baby's clothes, often embroidered with silver thread. The cutting of cloth, *meter tijera*, took place while women sang uplifting songs, *kanticas de parida*, to the expectant mother.

Naming according to Sephardic custom

A child is named according to an established priority after a living relative such as a grandparent. The firstborn son is named after the paternal grandfather; the second son after the maternal grandfather. The firstborn son is given the title *behor*, or *behora* for a girl. Names of sons also often reflect incidents around the birth concerning the family – *Nissim*, (*miracles*) could be given to a boy whose family were living in extreme hardship hoping for a change of fortune.

The firstborn daughter receives the name of her paternal grandmother and the second born daughter that of her maternal grandmother. After happy events, a girl can be named *Mazaltov* (good luck), *Fortuné* (good fortune), or *Bienvenida* (welcome). A daughter could be named after a biblical figure, for example, Rachel, Sara, Miriam or Rebecca. In times past the names of flowers were also popular, such as *Rosa* (rose), *Flor* (flower) or *Violetta* (violet). Other popular names were *Estreya* (star), *Luna* (moon), *Sol* (sun) or even precious stones; *Perla* (pearl), *Diamante* (diamond) or *Gioya* (jewel). As Rabbi Herbert Dobrinsky states in his book *A Treasury of Sephardic Laws and Customs*, women do not necessarily have Hebrew names, they may also have Spanish names. The exact name, whether Spanish or Hebrew, is used in the marriage contract or on any other official document.

Brit Milah – Circumcision ceremony of the newborn male

The first good deed incumbent on a father is the rite of circumcision of a newborn son, performed on the eighth day after birth. This takes place at the family's home or synagogue, when the godfather and godmother, *kitado* and *kitada*, are also announced. It is customary to give the honour of godparents for the first newborn male to the grandparents on the father's side and for the next male to the mother's side. At this ceremony, a special ornately embroidered cloth is draped over a chair – Elijah's chair, *la siya di Eliyahu Hanavi* – which is left empty. It is believed that the saintly prophet, Elijah, is an eternal witness, casting positive blessings over the ritual. The godmother carries the baby dressed in an embroidered white gown, *kamiza larga*, on a cushion and hands him over to the godfather, who holds the infant during the ritual. The surgeon, *mohel*, performs the circumcision during which the mother is not present and the baby is then named. A festive breakfast then takes place. Savoury and sweet treats are offered to the guests with the mother now present to take part in the celebrations.

Pidion Ha Ben – Redemption of the firstborn male child

According to the Law of Moses, *la Ley de Moshe*, the firstborn male child, if not born to a Cohen or Levy, belongs in spirit to the Priesthood, *Cohanim*, until the rite, *rehmido*, is performed on the thirty-first day after the child's birth. In this ceremony, the boy's father redeems his son by paying five silver coins to a Cohen who gives the baby boy a priestly blessing.

My son, Claude's Bar Mitzvah, Harare, 1981.

Claude's bar mitzvah with his father, Aldo Levy, second from the right.

Las Fadas/Fadamiento – **Naming of a newborn daughter**

For a baby girl, the *Las Fadas* ceremony takes place about a month after birth. *Las Fadas* is derived from the Spanish word *hadas,* meaning fairies, for it was the custom in medieval Spain to have the baby girl clothed in an exquisite white dress, blessed by 'good fairies', a tradition adopted by the Sephardim. Another ritual that often took place was known as *Las siete kandelas,* with seven candles lit – deemed to bring good luck in Jewish mysticism. The Rabbi recites blessings for her good health and happiness and announces her name. Festivities follow where guests offer a small gift along with their congratulations as they celebrate with a selection of homemade sweet treats. Traditionally, the baby is given an amulet symbolic of an open hand, *hamsa,* and a sprig of rue, which are placed on the cradle, believed to ward off the evil eye.

Bar Mitzvah – **Initiation ceremony on reaching manhood**

The *Teffilin* ceremony takes place on a Thursday, upon a boy reaching the age of thirteen, signifying the transition of a young adult to a fully-fledged member of the community. He is now said to be mature enough to be accountable for his own actions. The binding of the phylacteries, *teffilin,* at morning prayers, is symbolic of a lifelong obligation binding the young man to the Divine.

For my son Claude's *Bar Mitzvah* (Zimbabwe, 1981), we had the traditional celebratory dairy breakfast, *desayuno.* A delectable array of savoury pastries, vegetable bakes, festive bread rolls and *reshikas,* accompanied with a variety of cheeses and olives graced the table. A choice of marzipan-based sweets, rice and rose water-scented puddings, fruit preserves and a full repertoire of cakes, sweet pastries and biscuits were shared with family and friends. On the Saturday, a portion of the Torah, the *Perasha,* was read followed by great festivities for the rest of that day.

The special blessing made on congratulating the *bar mitzvah* boy is *Novio ke te veygamos en vida de padre i madre i todos justos i sauldosos,* "May we see you as a groom with your father and mother and everyone in the family healthy and well."

Bat Mitzvah – **Initiation ceremony on reaching womanhood**

It was only around my daughter Monique's twelfth birthday in 1984, that *Bat Mitzvah* ceremonies took place in our Sephardic community in Zimbabwe. This was groundbreaking for the descendants of the Jews of Rhodes.

Espozorio – **Engagement**

Like all rites of passage, a proposal of marriage in the Judeo-Spanish custom brings with it a flurry of feasting and merry-making, involving both the extended families and many of the community showering their blessings on the couple.

In Rhodes, an engagement was celebrated at the home of the bride-to-be, with a full complement of sweet treats offered especially to the parents of the groom, *novio,* as a gesture to sweeten the meeting of the two families at the engagement. Amidst great excitement the future in-laws would exclaim, *Vamos a ser kosuegros!,* "We're going to be in-laws!" The town crier, *kombidadoro,* would announce the engagement along the streets of the Jewish quarter. He would carry a silver tray, *mandada,* holding marzipan sweets, a sprig of rue, gold leaf paper, *varak,* and jewellery, including a gold chain, *kadena,* and a gold amulet, *shaddai,* with the mystical name of G-d engraved on it.

Nochada d'espozorio – **Evening engagement celebration**

The Rabbi was invited to read the nuptial agreement, *tenayim.* In the *kinian* ceremony, an exquisitely hand-embroidered white handkerchief was held by a member of

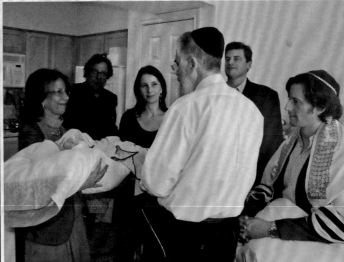

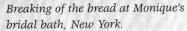
Breaking of the bread at Monique's bridal bath, New York.

Cutting of the layette celebration for Monique's first baby, New York.

Circumcision and naming of my grandson Nico, Boston, 2008.

both families, indicating the groom's promise to bind himself to his chosen fiancé. This was followed by the family wishing the couple good health and happiness, *salud i alegria*. The future father-in-law of the bride, *esuegro*, then handed the couple a simple gold ring, *anio d'espozorio*, engraved with the Hebrew letter *He*. The wedding date was then announced. Weddings are not permitted to take place during the month of *Marheshvan*, the month in which the biblical flood took place. Weddings can take place after the thirty-third day of the counting of the *Omer*, which is the forty-nine days between Passover and Shavuot. The rest of the year is considered an auspicious time for a wedding.

Banyo de novia – Bridal shower
On the Friday afternoon preceding the wedding on the Sunday, a 'bridal shower' is hosted by the bride's mother. A ritual bride's bath, *banyo de novia*, takes place, as was celebrated for my daughter, Monique, in New York in 2010. Traditionally in Rhodes, the groom would send a gift to his fiancé including toiletries, perfume and an embroidered towel. After the ritual bath, the bride-to-be, dressed in an ornate gown, is seated surrounded by her close girlfriends and the women of her family. For this occasion, a round festive bread stuffed with marzipan and often with an embedded gold coin or piece of jewellery concealed in the dough, is wrapped in foil and baked. The bread is broken over the bride's head by her mother. The womenfolk entertain the bride-to-be, *alegrar la novia*, wishing her a life without sorrow and adversity, *Blanka i kontenta ke estes siempre*. They sing ancient songs – *kanticas* and *romansos* – some extolling the bride's beauty, accompanied with musical instruments and the sound of tambourines. Sephardic sweet treats, Turkish coffee and refreshing drinks are offered. The marzipan served is

symbolic of wishes for her life to be as sweet as the marzipan, *Para ke la vida kon tu esposo sea dulse komo il masapan*. From then the future husband is not permitted to see the bride until they meet at the synagogue for the wedding ceremony.

As was the custom in Rhodes, before my wedding my parents prepared my trousseau, *ashugar*. This was kept in a trunk, *baul*, filled with lingerie and fine needlework linen, the equivalent of the 'bottom drawer' in English tradition. The Saturday before my wedding, my trousseau was displayed, *aparar el ashugar*, to family and close friends. My in-laws were especially invited to appraise the beauty of the trousseau, *apresiar el ashugar*. I was probably one of the last of my generation in my community to follow this custom.

La Salidura – Honouring the Groom
The Saturday preceding the wedding the groom attends the synagogue and is called upon to read a portion of the Torah. In Rhodes this was followed by a ritual honouring the groom, *la salidura*, with a reception held at his home.

Kasamiento – Marriage or *La Boda* – Wedding
On the island of Rhodes the town crier, *kombidadoro*, was entrusted with inviting the entire community in the Jewish quarter to the wedding and delivering gifts to the bride. A band of musicians, *tanyidores*, was sent by the groom to lead the bridal procession to the synagogue.

Family and friends were involved in the extraordinary preparation for the wedding feast. The food included a splendid array of handcrafted marzipan and sweet treats to augur a long, healthy new life for the couple. Other sweet pastries with nuts and seeds were served as a symbol of fertility.

Now, alas, the lively family activity of preparing food for the festivity has largely been replaced by catering chefs,

Claude and Danielle's wedding, New York, 2003.

Marriage document I hand-painted for Claude and Danielle's wedding.

though a few of us mothers cannot resist making marzipan-based sweets in the kosher kitchen of our Sephardic synagogue as I did for my children's weddings in New York. The marriage contract, *ketubah*, written in Aramaic, is traditionally decorated with artistic symbols and designs pertinent to the couple. I illustrated the *ketubot* for my children with symbols pertaining to their life, such as adding the African baobab tree as the tree of life.

It is customary for the bride's family to buy a new prayer shawl, *talleth*, for the groom for the wedding ceremony. Both sets of parents hold the prayer shawl over the bride and groom, *echar talleth*, who are blessed under a canopy, *huppa*, while they recite the seven blessings, signifying that the bride will now be under the groom's care and protection.

After the bride is presented with a plain gold wedding band by the groom, the couple sip the wine and are then given the sacred priestly blessing by a Cohen. The groom, with great exuberance, then stamps on a glass, representing the destruction of the Second Temple of Jerusalem destroyed in 69 CE, to recall that in times of joy we also remember times of sadness.

After the ceremony, marzipan and candied almonds, *bon bons*, are offered to the guests, who extend their profuse wishes, *Mazal alto ke tengan los novios*, "Good luck to the newlyweds." Great jubilation and celebration follows with folk dancing, *baylar chiftetelli*. After enjoying a banquet of Sephardic delicacies the guests wish the couple, *Siempre fiestas i alegrias*, "May there always be celebrations and happy events," as they take their leave.

Shabbat de Avraham Siv – Sabbath after the wedding
The newlyweds, family and friends attend a synagogue service where the husband is given the honour of reading a portion of the Torah – Genesis 24.1 – recounting the Story of Abraham selecting a wife for his son Isaac. Later, a lavish tea with a table laden with sweets, *mesa alegre*, awaits the congregation.

Hanukat HaBayit – Dedicating a new home
Moving into a new home is regarded with great reverence. Within thirty days of moving in, the homeowner recites a special blessing, nailing a *mezuzah* (a decorated tubular case enclosing a sacred parchment) to the right-hand doorpost of the entrance to the house. It is placed a third of the way down from the top of the doorpost slanting upwards, affording protection and bringing holiness into the new home. The folk belief was that it was auspicious to move into the new home before the full moon, not after, armed with flour, sugar, oil and eggs! *Se muda de kasa i entra por la primera ves se yeva, arina, asuker, aziete i huevos.*

La Muerti – Death and Remembrance
Our sages taught us that just as we bless the Almighty in our joy, so too must we bless Him in our sorrow. Jewish law requires that the burial takes place as soon as possible.

In Zimbabwe, I am still a volunteer, together with a few community members, who are well versed in the sacred rites relating to burial known as the *hevra kaddisha*. I believe we are one of the last Sephardic communities to sew shrouds by hand, *kortar i kuzir la mortaja*, as was the ancient custom of our ancestors. Women partake in the ritual of preparing the deceased woman for burial and men that of the deceased male.

In Sephardic custom, the ritual rending of the deceased family's garment, *kriah*, is enacted after the funeral by a member of the burial society. The mourning ceremony

My father, Sam, with his grandson, Claude, on his 70th birthday, Harare, 1983.

My mother, Marie, and me on her 85th birthday, Harare, 2011.

Monique with Mia, my granddaughter, November, 2011.

takes place at the home of the eldest child of the deceased. The immediate family then sits on cushions on the floor to start the seven days of mourning, *asentarse en siete*, a custom derived from the Bible, where it is described how, after Jacob died, Joseph mourned for seven days.

At the mourner's home, the mirrors are kept covered during the first week of mourning. A bowl is filled with water and a thick layer of olive oil. A three-pronged cork, with a cotton wick, is floated on the oil. On returning home from the funeral the wick is lit and kept burning throughout the seven days of mourning on which there is a daily memorial service, *Hashakvah*, reciting the 49th Psalm. The first meal, consisting of whole peeled hard-boiled eggs and bread, is eaten after the wine is sanctified. Those who make a condolence call comfort the family with the wish, *Mas por dengunos non*, "May you know no further sorrow".

At the end of the 30 days of mourning, there are readings that take place, *cortar el mes*. This is a custom derived from the Bible at the time when Moses died "the children of Israel wept for thirty days", after which the period of mourning ends. This day is said to have a Kabbalistic significance, where the soul of the deceased ascends to a higher level on its way to its "celestial place of rest". The wish *Para vosotros ki bevesh muchos anios*, "May you continue to live in good health" is expressed to the grieving family. This tradition is mirrored in Zimbabwe, with the *Nyaradzo* ceremony, which also takes place a month after the death. In Shona tradition, after this period, the deceased is believed to now be among one's ancestors and in a position to guide the family.

In our community, there is always a heartfelt outpouring of comfort and support to the bereaved family from relatives and friends. Food is prepared and brought to the house of mourning throughout the entire week. Male mourners recite the *kaddish*, prayers of praise, for eleven months, and those in mourning refrain from attending joyous occasions during this period.

The custom of placing the tombstone, *meter la piedra*, and the unveiling of the tombstone, takes place eleven months after the burial. This is followed by a tea at the mourners' home, marking the end of the mourning period. At the commemoration of an anniversary of death, the family is greeted with, *Bivos i sanos siempre*, "To life and good health always."

This is a brief glimpse of a few of the more significant traditions of our forebears from Rhodes, which hopefully will be maintained by generations to come.

My husband, Victor, and me on his 70th birthday, 2009.

MYRIAM PIHA
b. pre 1865 RHODES   d. 1944 en route from Rhodes to Auschwitz

M

VIDA CAPOUYA
b. 1879 Rhodes, Otto. Emp.
d. 1979 Cape Town, S. Africa
m. DAVITCHON HANAN
b. 1867, Rhodes
d. 1957 Elizabethville, Bel. Congo

SARINA CAPOUYA
b. 1899 Rhodes, Otto. Emp.
m. DANIEL ROUSSO
b. 1899 Rhodes
d. 1980 Atlanta, Georgia, USA

GUILSON CAPOUYA
b. 1900 Rhodes, Ottoman Empire
d.
m. MARCO GATENO

MYRIAM GATENO
b.
m. WALDMAN

DAVID GATENO
b. 1970

REGINA ROUSSO
b. 1921
m.
RALF TOURIAL
b. 1915

MORRIS ROUSSO
b. 1922
m.
CORRINE SCHUMAN
b. 1933

MARIE ROUSSO
b. 1920
m.
Dr BENJAMIN SAFFAN
b. 1928

JACK ROUSSO
b. 1927

SARAH TOURIAL
b. 1946
m.
MORTON GROSSWALD
b. 1947

MARGARET TOURIAL
b. 1947

DANIEL TOURIAL
b. 1951
m.
ANNIE

DAVID TOURIAL
b. c. 1954

DAVID SAFFAN
b. 1955
m.
MICHELLE RENO
b.

ROSE SAFFAN
b. 1957
m.
GORDON SINGER divorced m. ARTHUR LEVIN

JEFFREY TOURIAL
b. pre 1980

ROBERT TOURIAL
b. pre 1980

GEORGE TOURIAL
b. c. 1991

RYAN TOURIAL
b. c. 1993

HANNAH SAFFAN
b. 1992

SOPHIE SAFFAN
b. 1995

JACOB SINGER
b. 1993

RALF GROSSWALD
b. 1966

STEVEN GROSSWALD
b. 1970

MICHAEL GROSSWALD
b. c. 1973

STEPHANIE SINGER
b.

DANIEL ROUSSO
b. 1955
m.
NANCY POPKIN

ROBYN ROUSSO
b. 1958
m.
TONY LEVITAS

SARINA ROUSSO
b. 1960

EMILY ROUSSO
b. 1987

CRAIG ROUSSO
b. 1990

GRAHAM LEVITAS
b. 1991

CHLOE LEVITAS
b. 1999

JACQUES HANAN
b. 1920 Rhodes Is. Italy
m.
JULIA LEVY
b. 1928 Mersin, Turkey

NISSIM HANAN   m.   ESTREA LEON
b. Rhodes Is.   Rhodes Is.
d.

SAMUEL HANAN
b. Sept. 13, 1926. Rhodes Is.
Italy.
d. Aug 11, 1988. Harare, ZIMBABWE

SOLOMON HANAN
b. Rhodes Is.
d.

MOSSE HANAN
b. Rhodes Is.
d.

MATHILDA HANAN
b. Rhodes Is.
d.

VICKY HANAN
b. 1948 Elizabethville Bel. Congo
m. ALAN ATLAS Cape Town S. Africa

RACHEL HANAN
b. 1960, Milan Italy
m. BRIAN MICHAELS
b. 1958 Cape Town S. Africa

DAVID HANAN
b. 1953 Elizabethville, Belgian Congo
m. RARNI TURKIN
b. 1951 Cape Town S. Africa

MOISE LEVY m. BECKY SORIANO

LUCY LEVY

SARICA LEVY

VICO LEVY

y. Rhodesia
y. Rhodesia.

thville

SAMUEL LEVY
February 2008
on USA

Food & Customs for the Sabbath and other holy days

Sephardim observe the Sabbath and holy days with their own unique traditions and customs, including food. These customs have endured for centuries, providing succour and continuity over multiple migrations. Some Sephardic dishes carry symbolism and meaning in the context of Jewish holy days, providing a way of connecting with the sacred and spiritual in our heritage.

SHABBAT – The Sabbath: The seventh day of the week, the Sabbath, is a time of rest and spiritual rejuvenation, a respite from the challenges of daily life. It is celebrated from twilight on Friday until the appearance of the first three stars on Saturday evening. On the Sabbath, families and friends get together and celebrate with special meals.

In addition to preparing the Sabbath meal, great attention is given to preparing the home where the dinner table is laid with the finest cloth and tableware. Shabbat is ushered in with blessings in preparation for the symbolic coming of the Sabbath bride, whom the Sephardic poet Rabbi Solomon HaLevi Alkabetz mentions in his beautiful hymn, *Lecha Dodi*, still chanted in our synagogues in the same ancient stirring melody with the words "Come my beloved to greet the bride; let us welcome the presence of the Sabbath."

The woman of the home prepares the Sabbath candle before sunset. In Rhodes it was customary to fill a small glass bowl with a little water and a thick layer of olive oil. A three-pronged cork with a cotton wick, *mecha*, is placed so that it floats on the oil. At dusk the wick is lit, *asiender la kandela di Shabbat*, with blessings and heartfelt prayers made for the family. The wish for a peaceful Sabbath is made with the expression, *Shabbat Shalom*, to which the response is *Shabbat Shalom umevora*.

At the table, the man of the house recites a prayer sanctifying the wine, *kiddush*, and makes a benediction, *hamotzi*, over the festive bread, which for the Jews of Rhodes is an egg-enriched sweet bread called *roska*. Sephardim usually break the bread with their hands and in some Sephardic communities the pieces of bread are tossed to the guests rather than handed directly – symbolising the belief that the Divine is the source of food. Then, before the meal, as was done through the ages on the Sabbath eve, parents place their hands on their children's head to bless them.

Since this time of rest entails abstaining from any work or cooking, the Friday night meal and Saturday brunch are traditionally prepared before sunset on Friday. The Friday night meal includes a variety of dishes that taste good whether served warm or at room temperature the next day.

To usher out the Shabbat, the *Havdala* ritual takes place at the synagogue on the Saturday evening. This involves the lighting of a braided candle, a sniff of fragrant spice and a blessing made over the wine. On returning home from the Sabbath services, the customary wish for a good week is *Semanada buena!* On a Saturday evening a celebration, bidding farewell to the Sabbath, takes place, *Noche de Alhad*, meaning the Night of Sunday. Sweet confection and Turkish coffee are offered, auguring sweetness for the coming week.

A typical Friday Sabbath dinner may include:
Kiddush wine and braided festive bread (p182).
A selection of savoury pastries and pies (p187–202).
A variety of salads: Aubergine, bell pepper and tomato (p37); black-eyed bean (p41); potato, egg, olives and fresh herb (p54); aromatic carrot (p32); roasted baby beetroot (p42); garlic and potato dip (p46).
Entrée: A fish dish that is symbolic of good fortune and abundance, such as fish stewed in a fresh tomato sauce (p99), fried fish (p95) with egg-lemon sauce (p94) or fried marinated fish (p100) that can also be served cold the next day.
Macaroni and meat bake (p120), a stuffed vegetable dish (p132–145) or Ottoman-style braised meat with cannellini beans (p84) accompanied by any rice pilaf, the favourites being chickpea rice pilaf (p169); saffron rice pilaf (p168) or toasted noodles (p174).
Desserts: Fresh seasonal fruits and sweet treats are offered, including rice and rose water-scented milk pudding (p249); almond-filled, honey-drenched crescents (p214) or shortbread filled with dates and walnuts (p254), spoon sweets (p257–262), and baklava (p220).

At Saturday morning brunch, *desayuno*, after the synagogue service, the table is brimming with an array of savoury pies, vegetable and cheese gratins, hard-boiled eggs, along with braided festive bread, feta and kashkaval cheese, pickles and olives. Seasonal fresh fruit, rice and rose water-scented milk pudding, and spoon sweets are also Sabbath brunch fare.

ROSH HASHANAH – The Festival of the New Year: The New Year marks new beginnings and is celebrated with great joy. Rosh Hashanah falls on the first two days of the Jewish month of Tishrei, usually in September. It is ushered in with the blowing of the *shofar*, the piercing sound of the ram's horn. The 10-day period between the New Year and Yom Kippur is one of introspection and self-examination and culminates with the Day of Atonement. It is customary for the Jews of Rhodes to visit the resting places of their deceased family members on a Sunday a week before the New Year.

For the Rhodeslis, the customary greeting for the New Year is *Renova sovre nostros anyada buena i klara skritas en livros de vida*, "May we be blessed again with a Happy New Year and be inscribed in the book of life", or more simply, *Anyada alegre*, "Happy New Year".

Sweet-tasting food, auguring a New Year filled with joy and abundance, is offered, including homemade marzipan and white lemon-flavoured fondant, which is a symbol of purity. Some Sephardim avoid eating sour or bitter-tasting foods or those that are black in colour, such as olives, raisins and aubergine, as it is associated with mourning. New seasonal fruit is tasted with a blessing of thanksgiving, *Shehecheyanu*. Several foods are made in a rounded shape, symbolising continuity and wholeness, including the festive ring-shaped bread, stuffed vegetables, savoury pies and pastries, pumpkin coils, leek fritters and marzipan. It is customary to place sugar on the table instead of salt for a sweet year.

Symbolic foods for the New Year:
The Sephardim have a unique tradition of reciting blessings, *Yehi Ratsones*, before each of the symbolic foods eaten preceding the New Year dinner on the first and second nights. The festive dinner takes place after ritual blessings.

- **Apples** – Dipping a slice of apple in sugar or honey comes with the wish of renewal and a fruitful and joyful year, with the Ladino words, *Renova sovre nostros anyada buena i dulse d'el presipio d'el anyo asta el kavo d'el anyo.*
- **Dates** – Plump sweet dates are eaten in the hope that our enemies will cease to harm us.
- **Pomegranates** – Replete with hundreds of seeds – pomegranates are symbolic of the number of good deeds the Jewish people are obliged to fulfil. The hope expressed is that the coming year will be filled with as many good deeds as the seeds of the pomegranate.
- **Black-eyed beans** – Symbolic of abundance and fertility.
- **Pumpkin** – Symbolic of protection from harm and expresses the hope that we be remembered for our good deeds.
- **Leeks** – Tasted with the hope of cutting off all evil intent against us.
- **Swiss chard or beets** – Expresses the hope that our enemies be removed from our midst.

- **Head of a fish** – Symbolises the hope that we will lead new initiatives in the coming year.

A New Year dinner may include:
Round-shaped festive bread, (p182); apple slices served with white sugar or honey; pomegranate seeds sprinkled with orange blossom water; Medjool or other fresh plump dates.
Salads: black-eyed bean (p41); aromatic carrot (p32); boiled or roasted baby beetroot (p42).
Pumpkin and cheese-filled coiled pastries (p195); savoury turnovers with vegetable fillings (p200); candied pumpkin (p262).
Leek, potato and fresh herb fritters (p119).
Swiss chard-filled savoury turnovers (p200); flaky filo-like savoury pastries (p188); Swiss chard, fresh herb and cheese pie (p202); Swiss chard and chickpeas braised with veal (p79).
Entrée: Red snapper roasted on a bed of baby potatoes (p104); tomatoes and onions stuffed with meat (p143); Mediterranean vegetables stuffed with meat and rice (p139); slow-cooked lamb with potato (p157); fresh broad bean and veal stew (p75); white rice pilaf (p168).
Desserts: Fresh fruit platter; marzipan (p232) or marzipan filled with lemon fondant (p235); almond semolina cake soaked in a honey-citrus syrup (p216); almond filled honey-drenched crescents (p214); almond frangipane-filled filo triangles (p213); baklava (p220); candied quince paste (p261).

YOM KIPPUR – The Day of Atonement is about forgiveness: forgiving others for the wrongs they may have committed towards us, seeking others' forgiveness for our own shortcomings and seeking the forgiveness from the Almighty.

It is the most sombre and awe-filled day on the Hebrew calendar with a complete 25-hour fast for all adults over 13 years of age, and abstention of pleasurable activities from sundown to sundown.

In the synagogue, the deeply moving chant of the ancient hymn *Kol Nidre*, the commencement of the fast harking back to the 13th century, is sung. The Sephardic liturgy includes poems by Spanish medieval poets, Shelomo Ibin Gabirol and Yehuda Ha-Levy, where verses are sung in Ladino. Towards the evening, men cover their heads with their prayer shawls, while 30 blasts of the ram's horn, *shofar*, are blown with great fervour..

Pre-fast meal, *tomar tanit*:
Before sundown, a very lightly seasoned meal is eaten – such as chicken stewed in tomatoes with potatoes (p72) with a white rice pilaf (p168), followed by fresh fruit. Spices are avoided so as not to increase thirst. People try to hydrate themselves more than usual before the beginning of the fast.

OPPOSITE: *Sabbath with the family at our home in Harare, 2009.*

A typical breaking of the fast meal, *kortar il tanit,* **may include a table laid with:**

Melon-seed drink (p265).

Round-shaped festive bread (p182) often stuffed with marzipan (p232) or the travado nut filling (p214); bread rolls (p182) dipped in olive oil.

Feta and kashkaval cheese and sliced ripe tomatoes drizzled with extra-virgin olive oil.

Twice-baked bread rusks (p205); sesame-studded biscuits (p250).

Savoury pastries and pies (p187–202); Swiss chard, potato and cheese gratin (p124).

Fried fish (p95) with egg-lemon sauce (p94).

Orange Spanish sponge cake (p243); rice and rose water-scented milk pudding (p249); marzipan filled with lemon fondant (p235); seasonal fruit platter.

Chicken and rice soup (p65) is often served an hour or so after the meal.

SUKKOT: Sukkot is a harvest festival that also commemorates the travels that the Israelites made during their 40-year journey through the desert after they fled Egypt. This festival is a reminder that life is a transient and spiritual journey.

Immediately after Yom Kippur, there is great haste to prepare the *sukkah*, a temporary structure with at least three walls and a roof that offers shade but still allows one to see the sky through branches. The *sukkah* symbolises the temporary shelters that the Jews lived in during their desert journey. In Rhodes, families created a *sukkah* in their courtyards, *kortijo*. The interior of the *sukkah* is sumptuously decorated with a table, divans, a fine gold embroidered cloth (*cevri* in Rhodes), cushions and oriental rugs, *tapeties*. Myrtle leaves may be hung for their herbal fragrance, along with flowers, seasonal fruit and cinnamon ring biscuits, *biskotchos*.

Sukkot is a popular time for entertaining in the *sukkah*. Each night a tradition is followed where one of the seven forefathers – Abraham, Isaac, Jacob, Moses, Aaron, Joseph and David are welcomed to share the meal and the spiritual experience of the *sukkah*.

Sukkot is also the autumn harvest thanksgiving festival. At the synagogue, the daily *lulav*-waving ritual takes place with four symbols of the earth's bounty – the *lulav* (green palm), *hadas* (myrtle branches), *aravah* (willow) and *etrog* (lemon-like fruit, citron). Blessings are said with the *lulav*-waving mystical ritual, as if showering the land with G-d's kindness.

SIMCHAT TORAH: This festival, which takes place on the last day of Sukkot, celebrates the end of the annual cycle of reading the Torah. Two men are given the honour of reading the Torah, the Five Books of Moses. The men-folk walk around the synagogue seven times carrying the Scrolls of the Torah, followed by singing and dancing by all adults and children. In Rhodes, they would set out through the narrow cobbled streets of the Jewish quarter with much merriment.

A variety of stuffed vegetable dishes and nut and date-filled pastries, representing a bountiful harvest, are prepared for this festival.

HANUKKAH – Festival of Lights: Hanukkah celebrates the victory of the Maccabees over the Syrian-Greeks in 165 BCE and the rededication of the Temple in Jerusalem. According to legend, it is said that there was only enough pure olive oil to keep a *menorah* burning for one day. Miraculously, the flame was kept alight for eight days. Traditionally, we re-enact this miracle by kindling an eight-branched *menorah* over the eight days. The *menorah* is usually placed where it is visible from the outside of the home, near a window. In Rhodes, eight small glasses with a little water and a thick layer of oil on which wicks were floated and lit were used instead of a *menorah*.

Fried foods dominate the menu to emphasise the miraculous oil that is central to this holiday. Delicious leek, potato and fresh herb fritters (p119), fried fish (p95), doughnut puffs (p227), and pastry puffs topped with honey (p246). Almond and sesame seed brittle (p210), marzipan (p232), Turkish delight and halva are also some of the foods served at this festival.

TU B'SHVAT or *Las Frutas* – The Jewish New Year for the Trees: This festival is particularly important to the Sephardim and involves a ritual meal called *Las Frutas* (The Fruits). This was created by Jewish mystics in the 16th century, where four categories of fruit are served in successive courses, each accompanied by a glass of wine representing the different seasons. On this festival an abundance of sweet treats, including halva and marzipan, are offered. In Rhodes, children were encouraged to carry small bags of fruit and nuts, *bolsas de frutas*, on their visits to family. An expression was made *Ke bivas komo la agwa, ke tengas yena tu kasa, komo la portugal*, meaning "May you live as abundantly as running water, may your home and possessions be plentiful as this sweet round orange".

PURIM – The Festival of Lots: On the 13th of Adar 365 BCE, Queen Esther triumphed over the evil of Haman's decree to destroy the Jewish people at the Court of Ahasueros. Purim celebrates the miracle of Queen Esther saving her people, with feasting, rejoicing and re-enacting the story of Purim. In the synagogue, the reading of the Book of Esther takes place. It is especially a time for giving to the needy, where homemade cakes, biscuits and sweet confectionery, *platikos de Purim*, are given to relatives and friends. On the island of Rhodes it was customary to make *foulares* – strips of baked pastry criss-crossing over a hard-boiled egg, believed to be symbolic of the Ears of Haman or the rope used to punish Haman. Sumptuous feasts are held with wine, symbolic of the wine banquet Esther held. One of the favourite Ladino Purim songs is *Kuando Haman se emboracho*, meaning when Haman became drunk.

A typical Purim evening meal may include:
Savoury pies and pastries (p187–202).
Slow-cooked lamb with potatoes (p157).
Toasted noodles (p174).
Green beans braised with carrots and potatoes (p76);
Swiss chard and chickpeas braised with veal (p79).

Mesa alegre, known as 'the table of joy', is laden with sweet treats, especially almond-filled honey-drenched crescents (p214); almond semolina cake (p216); Passover wine biscuits (p245); almond and sesame seed brittle (p210); wine and liqueurs.

PESACH – Passover: Passover, which usually falls around March or April, celebrates the freedom of the Jews from centuries of bondage in Egypt and takes place a month after Purim. In Rhodes, the popular expression after Purim in Ladino was *Purim lanu*, *Pesach en la manu*, meaning "Purim has come and before you turn around, Passover is here". Before this holiday a good spring-cleaning takes place to rid the home of all traces of leavened foods, *hametz*, including utensils used during the year. Special cookware and porcelain are brought out especially for Passover.

Eating the unleavened flat bread, matza, as a reminder of the haste with which the Israelites left Egypt, commemorates this holiday. During the seven days of Passover all yeast-raised foods, grains and legumes are prohibited. Our everyday fare differs from that of the rest of the year. As rice plays a fundamental part in our cuisine most Sephardim do eat rice, unlike the Ashkenazi Jews.

The mystical view is that Passover is a metaphor for profound liberation, for healing and transcendence.

The Seder: The Seder meal and the order of the ritual on the first night of Passover recounts the story about the exodus from Egypt. As several generations of our family and friends gather around the celebration table, the *Haggadah* is recited in Hebrew, Ladino or English, relating the 3 600-year story of deliverance.

The Seder plate is set out according to the tradition of Ari (Rabbi Isaac Luria, of medieval Spain). Each little compartment on the tray contains one of the ritual foods that remind participants of certain historical truths. The ritual foods include: three matzot with the middle matza broken in half, enclosed in a special embroidered cover. A roasted lamb shank and a whole hard-boiled egg are both kept on display, symbolising the temple offerings and sacrifices. *Harosi*, the sweet fruit and nut paste, is symbolic of the mortar used by the Hebrew slaves to construct the pyramids. *Karpas*, parsley or celery, represents new growth also displayed with *maror*, Romaine lettuce, denoting the bitterness of slavery, and lastly white vinegar, that the lettuce is dipped in, representing the tears of captivity.

An empty chair and an extra cup of wine are also placed at the table, with the door left open, mystically awaiting the Prophet Elijah, as well as the poor who might wish to join the Seder.

Traditionally, a young person recites the Four Questions, which begin with the verse, "Why is this night different from all other nights?" Later, children also search for the middle portion of the matza, *afikomen*, which has been hidden. The lucky child who finds it receives a token reward.

A typical Passover evening meal may include:
Matza, served with sweet fruit and nut paste (p245).
Fried fish (p95) with egg-lemon sauce made with matza cake flour (p94).
Leek, potato and fresh herb matza fritters (p119).
Beef or chicken matza bake (p108, 109); veal, egg and herb-filled potato croquettes (p127) served with hard-boiled eggs (p113).
Slow-cooked lamb with potatoes (p157); broad bean and veal stew (p75) served with green spring salad (p48).
Dessert: Meringues with mastic (p239); marzipan (p232); spoon sweets (p257–262); Passover wine biscuits (p245); whole pear and almond preserve (p262); hot fresh apricots filled with almond paste (p231); Clementine and almond cake (p223).

For breakfast we eat matza fritters. Throughout the week matza is eaten dipped in the delicious sweet fruit and nut paste as a snack.

In Rhodes, traditionally the last day was celebrated by having a picnic in the country, bringing spring wheat back home with which to decorate tables for the meal on that evening. This meal, the first after Passover, always included both the first lamb and leavened bread.

SHAVUOT: This festival, which falls after Passover, commemorates the giving of the Torah to Moses at Mount Sinai, and is also a thanksgiving for the harvest. On the island of Rhodes a *Velada* ceremony took place on the first night, where men-folk studied and chanted special prayers and songs in Ladino and Hebrew. At sunrise women offered them warm savoury pies and pastries, hard-boiled eggs, feta and kashkaval cheese, olives and delicious rice and rose water-scented milk pudding. The homes of the Sephardim in the east Mediterranean are decorated in greenery, flowers and especially roses, which is why this holiday is often described as Festival of the Roses. A special festive sweet bread shaped into seven layered loaves is often made, called *los siete cielos*, meaning seven heavens. It is said that it represents the passage of the soul's ascent to eternal life and the seven weeks from Passover to Shavuot. A dairy and vegetable meal is usual fare for this holiday.

A typical Shavuot meal may include:
Festive bread (p182).
Egg dishes, fritters and gratins (p108–127).
A variety of cooked and fresh salads.
Rice pilafs and toasted noodles (p165–177).
Desserts: Fresh seasonal fruits and sweet treats are offered, including rice and rose water-scented milk pudding (p249); almond-filled, honey-drenched crescents (p214) or shortbread filled with dates (p254).

Getting to know your ingredients

The ingredients you select have as much to do with how your recipes turn out as to your cooking skill. Choosing top quality, fresh ingredients is also a pleasure in itself, particularly now that there is more access to organic foods and farmers' markets in most cities.

While preparing the recipes keep in mind that some ingredients such as lemons, onions, garlic, herbs and spices may vary in intensity and flavour. I encourage you to taste and adjust the seasoning while preparing the food, to suit your palate.

Most ingredients are relatively easy to track down in the usual places you do your grocery shopping, while others may require a visit to a Greek or Middle Eastern store. Buy spices, nuts and dried beans in small quantities so that they stay fresh.

Here are some hints I hope you will find useful when buying and using the ingredients for the recipes in this book:

CHEESE:
Feta: A moderately firm and crumbly, salty goat's milk cheese. It is excellent in chunks or crumbled in a salad or added to cheese mixtures for savoury pies and gratins. Be sure to store it in the brine it comes in to keep it moist. If it is bought in a block or you need more brine, dissolve ¾ cup of coarse or kosher salt in 1.2lt (2½pt) water. Use tongs to remove the cheese from the brine. If the feta is too salty, cover in cold water and soak for a few hours. I favour the Greek or Bulgarian feta.
Greek kefalotiri or Parmesan: Sharp, hard cheeses that are good for grating and are used in savoury pies, fritters and gratins. I like to finely grate hard cheese with a Microplane grater and leave uncovered on a tray at room temperature for a few hours to let it dry slightly, making the cheese taste stronger. Grated cheese can be stored in zip-lock bags in the freezer for later use.
Kashkaval or kasseri: Milder hard cheeses for those preferring a blander taste in cheese mixtures for savoury pastries and gratins.

EGGS: Large organic eggs are used in the recipes in this book. If you store eggs in the fridge, make sure they return to room temperature before using.

DRIED BEANS: I like to cook my own, even though they require lengthy soaking and cooking, as I find they are infused with the flavours of the aromatics I boil them with. Be sure to spread the dried beans on a tray and remove any grit and broken beans. Use the soaked beans at once or immediately refrigerate in their reserved cooking liquid in an airtight container for a few days or freeze with their cooking liquid for up to 2 months.

Chickpeas: These appear in various dishes in this book, as they are versatile, tasty and nutritious.
To cook: 1 cup dried chickpeas (250g/9oz) yields about 2½ cups cooked chickpeas. Cook the same way as the dried beans but in order to soften them add 1 tbsp coarse or kosher salt to the cooking liquid. Do not use bicarbonate of soda, as this tends to darken them.
To remove skins: You don't have to remove the fibrous chickpea skin because it is tasteless. However, they tend to float up to the top of your stew and aren't attractive so I like to remove as many of the skins as I can by putting the drained cooked chickpeas in a bowl of cold water and gently rub them between my palms. The skins fall off and float up.

Canned beans: You may prefer to use good quality canned beans or chickpeas to save on preparation time. Discard the brine and rinse the beans thoroughly before use. As these beans are already cooked, add them towards the end of cooking.

NUTS & SEEDS: All nuts and seeds should be bought as fresh as possible as they quickly turn rancid due to their high oil content. Store in an airtight container in the fridge or freezer.

Almonds: Buy them with their skin on to retain their flavour and freshness.
To blanch and peel: Place shelled almonds in a bowl with enough boiling water to cover. Leave for 5 minutes or until their skins have loosened. Drain and immediately slip off their skins by squeezing each nut between your index finger and thumb to pop the nut out of the skin.
To grind: When ground almonds are required, process the blanched and peeled almonds in a food processor in batches to avoid them becoming oily. Avoid ready-ground almonds as they do not have as much flavour.
To toast: Position a rack in the middle of a 165°C (325°F) preheated oven. Pat the freshly blanched and peeled

almonds dry with paper towels. Spread them on a baking tray and place in the oven. Toast for about 5 minutes or until the colour just deepens, stirring occasionally.

Pine nuts: These creamy-textured seeds of the pine tree add delicacy to Sephardic cuisine. Store untoasted pine nuts in the freezer to use as needed. There is no need to thaw them before using.

To toast: To enhance their flavour, gently toast them in a lightly oiled heavy-based frying pan over a medium-low heat for 8–10 minutes. Watch carefully and shake the pan often, as they tend to burn quickly. Remove from the pan before they have reached the desired colour as they will continue to cook even after you remove them from the heat. Lay them in a plate lined with paper towels.

Pistachios: These emerald nuts are sold in and out of their shells. Be sure to choose them raw and unsalted. To peel shelled pistachios follow instructions for almonds.

Sesame seeds: Used liberally in our savoury pastries, biscuits, festive bread and confectionery, these hulled 'white' sesame seeds have a nutty, rich flavour and a crunchy texture. To bring out their aroma, dry toast in an ungreased frying pan over a medium-high heat. Stir frequently for 5–10 minutes or until they begin to turn golden brown and the seeds start to pop.

SPICES:

Baharat: A generic name for store-bought Turkish spice mix, which includes ground cardamom, clove, black pepper, cinnamon, coriander, cumin, paprika and nutmeg. If not available, mix three parts of allspice and one part paprika.

Cinnamon: Ground cinnamon features in biscuits and many sweet dishes.

Cloves: Ground cloves impart a warm exotic flavour and should be used sparingly in baked cookies and sweet preserves as they easily overpower other spices.

Cumin: The favoured spice of the island of Rhodes retains its warm potency well and should be used sparingly.

Just a pinch of ground cumin is sufficient to give an earthy taste to meat dishes and kebabs.

Turkish red pepper flakes: From Maraş, Turkey, known as *kirmizi biber*, this imparts a slightly hot flavour. You can use 1 tsp of the milder Aleppo pepper instead of ½ tsp of Turkish red pepper flakes.

Mastic: These resinous gum crystals are from a type of Acacia tree, giving a chewy texture to meringues and adding flavour to the syrup drenched almond semolina cake and fragrant rice flour and milk pudding. Crush a mastic crystal with ½ tsp of granulated sugar in a pestle and mortar to prevent it from sticking to the mortar before adding to the chosen recipe. Store in an airtight container away from direct sunlight.

Pepper: Black pepper is best freshly ground from a peppermill. Finely ground white pepper is better suited for less robust foods.

Saffron: The red threads of the stigmas of crocus flowers tint food a rich yellow-gold and infuses rice pilaf with a smoky, delicate flavour.

Salt: I like using sea salt, preferably Maldon, which has a pure flavour, for all home cooking and a fine table salt for baking. I recommend salting lightly at the beginning of your cooking and adjusting the seasoning towards the end.

GREENS AND FRESH HERBS: Rinse salad greens and bunches of fresh herbs in a colander under cold running water. Shake out the excess moisture and use a salad spinner to remove remaining moisture. Transfer the rinsed greens or herbs to a dry tea towel to soak up excess water. Wrap them in paper towels and place each bunch in individual plastic bags. To store, refrigerate with the bags unsealed.

As bunches of fresh herbs are different in size, I have given the quantity in cups or tablespoons. For fresh thyme, rosemary, flat-leaf parsley and dill, gently pull your fingers backwards down the central stem, releasing the small tender stems and leaves. Discard the tougher stems.

Bay leaves: I prefer to use leaves from the east Mediterranean, as I find other types are usually too bitter and strong for these dishes.

Dill: Feathery fresh dill adds an anise-like fragrance to many savoury dishes and salads. Dill is usually added towards the end of cooking to retain its delicate flavour.

Mint: Wash the mint and chop it with a very sharp knife just before using so that the leaves do not darken.

Oregano: It is best to use the dried Greek or Turkish oregano for a more intense aromatic flavour.

Parsley, flat-leaf: The vivid green leaves and tender stems are chopped and used in profusion in many savoury dishes. It is also sprinkled in towards the end of cooking or as a garnish, adding colour and freshness.

FLORAL WATERS: Rose water is made from fragrant rose petals and can be used interchangeably with orange blossom water that is made from the distilled blossoms of Seville oranges. The best brands of floral waters are found in speciality or Middle Eastern stores. I find the reliable brands are *Cortas Lebanese* or the French *Monteux – Vallauris*.

FRUIT AND VEGETABLES:
Aubergines (eggplants): One of the mainstays of Sephardic cuisine, aubergines are amazingly versatile. Choose aubergines that are 'light' in weight for their size and firm, with a dark, smooth, glossy skin, as these are less likely to be filled with bitter seeds. Also look out for fresh unblemished looking stalks.

Celery: I like to use the tender inner stalks of celery hearts with some of the young leaves, which give a deeper flavour to the food.

Garlic: Select heads of garlic that are fresh, full and weighty. Store garlic at room temperature. I like to grate peeled cloves of garlic on a fine Microplane grater rather than chop them. When cooking, be careful not to allow garlic to colour and become bitter.

Lemons: The Sephardim have a predilection for the tart flavour of fresh lemon juice. Select thin-skinned organic lemons, as they tend to be juicier than the thicker-skinned ones. Lemon juice makes a refreshing dressing ingredient for salads and is the ultimate flavour heightener added to fish dishes and many stews near the end of cooking.

Quantities of freshly squeezed lemon juice are given in tablespoons and cups, as lemons vary in size and juiciness.
To grate and zest: Wash and dry the lemons well. If the juice is required, zest lemons before squeezing. For best results use a Microplane grater or lemon zester, being careful to avoid the bitter white pith.

Onions: White or yellow onions are generally used in cooking and sweeter red onions in salads and relishes.

Spring onions (scallions): Purchase fresh slender onions with bulbs no fatter than 1.5cm (½in). Rinse and trim off the root and use the white and light green parts.

Tomatoes: Tomatoes cooked with onions and garlic in olive oil are the basis of most Judeo-Spanish stews. Look for fully ripe, red tomatoes that will give the sauce an intensely rich and sweet flavour. Select the ripest Roma (plum) tomatoes only when in season for peak flavour. Good quality packaged Italian plum tomatoes in cans or jars, with no additives or seasoning, are a tasty substitute. I always have cans of whole plum Pomi or San Marzano tomatoes on hand. I lift the whole tomatoes from the can and crush them with my hand or chop them into the pan.

To peel: With a sharp paring knife, cut a shallow 'x' at the bottom of each tomato. Bring a large pot of water to a boil. Drop a few tomatoes in for 15 seconds for very ripe tomatoes, longer if less ripe. Remove with a slotted spoon and with a knife pull the skins away. Cut the skinned tomato in half and squeeze the seeds out if you like before chopping.

To grate: Halve the tomatoes, squeeze out and discard the seeds. Hold the coarse side of a grater over a shallow bowl. Grate the tomato on the cut side and discard the skin. You should have two cups thick grated tomato pulp from 1kg (2¼lb) ripe tomatoes.

Equivalents:
225g (8oz) = 2 medium tomatoes or 4 small plum tomatoes = 1 cup of chopped tomatoes.
A 400g (14oz) can = about 2 cups if you include the juice.

To slice or dice finely: Use a small serrated or sharp bladed knife.

To cook tomato-based dishes: Preferably use non-corrosive stainless steel or enamelled cast iron. Half a teaspoon of sugar added to the tomatoes counters any acidity.

Tomato paste (purée): I prefer Italian brands, which are rich and deep in colour. If only small amounts are required, buy the paste in a tube so it can be tightly sealed and kept in the fridge.

Vine (grape) leaves: Choose young vine leaves and blanch in small bunches in a saucepan of lightly boiling water for 30 seconds. If using thawed frozen vine leaves blanch for 1 minute. Leaves preserved in brine and sold in jars can be substituted for fresh vine leaves. In the U.S. I found the bottled leaves from California the best to use. If using brined, carefully separate each leaf and rinse first under water then blanch in boiling water for 3 minutes. Rinse under cool running water and drain.

BREADCRUMBS: Making these at home is easy – just put stale bread in a food processor and pulse. If buying from a store, look for breadcrumbs freshly made at the bakery.

OIL: Use natural cold-pressed extra-virgin olive oil for dressings and drizzling over food and olive oil for most stews. For deep-frying I find it best to use an oil that can be heated to a high temperature, such as grape-seed, safflower or sunflower. For shallow-frying use a vegetable oil, grape-seed, sunflower or canola oil. For baking I recommend a mild flavoured vegetable oil.

STOCK: Instead of making homemade chicken or vegetable stock, you can use a good brand of commercial organic chicken or vegetable stock or bouillon cube. If using a cube ensure it is flavourful, not too salty and that it does not have MSG. Usually add 2 cups of boiling water to 1 cube.

SUGAR: Always use granulated sugar unless otherwise stated.

Making sugar syrup: Use a clean, heavy-based pan and make the syrup with granulated sugar and warm water to help the sugar dissolve. Place the saucepan over a low heat and stir gently with a wooden spoon until the sugar dissolves. Do not allow the water to boil before the sugar has dissolved entirely and do not stir once the water starts to boil. Wash any crystals from the sides of the pan, using a pastry brush dipped in water.

Thread stage: In making sweets such as marzipan, a thread stage is required. As the sugar becomes slighter hotter and more concentrated, the syrup will feel tacky and a short thread about 1.5cm (½") in length will form between your wetted finger and thumb when they are pulled apart. A thread of about 2cm (¾") in length is considered a long thread.

Soft-ball stage: After the thread stage is reached drip the syrup from the spoon into a jug of cold water. At the soft ball stage the syrup will form into a little ball that will flatten on the bottom of the jug. It will feel soft and pliable.

Kitchen Tools for the Home Cook

Whether you are a beginner in the kitchen or an accomplished home cook, having the correct cooking tools and equipment is a must. Here are my personal suggestions that I hope will be invaluable in your cooking and baking endeavours.

BAKEWARE:

Baking tray (cookie sheet): You will need two or three large, flat metal trays that are rimmed and made of aluminium-coated steel as they are durable and retain the heat well. Choose light-coloured sheets as opposed to dark surfaces. This helps prevent scorching and promotes even browning of pastries and biscuits. Those with a non-stick surface are easier to clean but you can prevent sticking by lining the tray with non-stick baking paper or using a silicone baking mat.

Glazed earthenware or stoneware baking dishes: Shallow ovenproof dishes are ideal for baking vegetable and pasta gratins that can be served straight from the oven to the table. I prefer brightly coloured rectangular dishes, about 35 × 25cm (14 × 10in) and 6.25cm (2½in) deep, which add colour and interest to a table. Also useful is a set of individual ovenproof bowls or ramekins for rice and milk puddings.

Kitchen scales: A digital scale should allow you to weigh ingredients in any bowl or container. Choose one capable of weighing up to 2kg (4½lb).

Measuring cups and spoons: All cup and spoon measurements are level. Cup, metric and imperial measurements are given in this book. Follow one set of weights and measurements, they are not interchangeable. Dry ingredients are best measured in metal or plastic measuring cups. For measuring, sift the flour and then spoon the flour into the measuring cup, fill to overflowing, and then level the cup off with the back of a knife.

Measuring jug: Liquids are best measured in a heatproof jug (pitcher) with calibrated metric and imperial measurements and cups. I find a 2-cup (500ml/16fl oz) capacity the most versatile for measuring hot stock or when pouring rice puddings into individual bowls.

Mixing bowls: A set of about six glass bowls, made of tempered glass, in graduated sizes is indispensable. Glass has the advantage of not reacting with acidic ingredients like marinades, dressings and tomatoes and allows you to see how well the ingredients are blending. I find it useful to have at least one large, stainless-steel bowl for vegetable preparation or blending gratin mixtures.

Pastry board: Use a smooth hard surface, preferably a marble or other stone slab, to keep the pastry cool.

Rolling pin: My preference for rolling the dough for small savoury pastries is a tapered light-weight hardwood rolling pin. This makes it easier to roll out thin uniform circles of dough.

Pastry brush: Indispensable for brushing melted butter or oil directly onto dough or pastries, for greasing pans or glazing with egg wash. Be sure the brush has fine natural bristles.

Pastry cutters: Can be bought in sets, ranging in size from 2.5cm (1in) to 10cm (4in) across. Use one with plain edges for cutting the dough for savoury turnovers, cheese and potato tartlets and for marzipan-filled pastries. You can also use the rim of a thin glass, as our grandmothers used to do.

Spatulas: Silicone spatulas are invaluable for stirring, blending or folding ingredients and scraping out your pans and bowls. They withstand the heat and do not scratch cookware.

Wire cooling racks: Look for cooling racks made of heavy-duty metal that have feet so that steam and heat can escape from beneath fresh-baked cakes and biscuits, preventing moisture build up.

Wooden spoons: A long-handled sturdy spoon is needed for making marzipan and lemon fondant. Three or four smaller ones are useful for stirring sauces and syrups. As wood is porous, keep the ones for savoury and sweet foods separate.

COOKWARE:

Braising pan or casserole: An enamelled shallow, wide-based cast-iron pan with handles and a tight-fitting lid is ideal for braises and slow-cooked fish, meat, chicken and vegetable stews. I use 26cm (10in) or 30cm (12in) sized casseroles for the recipes in this book. They can go straight from the stovetop or oven to the table and retain the heat well. For cooking stuffed vegetables, I like to use All-Clad or WMF stainless-steel, heavy-based, shallow pans that have a glass lid.

Saucepans: I recommend aluminium-clad, stainless-steel pots and pans as they are durable, non-reactive to acidic ingredients, relatively resistant to sticking and are dishwasher safe. They will distribute the heat efficiently and are very responsive to temperature change. Select pans with a heat-resistant lid knob and handles, as well as a snug fitting lid. Some of the brands I have used successfully include All-Clad, WHF, Röslë and Silit. I usually have three round, straight-sided pans with high sides and tight-fitting lids; a 1.5lt (1.5qt) for sauce making and two medium pans 3lt (3qt) for cooking rice, vermicelli and vegetables.

For pasta and vegetables use a multi-purpose tall 6–8lt (6–8 quarts) pot with a well-fitting lid and perforated insert.

COOKING TOOLS:

Chopping board: Choose a large, tight-grained, hardwood board as it is more hygienic than other surfaces and is long lasting. I prefer boards that are 4cm (1½in) thick as they do not warp. Never submerge in water. For best upkeep I recommend thoroughly cleaning once a month with 4 cups water mixed with 1 tbsp vinegar and 1 tbsp coarse or kosher salt. Rinse well and air-dry, then wipe with grape-seed oil. Also handy to have are a few non-porous polypropylene flexible plastic mats that measure at least 30 × 45cm (12 × 18in). These are dishwasher safe so you can sanitise after each use. I recommend you reserve one board for meat, poultry and fish and a second for fresh herbs, vegetables and fruit.

Corer: Use an apple corer or a long thin *ma'anara* for hollowing courgettes and long aubergines, to prepare them for stuffing. These are available from Middle Eastern stores.

Electric mixer: Choose a free-standing electric mixer with a wire whisk for beating egg whites, a paddle whip for creaming butter and sugar and a dough hook for kneading. I have found that Kitchen Aid and Kenwood are durable and sturdy.

Food processor: Invest in a large, heavy-duty one.

Frying pan (skillet): I like to have two frying pans, one 23–25cm (9–10in) and one 30–35cm (12–14in). Make sure you find ones with flameproof handles and non-stick Calphalon surfaces, as they are easier to clean.

Grater: Hand-held rasp graters made under the brand name Microplane, which feature razor sharp stainless-steel cutting teeth, are ideal. For easy, precise grating, choose a fine one to zest citrus and grating garlic to a paste, a medium ribbon grater for soft cheese and onion and a coarse grater for tomatoes, hard cheese and feta required for savoury pies and gratins.

Grill pan: A cast-iron pan or griddle with ridges across the bottom is useful for indoor grilling. It will sear food with brown marks, resembling the cooking grid of a barbecue grill.

Ice-cream scoop: I like to use a 4.5cm (1¾in) ice-cream scoop to portion out even-sized amounts of the potato mixture for croquettes or the meat mixture for meatballs.

Knives: Good knives go a long way. You will need a knife with a sharp blade for chopping fresh herbs and a razor sharp serrated 11.5–13cm (4–5in) blade for cutting ripe tomatoes or segmenting citrus fruit. Also essential is an 11.5–13cm (4–5in) straight edge paring knife for peeling, trimming, slicing and chopping vegetables and fruit. I find Swiss Innox indispensable and the best tool in my kitchen. A multi-purpose 46cm (18in) well made and easy to grasp chef's knife is a useful addition.

Potato ricer: I prefer this device rather than a potato masher for a finer, fluffier puree for boiled potatoes used in Swiss chard, potato and cheese gratin, potato and cheese filling for pies and veal, egg and herb-filled potato croquettes.

Roasting pan: I like the sturdy enamelled cast-iron or stainless steel rectangular dishes for cooking poultry pieces and butterflied baby chickens or roasting a joint of lamb.

Skewers: Invest in sturdy stainless steel skewers for grilling kebabs. Select ones with a wide flat blade 30cm (12in) long as the minced meat adheres better and is more easily moulded to the skewer. I prefer to use the flat rather than round steel skewers for threading chunks of meat, chicken or fish, which prevents the food from spinning on the skewer while turning on the grill. Available at Middle Eastern stores.

Slotted spoon or wire skimmer: I find this the best tool for scooping out fried fish or other foods from hot oil.

Whisk: Have two in your kitchen – a balloon whisk for beating egg whites and cream, and a flat whisk for stirring sauces like the egg and lemon sauce, *agristada*, to smooth out any lumps that may form at the base of the pan.

Original pages from my mother's first recipe book, 1948.

Acknowledgements

O n one of my frequent trips to visit my family in New York, I was asked by my children, Claude and Monique, to appease their nostalgia by making one of the many Sephardic dishes they craved. While savouring the bean stew and tomato rice pilaf with gusto, the idea to write a book of recipes was born. Claude and Monique both wished for a compilation of the Sephardic dishes with which they had grown up in Zimbabwe. They also suggested that I document and include some of the customs of our community as a Sephardic descendant from Rhodes Island and Turkey living in Africa. Their request was the catalyst for the creation of this book.

I am truly indebted to the kindness and generosity of many dear ones who helped me compile this legacy.

My eternal gratitude goes to my father, Sam Hanan, of blessed memory, and to my mother, Marie, whose well of wisdom and love I tap into daily. My mother's passion for cooking, refined palate and pleasure in delighting others with her cooking inspired me at an early age. Her legendary meals were well-known in the community and set a high standard for me to follow. My father's deep love and pride in Sephardic culture continues today in his grandchildren and great-grandchildren. In particular, his approach to living life is best described by the Greek word *kefi*, a passion for life. The joy derived from entertaining loved ones with openhearted generosity is one that has been carried down through the generations.

I am forever grateful to my husband, Victor, for being an infinite source of strength. You were the cornerstone of bringing this book to life. Without your encouragement, patience and belief in this book I would never have persevered.

A monumental thanks to my children. To my son, Claude, and his wife, Danielle, my daughter, Monique, and her husband, Habib; thank you for your support, insight and hard work on all stages of this book. Many recipes, written works and photographs were a wonderful co-creative process between all of us.

My beloved grandchildren, Gemma, Bianca, Nico and Mia whose presence fill my life with joy. Your delight and enjoyment in savouring your favourite Rhodesli foods on my visits reaffirmed the need for this book. As the Ladino saying goes, "Children of my children are twice my children", *Ijos di mis ijos, dos vezes mis ijos*.

My cousins Vicky and Alan Atlas in Cape Town, for your support and feedback and for introducing me to Gerald and Marc Hoberman who so enthusiastically embraced the idea of this book and became my publishers. To Gerald and Marc, my profound gratitude for your elegance and vision. I could not have been in better hands. A special thank you to Mellany Fick, not only for your extraordinary talents as a designer, but for sharing this creative journey with me and to the Hoberman publishing team.

To Jane Gerber for your outstanding work on the History and Heritage of the Jews of Rhodes. To Leon Levy, of blessed memory, and the American Sephardic Federation, and especially Lynne Winters for your involvement with my art exhibitions over the past years.

To each of you, my treasured friends, and my wonderful extended Hanan family, too many to name, for your heartfelt support, my deepest thanks.

My editorial assistant, Lesley Frost, for your painstaking editing and meticulous attention, even following me to my laboratory, the kitchen! You guided me to the creation of my dream. To Radhika Boddapati and Kirsten Pistorius for so willingly stepping in to assist me.

Thank you to my foremothers and the countless mentors over the past years in our Zimbabwe community. In particular, those who worked with me in order to compile the community cookbook *Sephardic Cuisine* in December 1986; Ettie Mizrakhi, Ketty Dozetos, Ray Cohen and Sarah Piha.

Thanos Stavrianakis, my friend, who made it possible for me to cook freshly caught fish in his restaurant, the Archipelagos, in the old city on the island of Rhodes.

I also want to thank Lazarus Muoomba, Lingiwe Ncube, Leonard Chinganga, Esther Kamwara and Brown Jawara, the team at home, for revisiting the recipes so many times with me.

A heartfelt thank you to my sister, best friend and spirit guide, Vera, of blessed memory, with whom I shared this life for only 21 years, for your infinite love and joy.

Select Bibliography

Alexiadou, Vefa. *Vefa's Kitchen*. New York, USA: Phaidon Press Limited, 2009.

Angel, Rabbi Marc D. *Foundations of Sephardic Spirituality*. Woodstock, Vermont: Jewish Lights Publishing, 2006.

Başan, Ghillie. *Turkish Cooking*. London, UK: Anness Publishing Ltd, 2006.

Dobrinsky, (Rabbi) Herbert C. *A Treasury of Sephardic Laws and Customs*. New York, USA: Yeshiva University Press, 1986.

Dweck, Poopa. *Aromas of Aleppo: The Legendary Cuisine of Syrian Jews*. New York, USA: HarperCollins Publishers, Inc., 2007.

Gitlitz, David M. and Davidson, Linda Kay. *A Drizzle of Honey: The Lives and Recipes of Spain's Secret Jews*. New York, USA: St Martin's Press, 1999.

Goldstein, Joyce. *Sephardic Flavors: Jewish Cooking of the Mediterranean*. San Francisco, USA: Chronicle Books LLC, 2000.

Hoffman, Susanna. *The Olive and the Caper: Adventures in Greek cooking*. New York, USA: Workman Publishing Company Inc., 2004.

Kiros, Tessa. *Food From Many Greek Kitchens*. Australia: Murdoch Books, 2010.

Kochilas, Diane. *The Glorious Foods of Greece: Traditional Recipes from the Islands, Cities and Villages*. New York, USA: HarperCollins Publishers Inc., 2001.

Levy-Mellul, Rivka. *La Cuisine Juive Marocaine*. Montreal, Canada: Albert Soussan, 1983.

Mallos, Tess. *Middle Eastern Home Cooking: Quick, easy, delicious recipes to make at home*. Boston, USA: Periplus Editions (HK) Ltd., 2002.

Malouf, Greg and Lucy. *Turquoise*. Victoria, Australia: Hardie Grant Books, 2007.

Manasce, Elsie. *The Sephardi Culinary Tradition*. Cape Town, South Africa: The Sephardic Cookbook Corporation Publishers, 1984.

Marks, Gil. *Encyclopedia of Jewish Food*. Hoboken, NJ, USA: Wiley Publication, 2010.

Roden, Claudia. *The Book of Jewish Food: An Odyssey from Samarkand and Vilna to the Present Day*. New York, USA: Alfred A. Knopf, 1996.

Salaman, Rena. *The Greek Cook: Simple Seasonal Food*. London, UK: Anness Publishing Inc., 2001.

Sephardic Ladies. *Sephardic Cuisine*. Bulawayo, Zimbabwe: R Christian Press, 1986.

Shaul, Moshe; Rodriguez, Aldina Quintana; Ovadia, Zelda. *El Gizado Sefaradi*. Zaragoza, Spain; Libros Certeza.

Sternberg, (Rabbi) Robert. *The Sephardic Kitchen: The Healthful Food and Rich Culture of the Mediterranean Jews*. New York, USA: HarperCollins Publishers Inc., 1996.

Uvezian, Sonia. *Recipes and Remembrances from an Eastern Mediterranean Kitchen*. Northbrook, USA: Siamanto Press, 2001.

Wolfert, Paula. *The Cooking of the Eastern Mediterranean: 215 Healthy, Vibrant, and Inspired Recipes*. New York, USA: HarperCollins Publishers, Inc., 1994.

Glossary

almonds, blanched
almendras, blankeadas

almonds, ground
almendras, moulidas

almond shortbread
kurabyes

apples
mansanas

apricots
kayisi

artichokes
anjinaras

aubergines, diced
berendjenas, kuartikos

aubergine filling
handrájo

beans, black-eyed
fijónes

beans, borlotti
barbunyas

beans, cannellini/haricot
avas

beans, fresh broad
ava, freska

beans, fresh green
fasùlya

beans, fresh yellow wax
haunum, fasùlya

beef
karne de vaka

beetroot
pandjar

beverages
bividas

biscuits, rusks
biskotchos ou biskotchadas

biscuits, sesame
reshikas

bread
pan

breakfast, savoury pastries
desayuno

butter
manteka

cabbage
kol

carrots
safanorya

casserole (oven to table)
tendjeré

cauliflower
karnabit

celery, head of celery
apio, kavesa de apio

cheese, grated
keso, rayido

chicken
gayina

chickpeas
garavansos

chickpeas, roasted
bilibiz

chopped
machakado

cinnamon, ground
kanela, moulida

cloves, ground
klavo de komer, moulida

coffee cup
finján

coffee froth
kaymác

coffee, Turkish
kavé, Turko

colander
tefsín borakado

cook (to)
gizar, kuzinar

cooked
kócho

cover (to)
tapar

cover (lid of a pot)
tapon

cucumber
pipino

cumin
kimion

cut finely
kortar minudo

dates, pitted
datlis, sin kueshko

dill
anitó

dough
masa

doughnuts
bimuelos

drain
meter a eskurir

eggs, hard-boiled
huevos haminados

eggs, soft-boiled
huevos rifidán

fillings
gómo

filo
fila

filo pies
hojaldres

fish
peshkado

flour
arina

fritters
keftes

fruit, pip (stone)
fruta, kueshko

frying pan
sarten

garlic, cloves
ajo, dientes de ajo

garlic sauce
ajada

grape (vine) leaves, stuffed
oja di parra, yaprakes

grapefruit segment
gajo

grapes
uva

grate (to)
rayér

gratin
quajado

greens, vegetables
verduras

grilled
asado

honey
miel

kitchen
kuzina

kitchen cloth
kanyimazo de kuzina

knife
kuchiyo

lamb, leg of
kordero, pierna de

leeks
prása

lemon
limón

lemon and egg sauce
avgolemono, agristada

lemon juice
sumo de limón

lentils
lentejas

lettuce
lechuga

macaroni
makaron

marzipan
masapan

mastic
almastíga

meat
karne

meatballs
keftes de karne

meatballs in tomato sauce
albondigas

meat, minced (ground)
karne, moulida

milk
leche

mint
menta

noodles, strands
fidéyos, madeshas

noodles, toasted
fidéyos, tostados

nuts, chopped
muéz, machakada

oil, for frying
azeyte, para friyir

okra
bárnia

olives
azeytúnas

onion
sevoya

onion, spring (scallions)
sevoya freska

orange
portokál

orange blossom water
agua de flor

parsley, finely chopped
prishil, pikado minudo

pastry, to prepare
tomar la masa

pears
peras

peas
bizelyas

pepper, ground
pimienta

peppers, red
pimintones, kolorado

peppers, bell
pimintones

pickles
salamura, trushí

pine nuts
pinyones

pistachios
pistash, fistok

pomegranates
granada

pot, shallow sided
paylon

potatoes
patatas

pumpkin, butternut
kalavasa

pumpkin seeds, roasted
pipitas

radish
ravanos

red mullet
barbunya

rice
arroz

rice flour pudding
sutlach

rose water
agua de kondjá

sabbath
shabbát

sabbath bread
roska

salad
salata

salted bonito or tuna
palmida, lakerda

salted fish
salado

sardines
sardellas

saucepan
paylón

sesame seeds
susam

slice of bread
revanada de pan

soup
supa

spinach
spinaka

spoon, wooden
kuchara de palo

stews
komidas

stuffed vegetables
legumbres reynados

sugar
asúkar

sweet confection
dulses

Swiss chard, stalks
Pazí, ravos

tomatoes, grated
tomates, rayidos

tomato sauce
kaldo de tomat

vinegar
vinagre

watermelon
karpuz

yoghurt
yogurt

Stella's Paintings

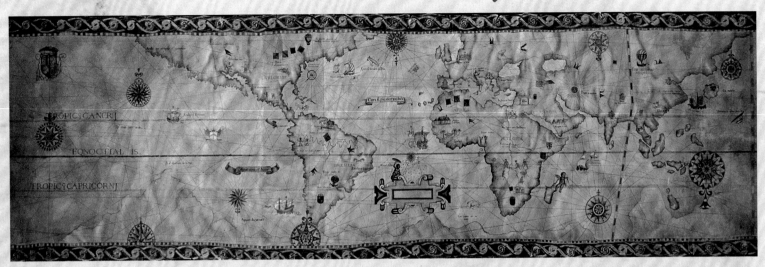

Sepharad 1492, 1992. 7 × 1.85m (276 × 73in), from the exhibition *Bendisiones de Vera* held by the Yeshiva University Museum and the American Sephardi Federation, New York, 1999. This work is on permanent exhibition at the Center for Jewish History, New York. (on the front and back endpaper)

Soul spirit, 2000. From the exhibition *Oracle Women*, Deutser Gallery, Jewish Communal Center of Houston, 2001. (page 62)

The Rhodesli Odyssey, 2011. (pages 128–9)

The Absent Healer, 2000. From the exhibition *Oracle Women ll*, American Sephardi Federation, New York, 2000. (page 269)

HANAN-CAPOUYA Family Tree, 2009. (pages 278–9)

Sabbath Bride, 1998. On permanent exhibition at the Beyachad Community, Johannesburg. (page 281)

*All paintings are oil on canvas.

Section Dividers

Meze & Salads (page 29)
Detail of an *anteri* garment, The Jewish Museum of Rhodes

Soups, Stews & Braises (page 63)
Detail of a *baul* – a decorated chest used to contain a bride's trousseau, which was known by the Ladino-speaking Jews of Rhodes as *ashuar*, The Jewish Museum of Rhodes

Fish (page 89)
Patterned cobblestone, Kahal Kadosh Shalom synagogue, The Old Town of Rhodes

Gratins, Fritters & Egg Dishes (page 107)
Antique baroque table wood inlay detail, Author's Home

Stuffed Vegetables (page 131)
Tablecloth detail, The Jewish Museum of Rhodes

Meat & Poultry (page 147)
Detail of a frieze from ancient Temple of Aphrodite, Rhodes c.3rd century BCE

Rice Pilafs & Noodles (page 165)
Architectural detail of historic building in Mandraki Harbour, Rhodes Island

Savoury Pastries & Breads (page 179)
The Deer symbol of Rhodes, depicted on the cobblestone streets in the Old Town of Rhodes

Sweet Treats & Beverages (page 207)
Tablecloth detail, The Jewish Museum of Rhodes

All the motifs on pages 136, 140, 167, 192 and 196 are taken from the synagogue in Rhodes Island.

General Index

Page numbers in **bold** type indicate photographs.

Recipe Index